CLASSIC TURKISH COOKERY

CLASSIC TURKISH COOKERY

Ghillie Başan
Photographs by Jonathan Başan

Foreword by Josceline Dimbleby

TAURIS PARKE BOOKS
LONDON • NEW YORK

Reprinted in 2005 by
Tauris Parke Books
6 Salem Road
London W2 4BU

Tauris Parke Books is an imprint of I.B. Tauris & Co. Ltd

First published in 1997.
Copyright © 1997 by I.B.Tauris & Co. Ltd
Photographs copyright © 1997 by Jonathan Başan

A full CIP record for this book is available from the British Library

ISBN 1 86064 011 7

Coordinating Editor: Sue Phillpott
Designed and typeset by Karen Stafford

Printed and bound in Hong Kong by South China Printing Co.

Frontispiece *Zeytinyağlı enginar* ARTICHOKES IN OLIVE OIL.

To the memory of Nazlı Başan (1911–91)

Nazlı Başan grew up in the Kıbrıslı Yalısı, which had been bought in 1840 by her great-grandfather, Kıbrıslı Mehmed Emin Paşa, first appointed Grand Vizier of the Ottoman Empire in 1854. Contrary to the custom of the time, the men and women of the Kıbrıslı Yalısı ate together, dining on both the traditional Anatolian fare and the sophisticated dishes of the Palace cuisine. Nazlı Başan thus became intimately acquainted with the wealth of tastes to be found in Turkish cooking, the secrets of which she revealed to me.

CONTENTS

Foreword by Josceline Dimbleby ix
Acknowledgements xi
Conversions and Equivalents xii
Map of Turkey xii–xiii

Introduction *15*

Essential Elements of Turkish Cuisine *23*
Yogurt and Cheese *43*
Meze and Salads *47*
Soups *79*
Breads, Savoury Doughs and Pastries *89*
Vegetable Dishes *103*
Pilafs *121*
Fish and Seafood *133*
Meat Dishes *149*
Poultry and Game *171*
Desserts *183*
Festive Sweets and Jams *203*
Drinks *211*

Glossary 219
Index 222

Foreword by Josceline Dimbleby

When I was barely twenty I arrived for the first time in Istanbul, after the long journey from Paris on the original Orient Express. It was only on boarding this historic train, for one of its last trips, that we learned that the restaurant car had already been taken off. So after eating nothing but platform sandwiches for three days my girlfriend and I, starving, rushed to the one address we knew, the Pera Palas Hotel, and ate our first Turkish meal completely alone in the palatial dining-room. The *yalancı dolma* – stuffed vine leaves so different from those I had known at London's Mediterranean restaurants – were made with rice which had a bite to it, and were flecked with pine kernels and fresh dill.

I had been given one Istanbul telephone number by a friend in London. This call transformed my first experience of Turkey, and several others in the years to come. For it was to Emin Dirvana, Jonathan Başan's uncle, an ex-soldier and diplomat who was to become a firm friend from then until his death about thirty years later. A charming and courteous anglophile, Emin took us under his wing and showed us all of Istanbul. He was better than any guidebook, he knew all there was to know of the fascinating history and architecture of the city, and he had many personal anecdotes about his house on the Bosphorus and his grandmother's experiences during the days of the last sultan at the Topkapı Palace. But the icing on the cake was that he loved and knew about food, so that in between sight-seeing he introduced us to his favourite restaurants.

I still remember Konyalı, a businessmen's restaurant near the railway station. It was the kind of establishment I enjoy most: no pretensions, just a large room with white-clad tables, talkative customers with large and discerning appetites, swift service and well cooked Turkish food. This was where I first tasted *tavuk göğsü kazandibi*, one of Turkey's most surprising and, to me, irresistible desserts. This creamy milk pudding is made from an unlikely ingredient: breast of chicken. I was told that, ideally, the bird should be only just killed and still warm in order to produce the intriguing smooth texture, its silk-fine threads totally unidentifiable as chicken. I became addicted to this pudding, served with a dark-brown, almost burnt, top, and made Emin ask for it wherever we went.

Another restaurant that remains in my memory is the famous Pandeli in a room above the covered market. A meal here after our appetites had been whetted by a walk through the spectacular food markets was a treat indeed. Here I realized that the aubergine is the national vegetable of Turkey, since no other nation has so many or such good ways of serving it. At

Pandeli I learned how to make the best smoked-aubergine purée, as well as a luscious hot version incorporating melted cheese that they served with charcoal-grilled lamb or fish. Outside the market at the fish restaurants under the Galata Bridge I was thrilled at the ingenuity of *uskumru dolması*, a mackerel with all its bones carefully removed, leaving the fish whole so that when stuffed it looked almost alive again. The Turks quite rightly appreciate the fine moist texture of mackerel, and cook it in several different ways.

Some of our most enjoyable meals were eaten away from the noise and hubbub of central Istanbul in the garden of Emin's family home beside the Bosphorus on the Asian side. This lovely old house is one of the last remaining wooden *yalıs* that used to flank the Bosphorus. Several generations of Emin's extended family wandered in and out, and his brother's wife produced some delicious things for us to eat. I remember particularly crisp, light cheese pastries and a tender cake made with yogurt. But most of all I remember the plumpest, sweetest, juiciest deep-orange Bosphorus mussels, coated in an incredibly light batter made with beer and briefly deep-fried.

When the time came for us to leave Istanbul, we confidently told Emin that we proposed to travel down to the south of Turkey by local buses. But Emin would not hear of this; it was the early 1960s, there were few roads or hotels in the far south, no one spoke English and the idea of young foreign girls travelling alone was not a safe one. 'I will accompany you,' he said. He suggested that he would hire a car but we protested that we must experience the real Turkey. So for three weeks poor Emin was forced to travel on buses crowded with country people and their baggage, and often with some of their animals too. We insisted on staying at the oldest, cheapest hotels – yet again, for the 'atmosphere'. But the journey was beautiful, varied and always interesting. Through Emin we were able to communicate with people, to learn about their way of life and, of course, their food. He was clearly entertained by our conversations, and protected us from over-enthusiastic men. By the time we got back to Istanbul I knew that Emin would be a friend for life, that I loved his richly endowed country and that I would return to it many times.

Ever since that first visit I have experimented with Turkish ideas in my own dishes. I am almost as addicted to aubergines as the Turks themselves and, like them, I love the exciting surprise of stuffed ingredients. Frequently as I cook I come back to the Turkish favourites: pine kernels, little currants to add sweet to savoury, coriander seeds, fresh dill, rose-water for milky puddings, honey for filo pastry sweetmeats. For years I cooked only from memory, as there were few books to refer to. Now, with this evocative collection of recipes, clear guidance and beautiful photographs brought to us by Ghillie and Jonathan Başan, many more people will be able to experience the delights of Turkish cooking in their own homes. And I shall have even more than memories to inspire me.

Acknowledgements

While researching and photographing this book, we have run into a chain of infectious enthusiasm as people, some of whom we had never met before, tirelessly offered their assistance – sometimes pressing into our hands scribbled recipes and small packages of food, proudly identifying dishes from their particular regions of Turkey. To these people we offer our sincere thanks and hope that this book will help to identify Turkish cookery on the culinary map.

We would particularly like to mention our good friend Hasan Selamet for his artistic direction and willingness to share his intimate knowledge of Istanbul and its food; Serdar Palas, for his guidance and culinary input; Kenan Eren, for his companionship in eastern Anatolia; Taşkut Adanır of May, Istanbul, for the loan of his Anatolian artefacts; Sibel İren for the use of her plate collection; Edith Oyhon for her pharmacological tips; Deniz Restoran and Boncuk Meyhanesi, Istanbul; Bülent Barım of Mantıtheque, Istanbul; Osman *bey* of Kimene in the Çiçek Pasajı, Istanbul, for years of food and gypsy music; Volkan Öztaş and Ismail Seymen of Yaşar Kuru Yemişci in the *Mısır Çarşısı*, Istanbul; Mustafa Günder of Şömene, Ürgüp; Hüseyin Dengel and Yildiray Şıh of Gemibaşı, still the best restaurant in Bodrum; Zahide Şibik for her warm welcome in Avanos; and Belkis Aksunkur and the late Emin Dirvana for their stories of old.

We would also like to thank those few who have been involved in this book in their own special ways: Aziz and Mo Başan for their constant support and help with the research, and their cook Sevim *hanım*, who patiently prepared special dishes for us; Cem Kum for his infallible knowledge; Alex and Anne Caroline Peckham whose vociferous enthusiasm over the years has encouraged us to keep going; John and Karon Hammond, whose home became our office; Bill and Frances Fulton for plugging it to all their friends; Shaan and Angela Singh for taking care of us in London; Clarissa Dickson Wright, who has generously shared her expertise; and veteran publisher Tom Rosenthal, and Yvonne McFarlane, for believing in us at the beginning of this, and other, projects.

Last, we would like to thank Josceline Dimbleby for her interest in, and lively contribution to, the book; the team at I.B. Tauris for their patience and enthusiasm under often difficult and remote circumstances; the designer, Karen Stafford, for shaping the words and photographs into a book; and the editor, Sue Phillpott, whose guidance made it painless and whose thoroughness made it better.

CONVERSIONS AND EQUIVALENTS

The measurements given within the recipes should be treated as guidelines, the best measurement of all being personal taste.

Weight measurements are provided in imperial and metric. These correspond closely with US measurements, e.g. 1oz equals approximately 30g.

For liquid measurements the simplest conversion to US equivalents is:

IMPERIAL	AMERICAN
½ fluid oz	1 tablespoon
8fl oz	1 cup
10fl oz (½ pint)	1¼ cups
16fl oz	2 cups (=1 US pint)
20fl oz (1 pint)	2½ cups (=1¼ US pints)
30fl oz (1½ pints)	3¾ cups
40fl oz (2 pints)	5 cups

The following weight-to-cup conversion table is a rough approximation only:

IMPERIAL	AMERICAN
2oz	¼ cup
4oz	½ cup
8oz	1 cup
16oz	2 cups

ENGLISH TO AMERICAN USAGE

aubergine	eggplant
cornflour	corn starch
courgette	zucchini
double cream	heavy cream
grill	broil
icing sugar	confectioner's sugar
marrow	large zucchini
minced	ground
plain flour	white all-purpose flour
pulses	dried legumes (lentils, beans, chickpeas)
self-raising flour	cake flour plus 1 teaspoon baking powder
sheep's trotters	sheep's feet
strong plain flour	unbleached bread flour
sultanas	yellow raisins
wholemeal flour	whole wheat flour

Turkey

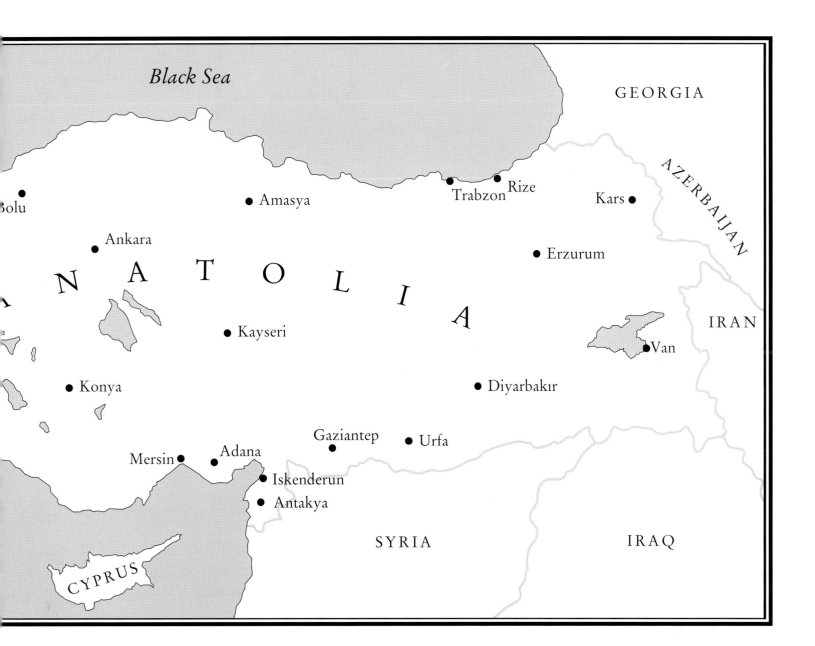

INTRODUCTION

The Turks love to eat. Ask a Turk about his food and his eyes light up as he warms rapturously to his theme. It's not the dish that matters but the taste, the smell, the passion, the pleasure.

That pleasure is reflected in the dazzling arrays of fruit and vegetables proudly displayed in the markets; it is in the smile of the fishermen cooking their catch in small boats bobbing at the edges of the Bosphorus; it is radiant in the hospitality of deepest Anatolia; and it grows strong in the natural wealth of the land.

Life in Turkey revolves around food in many pleasurable ways. It oozes from the pores. Its aromas sting the air. *Kokoreç*, lambs' intestines stuffed with offal and spices, crackle in the streets; *midye tavası*, mussels fried in beer batter, sizzle on the boats; large spits of tubular *döner* grill inside the open windows of kebab houses; syrupy *baklava* beckon from specialist sweet shops; trays of mouth-watering, habit-forming *meze* play havoc with willpower; and the enticing smell of freshly baked *simit*, bread rings, teases the nose. There is always time to stop and eat.

Moreover, the offering and sharing of food are an expression of friendship, and it is impolite to refuse. Once when visiting a *hamam* for a private steam, I happened upon a wondrous and memorable scene. With clogs clacking and bare breasts flapping, scantily clad mothers and grandmothers manoeuvred their way over the slippery marble through the steam to invite me to join them. Spread across the central platform were containers of savoury pastries, olives, cheese, peeled fresh tomatoes and cucumbers, figs and grapes. This was a *hamam* picnic, a spread that could have matched any Ottoman feast. The magical – if somewhat wet – scene culminated in a crescendo of singing and dancing, while the children splashed delightedly in the water.

GOLDEN HORN, ISTANBUL

Every man, woman and child has something to say about their food, and they dispute vigorously over claims for regional specialities. When making inquiries about the origins and methods of a particular dish, I find myself surrounded by joyful faces eager to share their passion. As the pitch rises, more people appear from open doorways and across the street. And as I slip away I am none the wiser, for the gathered crowd, in their keenness to define local variations of the same dish, is now engaged in a good-humoured brawl.

To me the attraction of Turkish cookery lies in its simplicity; its strength is to be found in its traditions and diversity. A vibrant cuisine, it is about colour, balance and taste. Recipes and ideas have been passed down from generation to generation, always changing and resurfacing. I have tasted food in parts of Anatolia that my friends in Istanbul have never heard of and, in Istanbul, I have sampled dishes that I have never seen again.

It could be said that the history of Turkey is that of its cuisine. A continuity of movement has been maintained since the early pastoral nomads roamed westwards from Central Asia in search of lush pastures. Today it is the Anatolian workers, farmers and their families who migrate westwards to Istanbul in a quest for wealth, for a better life. And with them travels a piece of their culture, a taste of their cuisine. Movement and survival are in the blood of the Turks, and have thus been at the root of Turkish cooking.

FERRY BOATS BELOW TOPKAPI PALACE

The direct forefathers of the modern Turk, the *Oğuz* Turks, migrated from the Turan Basin in Central Asia and arrived in Anatolia in the tenth century. Like so many tribes before them, they would have acquired the tastes and foods of the lands in which they wandered. Yogurt, unleavened bread, the milk and meat of horses, mules and wild animals, would have been their main source of food. Once they established military might by using horses in warfare, the *Oğuz* went from strength to strength. A nation of twenty-four tribes, they created a warrior aristocracy, formed the *Selçuk* (Seljuk) Empire in the eleventh and twelfth centuries and established the *Osmanlı* (Ottoman) Empire in the fourteenth.

Although there are records from the Seljuk period referring to feasts of rice, stewed vegetables, pigeon and kebabs, it was not until the opulence of the Ottoman Empire that food really began to play a significant role. Once Mehmet II (1444–6/1451–81) conquered Constantinople in 1453, by dragging his ships overland, it became the centre of the Ottoman Empire and all culinary activity. He held great feasts at the Topkapı Palace and filled his kitchens with specialist chefs such as the *baklavacı*, the maker of syrupy pastries, the *börekçi*, maker of savoury pastries, and the *köfteci*, maker of meatballs, all of whom experimented and devised the first sophisticated recipes. This marked the beginning of the celebrated *Saray* (Palace) cuisine.

The men responsible for such culinary creativity came from Bolu, a forested mountainous area more hospitable to hunters than to chefs. The forests of Bolu were adopted as the official Ottoman hunting grounds and, so the story goes, the sultans and noblemen were so impressed with the food prepared by the local men that they took them back to Istanbul to cook in the Topkapı Palace and the houses of the wealthy. Small family industries sprang up as the chefs took their sons on as apprentices, leaving the women behind to till the fields.

In the sixteenth century when Europe still had no sophisticated culinary identity, the Palace chefs continued to push at the boundaries of creativity. The glorious rule of Suleyman the Magnificent (1520–66) was peppered with lavish and indulgent banquets. He was the first to bring the harem into the Palace – which may have yielded such descriptive names as *kız memesi*, young girls' breasts, and *kadın göbeği*, ladies' navels, for the popular syrupy desserts. It was a time when cooking was regarded as an art and a pleasure: sentiments that have survived.

As the Ottoman Empire proceeded to conquer vast territories, so the cuisine expanded. In their distant outposts, the generals of the Ottoman army would have clung to their culinary habits, for which the Topkapı Palace was the role model. They would have adapted the recipes to their new environments, adopting the best of the local cuisines they had invaded. In this way a degree of cross-fertilization occurred which would gradually have been fed back to the Topkapı Palace in Istanbul. It is because of this adaption and adoption

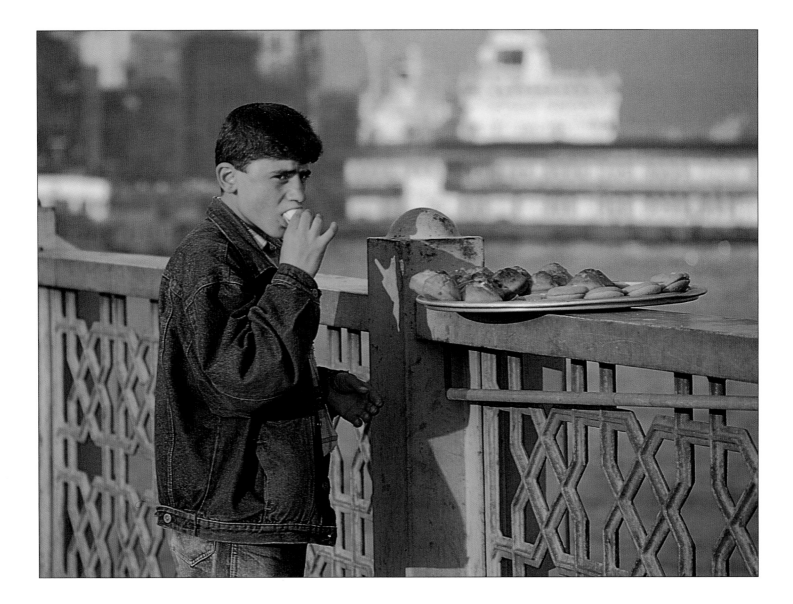

that a common food vocabulary developed and we find variations of *dolma*, *köfte*, *kebab*, *börek*, *baklava*, yogurt and Turkish coffee in Greece, Egypt, Hungary, Bulgaria, Romania, parts of North Africa and parts of Russia and former Yugoslavia.

Although the traditions and tastes of Turkish food have a long and interesting history, many of the key ingredients that have become so intrinsically part of Turkish food have, in fact, relatively recent origins. In the sixteenth and seventeenth centuries, when Istanbul and Madrid shared the political stage, tomatoes, potatoes, maize, sweet and chilli peppers, beans and sunflowers reached Istanbul from the New World. These new vegetables and grains were quickly incorporated into the cuisine of Istanbul, from where they spread out into the

countries of the Empire. Much of the cooking that we take for granted as Mediterranean owes its existence to this period of trade between Spain and the Empire.

The origins of Turkish food have been the subject of much debate, but its influence is unquestionable. For over four centuries it dominated the vast culinary terrain of the Ottoman Empire. But it must be remembered that it was only the food of Istanbul, of the Palace, that spread across the Empire. With their westward vision, the Ottomans didn't touch central Anatolia until the seventeenth century, and they never penetrated eastern Anatolia. Thus, tradition prevailed in parts of Anatolia and much of its inspired cuisine remained unknown.

Today Turkey's culinary legacy is a tapestry of tastes and pleasure, seasoned with Ottoman indulgence and refreshed by Anatolian inspiration. This book offers you an exciting blend of the sophisticated and the traditional, some of the recipes appearing in print for the first time. The philosophy is simple: dip heartily into the earthy flavours, calmly savour the sensual tastes, let them dance on your tongue and paint images of the East in your mind.

ESSENTIAL ELEMENTS OF TURKISH CUISINE

Turkey stretches from the southeastern end of Europe to the edges of the Middle East. Anatolia, the Asian part of Turkey, is divided into seven geographical regions: the Aegean, the Marmara, the Black Sea, eastern Anatolia, southeastern Anatolia, the Mediterranean and central Anatolia. It is a land of enviably rich produce and a cornucopia of tastes. It is where the flavours of the Mediterranean set and the aromas of the East rise with the muezzin as he calls the faithful to prayer.

In the villages of Anatolia meals are often eaten from a communal pot, off a communal tray on the floor, a tradition that stems from the leather sheet placed on the ground by the early pastoral nomads of Central Asia – the ancestral tablecloth. In the Topkapı Palace in Istanbul where one might expect elaborate dining-rooms, the sultans too sat on the floor and ate off trays or small, low-set, portable tables which were laid out in different parts of the Palace.

The traditional Turkish kitchen is very simple. Sophisticated utensils are not required – a sharp knife and nimble hands form the basic tools. Spoons and bowls are carved out of local wood and the cooking pots, water jugs and yogurt urns are beaten out of copper and tin-lined, each one representing a local shape or design – the yogurt urn from Trabzon takes the form of an elegant tulip, a complete contrast to the stout ice-bucket shape of the yogurt urn from Van. Bread is eaten with everything, garlic is crushed with salt, spices are freshly ground, and only the freshest seasonal produce is used.

To get the most out of Turkish food it is important to adapt your concept of eating. Throw away all ideas of three-course menus and 'meat and two veg', use the ingredients liberally and eat imaginatively, exploring the dishes in this book in any sequence, or several of them together.

Karışık turşu MIXED PICKLES

The basic elements of Turkish cooking can be found in the markets all over Turkey where all roads lead to the *Mısır Çarşısı*, the Egyptian Bazaar, an Aladdin's cave of foodstuffs in Istanbul. In Europe and the United States most of the ingredients can be found in a combination of cosmopolitan supermarkets, health food shops, Middle Eastern stores and delicatessens selling ethnic foodstuffs.

Many of the more common words relating to Turkish cookery are to be found in the Glossary on page 219.

AUBERGINES

If one vegetable could sum up Turkey, it would be the aubergine. Originally from India, aubergines are sometimes referred to as the poor man's meat. They pop up everywhere, prepared and cooked in infinite ways. During the Ottoman period, the Topkapı Palace

alone was known to produce aubergines in forty different ways. Available all year round, they range from the bulbous and gourd-like to the long, slender variety which sometimes stretch to the length of a forearm. The rounder ones are good for grilling over charcoal, while the longer present a perfect shape for stuffing.

Many *meze* dishes (see p. 47) require the softened flesh of grilled aubergines, which has a strong, smoky taste. To grill, the aubergines are placed either over hot charcoal or directly in the centre of a high gas flame. When grilled over charcoal the cooked skin toughens, which makes it easy to slit open and scoop out the flesh, whereas the gas flame burns the skin until it is almost papery, and more difficult to separate cleanly from the flesh. When you use the gas-ring method, it is easier to remove the skin from the flesh while holding the aubergine under a running cold tap. Then you squeeze it to drain off the excess water.

Before being fried, the aubergine is peeled lengthways in strips, like the stripes of a zebra, sliced or left whole, and soaked

DRIED AUBERGINES AND PEPPERS

in salted water for an hour to soften the flesh and remove the bitter juices. As well as removing some of the tough skin, the 'zebra stripes' procedure allows the salted water to penetrate. If dealing with slices, you then squeeze them in the same way that you would wring a pair of socks, to remove the excess water.

Strings of dried aubergines hang in the markets like chunky necklaces and, once reconstituted in water, are stuffed with rice and cooked in olive oil or stuffed with whole chilli peppers and pickled, specialities of Gaziantep and Antakya in southeast Anatolia. And from Antalya comes an unusual speciality of aubergine jam, *patlıcan reçeli* (p. 208), which, surprisingly, tastes of bananas.

CHARCUTERIE

Turkey has its own hung and cured meats made from veal and beef. The most common are *pastırma*, a cured fillet of veal encased in *çemen*, which is a thick dark-red paste made from ground fenugreek, cumin, *kırmızı biber* (p. 38) and garlic; and *sucuk*, a spicy beef sausage often flavoured with cumin, which looks like a salami. Both vary from region to region – sliced and eaten as a snack, stuffed into savoury pastries or cooked with vegetables such as beans and lentils, and eggs. *Mıhlama*, a dish made during Ramazan, consists of *pastırma* fried with onions, then swept into a ring leaving room for eggs to be dropped into the middle.

CHEESE

Beyaz peynir

The principal one is *beyaz peynir*, a white cheese usually made from cow's milk. There are many varieties, including *köy peyniri* (p. 45) which is made freshly every week in the villages. *Beyaz peynir* differs in its salt and fat content from region to region and everyone has their own preference – from the dry, white, firm cheese to a softer yellowy one. Urfa is known for its balls of *tuzsuz*, saltless white cheese, Van for its soft white cheese flavoured with local mountain herbs and stored underground, and Cappadocia for its powerful, dry, crumblier version which is matured underground for months. Some are better for cooking, others delicious to eat with jam for breakfast. Blocks of white cheese are stored in brine, and if a cheese is particularly salty it may be soaked in water for a few days before eating.

Others include *kaşar peyniri*, which is a hard, tangy, pale-yellow cheese made from sheep's milk; *lor peyniri*, a deliciously creamy whey cheese traditionally made from the milk of nursing cows and sheep; *tulum*, which is made and stored in the stomach or skin of a goat; *mihaliç*, a rich unsalted cheese made from sheep's milk; and *dil peyniri*, a mild cheese which, fascinatingly, peels off in thin strands.

CAPPADOCIA

FRUIT

From the fertile plains of Bursa to the lush valleys of Erzurum, Turkey's fruit basket is plentiful – juicy peaches and apricots, black and white mulberries, dates, pomegranates, apples, quince, oranges and tangerines, grapes, melon and watermelon, figs, cherries and bananas. A surprising variety of fruit grows in the arid soil of Cappadocia, a volcanic landscape of caves, including troglodyte dwellings, in central Anatolia. For centuries the fruit has been stored in the caves carved into the rock formations, where the cool, dry atmosphere matures it, enhancing the flavour without losing any of the texture.

All fruit is enjoyed in its fresh form, and most is cooked with sugar to make jam or *pestil*, a hard, thin strip of dried cooked fruit which is chewed for its flavour. White mulberries are dried and eaten like popcorn, apples are dried and used in tea, and, in Adana, oranges are turned into wine. Apricots, cherries, figs, grapes, lemons and pomegranates feature in a variety of ways.

APRICOTS The succulent, furry, sweet-scented apricots are as popular in their dried form as they are fresh. A fragrant jam is made from whole fresh apricots and the dried fruit is used in compotes, stuffings and desserts. At the end of the summer, the flat roofs of central Anatolia are carpeted with apricots drying in the sun, many of which are then exported to Europe.

CHERRIES The sweet cherry, _kiraz_, is usually enjoyed fresh, while the sour cherry, _vişne_, is cooked in casseroles, rice dishes and puddings, and is also made into jam and _vişne suyu_ (p. 213), a refreshing cherry drink. The sweet cherry is believed to stimulate the metabolism – 'If the mulberry didn't follow me, I would turn people into my stalk,' the cherry claims in Turkish lore. Dried cherry stalks have diuretic properties and, when infused in hot water, act as a herbal remedy for high blood pressure. The pale kernels of the black cherry are ground into a fine flour, _mahlep_, which is used as a flavouring in breads, biscuits and cakes.

CURRANTS Appropriately named _kuş üzümü_, 'bird grape', the tiny black seedless currant has endless uses. Traditionally used to sweeten dishes instead of sugar, currants are added to stuffings, _köfte_, fish and lamb casseroles, tomato sauces, breads, rice dishes and puddings. Some dishes require them to be plumped up in a little water before using.

FIGS When fresh, a golden nectar oozes from the deep purple skin of the fig, inside which is a flaming-red soft flesh. Unripe green figs impart a delicate honey flavour when cooked with sugar, to make a unique syrupy jam, _yeşil incir reçeli_ (p. 208). And in Bursa an unusual winter jam is made with dried figs and pine nuts, _kuru incir reçeli_ (p. 207). Dried figs are also used in compotes, stews and desserts.

GRAPES Like other Mediterranean countries, Turkey produces a variety of firm, sweet black and green grapes. Delicious fresh, they are also used to make a growing selection of wines, the best of which come from Ankara. They also form the basis of _üzüm pekmez_ (p. 220), a grape syrup which is often mixed with _tahin_ (p. 221) to make a popular spread for bread.

LEMONS Shiny yellow lemons add a bright splash to every market and table spread. They can be served with practically every _meze_ (p. 47) or vegetable dish, as the acidity cuts the heaviness of the olive oil. They are used in dressings and sauces, and squeezed in vast quantities to make a refreshing lemonade. Lemon juice is beaten with egg yolks to thicken thin soups and to make a tangy sauce for poached vegetables: beat the juice of half a lemon with two egg yolks over a low heat, add some of the poaching liquid until the dressing is

of pouring consistency and serve hot. Before lemons arrived in Turkey from India, pomegranates served the same purpose, and still do in parts of Anatolia.

POMEGRANATES A glamorous fruit encased in a tough, leathery skin, the pomegranate is often depicted in abstract form in Anatolian designs on plates, carpets and tiles. The trove of ruby-red grains concealed within the fruit symbolize fertility, good fortune and the continuation of life. It is also considered a cleansing fruit, able to raise the soul and banish negative feelings. You can cut it in half and squeeze it on a lemon press, then use the juice as a pleasant alternative to lemon juice in dressings and marinades. A refreshing pomegranate-juice drink is made in some Anatolian villages where they also make *nar pekmez* (p. 220), a dark pomegranate syrup which has a sweet-sour taste – good for sharpening dressings and marinades.

GARLIC

An essential ingredient in all Mediterranean and Middle Eastern cooking, garlic is used in both its fresh and dried forms. It is also pickled whole in its skin. It is believed to ward off the evil eye and to contain healing properties beneficial to the circulation of the blood. The lavish use of garlic and other strong tastes in Anatolian cooking contrasts with the smoother tastes of the Istanbul Palace cooking, which uses only small quantities of garlic, in specific dishes. Garlic is best crushed to a pulp with salt, which acts as an abrasive – by means of a mortar and pestle for the best effect – and then used according to personal taste.

HERBS

There is no shortage of fresh herbs in the mountains, valleys, markets and gardens of Turkey. In the summer heat the air of the Aegean and Mediterranean is intermittently scented with an enchanting pot-pourri of wild sage, basil, oregano and thyme, interspersed with dreamy wafts of eucalyptus and pine.

Herbs are used in large quantities, fresh and dried, to flavour and balance dishes. In addition to spices, herbs were traditionally believed to contain 'warming' and 'cooling' properties similar to the Yin and Yang theory of China. During the Ottoman period, the Palace chefs devised recipes by carefully balancing the herbs and spices to 'warm' or 'cool' the blood. The combination of fresh parsley, dill and mint has become widely used as a warming triune for 'cold' vegetables such as marrows, carrots and lettuce.

BASIL (REYHAN) A wild basil that grows all over the hills of the south Aegean and Mediterranean coasts. It is particularly pungent and dark in colour, and is used in both its fresh and dried forms to enhance local fish dishes, seafood salads and vegetable dishes.

CORIANDER (KİŞNİŞ) The seeds are crushed or ground to a powder, and added to many of the highly flavoured dishes of southern Anatolia. The leaves are used only in a few east Anatolian dishes that have been influenced by the cooking of the _Çerkez_ (Circassians).

DILL (DEREOTU) With its long feathery plumes, dill is one of the most traditional of the Turkish herbs. It is used fresh, on its own, with fish or in the 'warming' trinity mentioned above to balance vegetable dishes.

MINT (NANE) The strong-smelling leaves are used both fresh and dried in salads, vegetable dishes and casseroles, or combined with yogurt to make the refreshing dip, _haydari_ (p. 57).

OREGANO (KEKİK) Grows wild along the Aegean coast, and in the west, south and central regions of Anatolia is used frequently in its dried form in salads, fish dishes and grilled meats.

PARSLEY (MAYDANOZ) Always flat-leaved, very tasty, packed with vitamin C and used in large quantities. It is often served with hot kebabs to cut the spice, and is delicious on its own as a salad. It is also chewed to freshen the breath.

SAGE (ADI) Grows wild in southern Turkey, and is particularly fragrant. The dried leaves are mainly used to make an aromatic, cleansing tea.

THYME (DAĞI KEKİK) Called 'mountain oregano' as it has a similar smell, and grows wild in the hills and mountains of the southern Aegean and Mediterranean. Used in its dried form, it flavours local fish and meat dishes and is drunk in a herbal tea as an aphrodisiac.

ROSEMARY, MARJORAM, TARRAGON and _BAY_ also grow in the south and west of Turkey, but feature in only a few fish dishes and soups.

HONEY

The hills, valleys and plains of Anatolia burst into colour in spring, providing a haven for botanists and bees. The pine-wooded coastline of the Aegean and Mediterranean thrums with buzzing activity from spring through summer. Needless to say the honey of Turkey is fragrant and rich in natural shades of black, dark brown, deep yellow, creamy white and bright gold. The dark nectar from the pine forests of Marmaris is much sought after, in both comb and runny form. And the infamous _deli bal_ of Kars, extracted from the wild forest and mountain flowers of eastern Anatolia, is full of surprises: its fiery kick at the back of the throat brings with it slight hallucinatory sensations. Believed to sweeten life and ward off sadness, honey is used in cooking and in desserts, but it is best of all eaten in sticky dollops on fresh bread or trickled over thick yogurt.

MARROWS

Early Seljuk, Mevlani and Ottoman records refer to marrows cooked and stuffed in numerous ways. A dish of marrows stewed in grape juice was served at the banquets of Mehmet II (the Conqueror), who paid a great deal of attention to the culinary affairs of the Palace. The most commonly used member of the marrow family is the slender green courgette, complete with bright yellow flower frill, which is also stuffed and eaten, early in the season (see _kabak çiçeği dolması_, p. 113). Considered a 'cold' vegetable, every type of marrow is traditionally 'warmed' with a balance of mint and dill. Like the seeds of sunflowers and pumpkins, marrow seeds are roasted and salted and eaten like nuts or popcorn. And in the Mediterranean region marrows are made into a local sweet, _kabak helvası._

NUTS

The Turks adore nuts. They are stuffed into vegetables and fish, pounded into sauces, layered into sweet pastries, and added to *helva* (p. 203) and *lokum* (p. 204). They even form the basis of a nourishing, strengthening remedy for thin children who, each morning, are given a spoonful of chopped pine nuts, walnuts and raisins mixed with ground cinnamon.

ALMONDS (BADEM) A symbol of beauty, depicted in some ceramic designs from Iznik and Kütahya, almond trees grow along the Aegean coast and the Sea of Marmara. Enchanted by their beauty and fragrance, the Palace chefs cooked almonds with lamb and fish, turned them into puddings and marzipan, and baked them into biscuits and cakes. In spring whole unripe almonds are eaten along with their velvety green skins.

CHESTNUTS (KESTANE) Winter treats include freshly roasted chestnuts sold by street vendors, and boxes of succulent *kestane şekeri*, the Bursa version of marrons glacés. Both nourishing and filling, chestnuts are sometimes used as a substitute for potatoes and as a filling for vegetables.

HAZELNUTS (FINDIK) Grown mainly on the Black Sea coast; once harvested, they are dried by the sides of the roads. The most versatile of nuts, they are pounded into *tarator* (p. 221) sauce for vegetables and fish, baked into biscuits, used in puddings, *lokum* (p. 204) and *helva* (p. 203), and combined with chocolate. Hazelnuts are Turkey's largest nut export.

PINE NUTS (ÇAM FISTIK) The smallest and most subtle of nuts are those from the pine trees that grow along the Aegean and Mediterranean. With a woody smell and a mild taste of pine, these nuts are used for stuffings, rice dishes, puddings and the festive sweet *un helvası* (p. 205).

PISTACHIOS (ANTEP FISTIK) Famous for the green colour they impart to dishes, pistachios are popular in desserts and sweets. They are particularly delicious eaten warm, freshly roasted and salted. Turkish pistachios have now been adopted in parts of the United States where the climate and soil are similar.

WALNUTS (CEVİZ) The king of nuts: the fruit of the solid, ancient trees that grace the landscape of eastern, central and western Anatolia, including the environs of Istanbul. They are the favoured nut of Istanbul cuisine, used in many sweets and syrupy pastries and pounded into a heavier version of *tarator* (p. 221) sauce to accompany deep-fried seafood.

OLIVES

Basically, the green olives are the unripe fruit whereas the black ones have ripened on the tree. Both green and black olives are stored in brine or marinaded in olive oil and served as *meze* (p. 47), or with *beyaz peynir* (p. 219) for breakfast. Parts of the Aegean and Mediterranean, particularly around Kuşadası and Ayvalık, are dotted with lush olive groves, and the cuisines of the area incorporate both green and black olives in some special fish dishes and bread doughs. The hardy olive trees, which are able to survive in poor soil, grow in different geographical pockets of Turkey, thus producing fruit as diverse as the regions they grow in: large juicy, purple olives; succulent reddish-green, sweet olives; thin, unripe, bitter ones; roundish, wrinkled black ones.

Freshly picked black olives are sprinkled with coarse salt and kept in containers for up to a week. During this time they must be turned regularly in the salt – to crinkle the skin and soften the flesh, which turns brown at the same time. After this process they can be eaten; or tossed in olive oil and herbs, drained, and stored in jars in a cool place. Black olives are delicious marinaded in olive oil with fresh mint, and some of the fleshier green ones are scored before marinading, to soften them. When olives are eaten as *meze*, a little fresh lemon juice squeezed over them lifts and refreshes the taste. The cleaned and polished olive stones are strung together to make smooth *tespih*, the prayer beads flicked between the finger and thumb of every devout Muslim.

OLIVE OIL
AND COOKING FATS

If there were a rule for cooking with oil in Turkey, it would be to promote the use of olive oil in all dishes where the oil adds something to the dish and to reserve the lighter, less flavoured sunflower oil for deep-frying. Olive oil is used lavishly in areas where it is easily available, but in parts of central and eastern Anatolia, where it is scarce or expensive, both the Turks and the Kurds cook with sheep's tail fat (*kuyrukyağı*, p. 220), a distinct rancid-tasting clarified butter, or a fresh creamy butter, made from the milk of cows, sheep or goats and, occasionally, from the milk of water buffalo.

Although Turkey is fast becoming a major producer of olive oil, it is relatively new in the country's culinary history. Its original role was as a lighting fuel for the mosques, but it was gradually incorporated into the Palace cooking during the late seventeenth and eighteenth centuries. At first it was used sparingly, reserved for vegetables, but it is now used in most *meze* (p. 47), fish and chicken dishes. Olive oil plays a central role in the preparation of the popular *zeytinyağlı* vegetable dishes (pages 116–19), where the ingredients are cooked in a substantial quantity of oil. For those passionate about their food, olive oil imparts a warm, fruity taste and balance to most cold dishes, whereas the sheep's tail fat and clarified butter fire most soups, pilafs and meat dishes with the favoured pungency.

The quality of the oil is of dramatic importance, as an inferior one can severely alter the taste of a dish. Wherever olive oil is used, the dish will greatly benefit from a high-quality virgin olive oil. If you can get your hands on a good brand of fresh Turkish virgin oil you will swoon like the legendary imam (see p. 107). It is so delicious you can just dip your bread in it.

ONIONS

There are red, purple, pink, golden and white onions, spring onions and shallots. Sometimes sweet, the red and pink onions snap and zing with the aroma of hot soil and form the basis of many dishes. The juice of all the large roundish onions is used to marinade meat and fish. First, the onions are grated, then crushed to a pulp with salt and left to weep; then the pulp is pushed through a sieve to extract the juice. Large white onions are stuffed with minced meat and rice, the long reeds of spring onions are chopped into salads and *meze* dishes, and shallots and other tiny onions are cooked whole in casseroles or skewered on kebabs.

PEPPERS

There are sweet peppers and hot peppers. The sweetest are the large red and yellow bell-shaped peppers, which are delicious grilled. The small green bell peppers are picked unripe as, thinner-skinned, they are ideal for stuffing with rice and minced meat. Similarly, small red bell peppers from the southeast of Turkey are hung up and dried, which makes them easier to stuff once reconstituted in water. The pale-green, sweetly perfumed *çarliston biber*, shaped like Turkish slippers, are best grilled or fried whole and served with garlic-flavoured yogurt, *kızarmış biber* (p. 53), pickled whole, or sliced into a refreshing salad. The long, twisted bright-green and red chilli peppers, ranging from pleasantly to uncomfortably hot, are chopped into salads or grilled with kebabs. The tiny green and red match-stick chillies from the south and southeast can be breathlessly hot – they are used sparingly in meat and fish dishes, or pickled. And long strings of mild, horn-shaped chillies from the south and southeast are hung up to dry, roughly chopped, and then crushed or ground into the ubiquitous spice, *kırmızı biber* (page 38).

PICKLES

There are pickle houses in almost every town and village. Individual vegetables are pickled whole or in large chunks; some are stuffed and others are sliced and wrapped around whole bulbs of garlic or hot peppers; in some parts of Anatolia unripe apricots are pickled. The locals on the Black Sea coast maintain that if a fish is not worth pickling, it is not worth eating. The method of pickling does not vary much – usually a combination of white wine vinegar and salt is used – and the pickles are never sweet. Attracting customers with its colourful array of jars in the window, the pickle shop is much frequented, particularly on hot days when the pickling liquid quenches the thirst. Pickles are also served with grilled meats and tripe soup, *işkembe çorbası* (p. 81) or as *meze* (p. 47).

RAKI

The national alcoholic drink, *rakı* can be made from dried raisins, dried figs or fresh grapes. It is distilled once or twice and flavoured with aniseed. Popularly known as *aslan sütü*, 'lion's milk', it turns cloudy when water is added. Traditionally drunk by men, it goes well with *meze* (p. 47), grilled fish and meat as it opens up and refreshes the palate. It can be drunk in three ways: as a shot; in a tall glass mixed with water and ice; or in two glasses – one containing a measure of *rakı*, the other water – drunk alternately and cooled with ice. Some people add liquid *mastika* (p. 220) to their bottles of *rakı*, which gives it a chewy twang and knocks back the spirit.

Rakı and *leblebi* ROASTED CHICKPEAS

ROSES

Roses grow wild all over Turkey and are cultivated in parts of Anatolia for rose oil, rose-water and rose-scented cologne. From May onwards the hills and plains around Isparta are full of colour and fragrance. For centuries in the Middle East and India, the scented petals of pink and red roses have been infused in oil, milk, sugar and water for culinary pleasure. The petals of the old-fashioned cottage garden rose possess the best colour and fragrance for flavouring pastries and puddings and for making the delightful rose-petal jam, *gül reçeli* (p. 207). Scented rose-water is lavishly splashed into or over sweet pastries and milk puddings.

SPICES

Allspice, cinnamon, cumin and *kırmızı biber* are the leading spices of the Turkish kitchen. As the route of the early spice trade from China and India first entered eastern and then central Anatolia, the food of these areas began to incorporate a much heavier and more varied use of spices compared with the more restrained flavours of Istanbul. This adoption of new spices in Anatolian cooking and, later, in that of Istanbul, along with the arrival of chilli peppers from the New World, led to a number of spices being labelled *yeni bahar*, 'new spice': this could refer to paprika in Istanbul, to allspice in Antalya, or to coriander in Van. The traditional Turkish kitchen is incensed with spicy, sensual aromas considered sexually stimulating as well as beneficial to the digestion. The smell and taste of spices are believed to induce the appetite and to heighten the pleasure of the food. Whenever possible, spices should be bought in their seed, bark or fruit form and crushed or ground freshly when needed. This way, they retain their flavours longer than do the commercial powder forms. For a stronger, pungent flavour some spices are roasted by dry stir-frying in a heavy-based pan over a high heat or by placing them on a tray in a hot oven.

ALLSPICE (YENİ BAHAR or DOLMA BAHAR) The ground or crushed aromatic berries are most often used in vegetable, rice and fish dishes. It is the main spice used in the cold stuffed vegetables, *yalancı dolma*, and for this reason it is sometimes referred to as *dolma bahar*, 'dolma spice'.

ANISEED (ANASON) The most important role of aniseed is in the flavouring of *rakı* (p. 36). Ground aniseed is also used in some vegetable and fish dishes, and is sometimes combined with nuts and dried fruits in sweet and savoury dishes.

CARDAMOM (KAKULE) Rarely used in Turkey. In parts of Anatolia it is sometimes used in sweet dishes or added to Turkish coffee to enhance the flavour, but that's about it. Where it is used to flavour sweets in Persian and Indian cooking, it is replaced by vanilla and rose-water in Turkish food.

CINNAMON (TARÇİN) One of the most playful and amenable spices in Turkish cooking. Regarded as a 'warming' spice, it enhances rice, vegetables, fish, lamb, chicken, tomato sauces, desserts and milk puddings.

CLOVES (KARANFİL) Crushed or whole, cloves are mainly used in meat casseroles, sweets, breads and pastries. Whole cloves are chewed to freshen the breath.

CORIANDER (KİŞNİŞ) The seeds, like the leaves, add a particular flavour to some fish and meat dishes of southern and eastern Anatolia. Although available in Istanbul, coriander seeds are rarely used in its cuisine.

CUMIN (KİMYON) A popular spice used in a variety of meat and fish dishes, and increasing in dominance as it travels south and east where it is also used in vegetable dishes and salads. The seeds are believed to aid digestion.

FENUGREEK (ÇEMEN OTU) Mainly found in its ground form in a few vegetable and fish dishes from southeast Anatolia, and the seeds are sometimes used to flavour bread. Its most important role is in *çemen*, the paste that encases *pastırma* (p. 26).

NIGELLA (ÇÖREOTU) A useful small black aromatic seed that looks as if it has been charcoaled, it is sometimes inaccurately referred to as black cumin. It is called *çöreotu* because it is sprinkled on the *çörek*, a sweet bun eaten during Şeker Bayramı, the Sweet Festival immediately after Ramazan. It is most often sprinkled over bread to give it a slightly peppery lift, but it can also be added in small quantities, finely ground or in seed form, to salads and plain vegetable dishes. In the Mediterranean region it is mixed with coriander seeds, cumin seeds and Turkish saffron to make a distinct spicy mix for fish dishes.

POPPY SEEDS (HAŞHAŞ) Sprinkled in the usual way over breads and rolls, poppy seeds are also used in meat and fish dishes. Roasted poppy seeds impart a subtle flavour to light sauces and yogurt dressings.

RED PEPPER (KIRMIZI BİBER) Sometimes sweet and mild, sometimes piquant and occasionally hot, *kırmızı biber* is the most useful spice of all. A type of chilli pepper originally from Mexico, it is roughly chopped and crushed into flakes or ground to a powder, *pul biber*, and ranges from a tomato colour to a deep red. There are several different types of *kırmızı biber* to choose from, varying in strength and oiliness. The best is crushed and rubbed with oil, which keeps it fresh and helps to impart the flavour immediately, without cooking. The oiled flakes can also be roasted in a heavy-based pan over a high heat or baked in the oven until almost black, which gives them an interesting kick and increases their strength. The uses and strength of *kırmızı biber* alter according to the regions, dominating the tastes of southeastern Anatolia – starting with the hot and spicy *Adana kebabı* (p. 153).

Kırmızı biber OILED AND ROASTED RED PEPPER

Large sacks of *kırmızı biber* lie bewitchingly stacked at markets, encouraging shoppers to taste and compare one sack with another until the right flavour and the right oiliness for each person or purpose are found. This is the easiest and most pleasurable way to buy any spice, but it is also sold in a mix of approximately 90 per cent hot chilli pepper crushed with 10 per cent sweet pepper. The very hot commercial red pepper is only sold finely ground. There is also a commercial *köfte* spice, ready-mixed and finely ground, which consists mainly of sweet red pepper, hot red pepper, black pepper, dried mint, dried oregano and ground cumin.

Delicious with yogurt and often mixed into melted butter as the final touch to a dish, *kırmızı biber* is a must for the Turkish kitchen. The same, or similar, dried red peppers sometimes found hanging in Italian and Middle Eastern stores can be crushed and oiled at home. Otherwise a difficult spice to match, it can be replaced with a personalised mix of sweet paprika and cayenne.

SAFFRON (SAFRON) Turkish saffron is an imitation saffron made from wild flowers in the southeast of Turkey. It looks similar, but doesn't have a great deal of flavour. It is mainly used for its colour in a few rice dishes and in hot yogurt soup. Real saffron, the delicate spice from crocus flowers, is used in special dishes such as *zerde* (p. 195) but it comes from India and Iran.

SESAME SEEDS (SESAM) Sesame seeds are pounded into a thick oily paste, *tahin*, which is used in sauces and fillings and is spread on bread when sweetened and lubricated with *pekmez* (p. 220). Sesame oil is produced in modest amounts, occasionally used in fish and vegetable dishes, but it is not a particular feature of Turkish cooking. The seeds are also sprinkled over *simit* (bread rings, p. 93) and the toasted seeds are added to a meat spice mixture of ground sumac and dried thyme.

SUMAC (SUMAK) A deep-red, slightly sour spice, *sumak* comes in berry form or ground. The berries, which grow wild all over Anatolia, can be soaked in water, then pressed to squeeze out the juice which is used as a marinade for fish and chicken. Ground *sumak* is sprinkled on salads, grilled meats, fish, soups and rice dishes to give them a tangy lift. An aromatic mixture of ground *sumak*, dried thyme and roasted sesame seeds is also used with grilled meat or quick-fried meat dishes.

SPICE MIXES

FISH SPICE nigella seeds, coriander seeds, cumin seeds, Turkish saffron

KÖFTE SPICE ground sweet red pepper, ground hot red pepper, ground black pepper, ground cumin, dried oregano, dried mint

MEAT SPICE (grilled and fried meats) ground *sumak*, roasted sesame seeds, dried thyme

SUNFLOWERS

Originally from the New World, giant sunflowers now grow all over Turkey. At harvest time carts laden with the freshly cut sunflower heads dot the countryside, and the flat spaces running beside the narrow country roads, normally reserved for tractors, horse-drawn carts and herded animals, are spread with the drying heads until the seeds are released from the pods. The seeds are then roasted and eaten as a snack which, like melon, marrow and pumpkin seeds, are particularly popular with children. The light sunflower oil made from the crushed and pressed seeds is used for cooking a variety of dishes in Istanbul, but in the rest of Turkey it is mainly used for deep-frying.

TOMATOES

The big round tomatoes and plum tomatoes have slipped into the cuisines of Turkey and the Mediterranean as if they had always been there. Another gem of the New World, they arrived in the seventeenth century in Istanbul, from where they spread across the Ottoman

Empire and along the Mediterranean. Tomatoes are now one of Turkey's biggest food exports – tinned whole or chopped, dried and pressed into a thick paste or purée, or transformed into tasty *keçup*, which is similar to, and can be replaced with, a commercial ketchup. Plump and juicy, tasting like tomatoes should and polished and piled up into pyramids in the markets, they are used endlessly in salads and sauces. When cooking with tomatoes it is best to substitute tinned chopped tomatoes if the only alternative is pale and tasteless ones.

VINE LEAVES

The fresh leaves are sold in the markets at harvest time, but they can be found all year round preserved in brine. Before being used, the fresh leaves need to be softened by being tossed into a pan of boiling water for a few seconds, then refreshed in cold water. The preserved leaves must be soaked in several changes of cold water for at least an hour to remove the salt. Harbouring an unusual malty flavour, vine leaves are wrapped around pieces of cheese, seafood, fish and chicken before baking or grilling. Fresh, preserved and poached leaves are also wrapped around small homemade cheeses to keep them moist. The packages of vine leaves stuffed with an aromatic rice, *yalancı yaprak dolması* (p. 75), are legendary.

YOGURT

Yogurt plays an important role in Turkish food, and the Turks are one of the world's largest consumers. It is an old, nourishing friend passed down from the ancient pastoral nomads of Central Asia. Rich in minerals and vitamins, it provides an easily digestible source of calcium and contains antibiotic properties. The standard set yogurt, called *sıvı tas* (p. 44), varies in consistency from place to place. It is blended with water to make the refreshing drink called *ayran* (p. 212) and forms the base of most yogurt sauces. By hanging *sıvı tas* in a piece of muslin and leaving it to drain overnight, you get *süzme* (p. 44), which is a thick, creamy yogurt that lends itself to savoury dips with garlic and herbs, and is delicious eaten on its own with a sprinkling of icing sugar (a speciality of Kanlıca on the Asian shore of the Bosphorus), a dusting of cinnamon, puréed fresh fruit, or with a dollop of rich honey.

YOGURT AND CHEESE

Yogurt and white cheese are used every day. If they do not figure in the preparation of a dish, the yogurt will certainly be drunk in *ayran* (p. 212) and the cheese will be eaten with black olives and jam or honey for breakfast. The origins of both can be traced back to the nomadic peoples of Central Asia, who would have made yogurt and cheese from the milk of their horses and sheep. Now both are made from the milk of cows, sheep or goats.

It is satisfying to make your own but you can buy thick-set yogurt in most supermarkets and, if you cannot find Turkish cheeses for the recipes in this book, you can replace *beyaz peynir* with feta, and *köy* and *lor peyniri* with ricotta.

Unless otherwise stated, all the recipes that include yogurt call for the use of *sıvı tas* (p. 41), which is like standard set yogurt.

Köy peyniri VILLAGE CHEESE

Sıvı tas
SET YOGURT

Use 1 heaped tablespoon of fresh live yogurt to 1 pint/600ml of milk (for creamy yogurt, use full-fat live yogurt and full-fat milk; for thick yogurt, add 1–2 tablespoons of powdered milk to the milk boiling in the pan).

✧ Bring the milk to the boil in a large pan. As it bubbles and froths, turn the heat down and leave it to simmer for 2–3 minutes. Turn off the heat and leave the milk to cool to a temperature that is bearable to your finger dipped in it for a count of 10. Beat the yogurt in a bowl and strain a little of the milk into it. Beat well and gradually strain the rest of the milk into the yogurt, beating all the time. Cover the bowl with cling film or a plate, wrap it in a blanket or thick towel and put it in a warm place for at least 6 hours (or overnight). Once it has fermented and thickened a little, put it into the fridge for a few hours to set.

Süzme
THICK CREAMY YOGURT

✧ To make *süzme* (see p. 41), line a colander with a piece of muslin or cheesecloth, pour the *sıvı tas* into the middle and quickly gather together the corners, then tie them to a rod suspended over a bowl or over the sink. Leave to drain for 5–6 hours (or overnight). The consistency should be like cream cheese.

A plain, hard white cheese can be made from the drained liquid of süzme. Boil the liquid for two minutes while boiling double the quantity of milk in a separate pan. Pour the liquid into the boiling milk, turn off the heat and let clumps of cheese form on the surface. Strain and drain as above. Sprinkle the cheese with salt before eating.

Köy peyniri
VILLAGE CHEESE

This is a recipe for the soft white cheese that is made every week in the villages of Anatolia.

The standard beyaz peynir, made in a similar way, is left to dry out before it is stored in salty water for six months to a year to mature. To determine the correct quantity of salt required, bring water to the boil in a pan, add salt, then crack a fresh egg into the water. If the egg sinks more salt is needed; if it floats, leave the liquid to cool before pouring it over the cheese in a container for storing. Then keep it in a cool place to absorb the salt, which also hardens the cheese.

If you have difficulty obtaining liquid rennet, it is just as easy to make this cheese by using the same quantity of lemon juice added to boiling milk to curdle it. This method is quicker, as you can strain the curdled milk immediately and leave it to drain overnight ready for breakfast.

MAKES APPROXIMATELY 12oz/350g OF KÖY PEYNİRİ

4 pints/2.4 litres milk

1 tablespoon salt (more if you like a salty cheese)

4 tablespoons essence of rennet

✧ Pour the milk into a deep saucepan and heat it gently without a lid on. Stir in the salt and rennet and continue to heat gently until the milk is hot to the finger. (Be careful not to boil it.)

✧ Turn off the heat, cover the pan with a cloth and leave it undisturbed for at least 6 hours (or overnight). In this time the milk will separate into curds and whey.

✧ After 6 or more hours place a sieve or colander over a sink or bowl, line the colander with a piece of muslin and pour the milk mixture into it. Leave it to drain for another 6 hours (or overnight). When the mixture has completely drained you should be left with a lump of soft creamy cheese, which is perfect for cooking and delicious to eat just as it is.

✧ Store the cheese in a cool place.

MEZE AND SALADS

Most Turkish meals begin with *meze*, which literally translates as 'a pleasant taste' and is probably derived from the Arabic word *mezaq*, which means 'the taste, the savour of a thing'. Designed to tickle the palate and soak up wine and spirits, *meze* became a custom indulged in, and perpetuated by, early travellers and traders. The conversion of the Turks to Islam in the eleventh century may have curbed the drinking of spirits amongst devout Muslims, but the *meze* tradition survived. It was later refined and taken to new heights by the Palace chefs of Istanbul, who were reputed to have produced at least two hundred different types. In Istanbul some of the best *meze* and salads can be found in the traditional *meyhane* restaurants (from the Persian *mey*, wine, and *hane*, house), which have recently been transformed from male drinking dens into atmospheric taverns specializing in Anatolian cooking.

Meze and salads, both designed to increase the appetite for the ensuing courses, often go hand in hand. In a Turkish home the *meze* dish may be eaten as a first course, and the salad may accompany the main dish of beans, fish, vegetables or meat. In a restaurant, small portions of a wide selection of habit-forming dishes, presented on a large tray, are served as the starter to the meal. This may include an infinite variety of *ezme*, which consists of any vegetable mashed to a pulp and mixed with garlic and yogurt; *zeytin salatası*, finely sliced black and green olives tossed in lemon juice and fresh mint; *kızarmış peynir*, cubes of white cheese rubbed in olive oil and dried oregano, and then grilled until brown and buckled; *lekerda*, thin slices of smoked tuna; *çiroz*, dried, salted fillets of mackerel; *ahtapot salatası*, a salad of charcoal-grilled octopus marinaded in olive oil, lemon juice and fresh dill; cubes of *beyaz peynir* soaked in olive oil and sprinkled with dried oregano and *kırmızı biber* (p. 38); or simply refreshing strips of peeled cucumber sprinkled with salt to bring out the taste.

The key to eating *meze* and salads is in the understanding of their flexibility, which is most easily controlled by the quantity served. They can be presented as nibbles with a drink, as a first course, as a light lunch, or as a tantalizing buffet spread. Easy to prepare, perfect with a bottle of wine, beer or *rakı* (p. 36) and in the company of good friends, *meze* could become fashionable on Western tables.

Semiz otu salatası and *sigara böreği* LAMB'S LETTUCE SALAD AND CHEESE PASTRIES

Kavun ve peynir
MELON AND CHEESE

A popular summer snack or nibble, delicious with wine, rakı or cocktails. Use a ripe honey-dew or galia melon and, if you cannot find beyaz peynir (p. 219), replace with a moist feta. Cut both the melon and the cheese into bite-size cubes and place them side by side on a plate. Using a fork or small sticks, pick up a piece of melon with a piece of cheese and enjoy the refreshing flavours.

Patlıcan ezmesi
SMOKED AUBERGINE WITH YOGURT

Simple to make and soothing to taste, this is the ultimate quick fix of aubergine and garlic. To make it properly, it is essential to burn the aubergine over charcoal or directly over the flame of a gas cooker. The flesh is then chopped to a pulp and mixed with apple vinegar or lemon, olive oil, garlic and yogurt. Sometimes chopped tomato, parsley, dill, chopped or ground walnuts, or tahin (p. 221) are added. But to get the full benefit of the smoked aubergine, there is this simple way:

SERVES 2–4

2 large aubergines
3 cloves garlic, crushed with salt
juice of ½ lemon
1 tablespoon olive oil
2 tablespoons thick yogurt
salt and freshly ground black pepper

✧ Place the aubergines directly over the charcoal grill or gas flame, using the stems to turn them from time to time. The grilled aubergines are ready when they become soft and squishy, sometimes oozing a little juice. If you are using a gas flame, they are ready when the skin becomes burnt and flaky.

✧ Move the aubergines to a wooden board and slit them open lengthways, using a sharp knife.

✧ Carefully scoop out the hot flesh, removing any flecks of burnt skin, and put the flesh into a bowl.

✧ Use a fork to mix in the olive oil, lemon juice and garlic and bind with the yogurt.

✧ Season it to your taste, and serve while still warm with fresh bread.

Havuç ezmesi
CARROT PURÉE WITH YOGURT

A Turkish carrot can be as long as a flute and as sweet as honey. Used in many meat and vegetable dishes, they are particularly pleasant as meze. This can vary from a simple arrangement of long strips of carrot, dressed in salt and lemon juice, sprouting out of a jug like a vase of rigid flowers, to slices of carrot deep-fried and served warm with cool garlic-flavoured yogurt. Variations of havuç ezmesi, like the one from Istanbul using beyaz peynir (p. 219) and chopped parsley, can be found all over Turkey. This refreshing version is from the Marmaris region.

Patlıcan ezmesi SMOKED AUBERGINE WITH YOGURT

<u>*SERVES 4*</u>

4 large carrots, peeled and sliced

1 teaspoon caraway seeds

1 tablespoon olive oil

2 tablespoons lemon juice

salt and freshly ground black pepper

<u>*FOR THE SAUCE*</u>

4 tablespoons thick yogurt

1 tablespoon lemon juice

3 cloves garlic, crushed with salt

1 tablespoon fresh mint and dill, chopped

salt

✧   Steam the carrots until soft.

✧   Prepare the sauce. In a small bowl mix the yogurt with the lemon juice, garlic and herbs. Add a little salt to taste.

✧   In a bowl mash the cooked carrots with a fork and add the lemon juice, olive oil and caraway seeds (or blend together in an electric mixer). Season to taste.

✧   Spoon the carrot mixture on to a serving dish and make a well in the centre. Spoon the yogurt sauce into the well and serve immediately with bread, while the carrots are still slightly warm.

Havuç ezmesi CARROT PURÉE WITH YOGURT

Kısır BULGUR PATTIES

- ❖ Drain the *bulgur*, squeeze it dry and add the chopped ingredients, tomato purée and olive oil. Knead the mixture with your hands and season it to your taste. Leave it to sit until you are ready to use it.

- ❖ Take a small amount of the mixture into your hands and press it into a bite-size ball, indent it in the middle with a finger and place it on a small lettuce leaf. Serve with wedges of lemon – squeeze the juice into the indentation and eat the *kısır* in the lettuce leaf.

Kısır
BULGUR PATTIES

A speciality from the southeast of Turkey, kısır *can be served as a salad, particularly good with grilled meats or moulded into balls, and served nestling in small lettuce leaves and eaten with your fingers. It is regarded as a welcoming dish in the homes of Antakya and Gaziantep, where it is made with pomegranate juice instead of lemon.*

SERVES 4–6
3oz/90g *bulgur* (p. 219), soaked in boiling water for one hour
4–5 spring onions, finely chopped
4 cloves garlic, finely chopped
1 green chilli pepper, finely chopped
2 tablespoons tomato purée
1–2 tablespoons olive oil
2 tablespoons fresh parsley, chopped
3 tablespoons fresh mint, chopped
salt and freshly ground black pepper
Approximately 12 small lettuce leaves

Yoğurtlu patlıcan
FRIED AUBERGINE WITH YOGURT

A deliciously simple and soothing dish. A similar one can be made with fried courgettes or fried carrots. Sometimes all three are fried in an egg batter first, and they can be cut into any shapes or sizes. Anywhere you go in Turkey you are likely to come across some variation of this dish. A swirl of tomato keçup *(see p. 41) in the yogurt sauce sweetens and distinguishes the Bozburun version.*

SERVES 2–3
2 big aubergines
sunflower oil for frying
FOR THE SAUCE
½ pint/300ml thick creamy yogurt
6 cloves garlic, crushed with salt
1 tablespoon lemon juice (or more, to taste)
salt and freshly ground black pepper

- ❖ Partially peel the aubergines in zebra stripes (see p. 25), cut them in half lengthways, then slice each half into half-moon shapes. Soak them in a bowl of salted water for an hour. Using your hands, squeeze them dry as you would when wringing socks.

✧ Heat the sunflower oil in a frying pan and fry the aubergines until golden-brown. Drain on absorbent paper, then lay them on a serving dish.

✧ Make the sauce. Mix the yogurt with the lemon juice and garlic, add salt to taste and spoon it over the aubergines while still slightly warm, or when cold. Serve with bread.

Semiz otu salatası LAMB'S LETTUCE SALAD

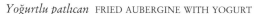

Yoğurtlu patlıcan FRIED AUBERGINE WITH YOGURT

Semiz otu salatası
LAMB'S LETTUCE SALAD

In Turkey this salad is made with thick, meaty lamb's lettuce leaves, but it also works well with smaller thin leaves. Gather together enough small heads of lamb's lettuce to fill your salad bowl and toss them in a little olive oil and lemon juice, seasoned with salt and freshly ground black pepper. Mix 2–3 tablespoons of thick yogurt with 2 cloves of crushed garlic, and add to the bowl. Toss well and serve.

Anadolu patlıcan
BAKED AUBERGINES WITH MINT YOGURT

A simple dish from central and eastern Anatolia. The aubergines are halved and put into the still-hot ovens, once all the bread has been baked. The warm, softened halves are then filled with a cool mint-flavoured yogurt and eaten like a melon with a spoon. It is delicious and refreshing with any shape or size of aubergine, but the tiny thin ones work particularly well as meze.

SERVES 4

4 small aubergines

4 tablespoons thick creamy yogurt

2 tablespoons lemon or pomegranate juice

2–3 cloves garlic, crushed with salt

small bunch of fresh mint, roughly chopped

salt and freshly ground black pepper

✦ Preheat oven to 400F/Mark 6/200C

✦ Wash the aubergines and place them in the oven on a baking tray for 15 minutes. Take them out and slit them lengthways, still attached at the bottom so that they open out like wings (if using 2 large aubergines, separate the halves – one is enough per person). Lay the aubergine wings on their backs and bake in the oven for a further 20–25 minutes, or until the flesh is soft enough to press in the middle to form a dip.

✦ Mix the yogurt with the lemon juice, garlic and mint and adjust the salt. While the aubergines are still hot, slit the toughened surface of each half with a knife and press the flesh down with your fingers until it resembles a hollowed-out boat. Fill the hollows with the yogurt mixture and eat with a spoon, scooping up the hot flesh with the cool yogurt until only an empty aubergine skin remains.

Kızarmış biber
GRILLED PEPPERS WITH YOGURT

If you can, use the long, perfumed and slightly piquant pale-green çarliston *peppers for this dish. It also works well with the sweeter bell peppers, cut into halves or quarters.*

SERVES 2–3

12 çarliston peppers, or 2 sweet bell peppers

4 tablespoons thick creamy yogurt

2 tablespoons lemon juice

3–4 cloves garlic, crushed with salt

salt and freshly ground black pepper

✦ Grill the peppers until soft and buckled. Mix the yogurt with the lemon juice and garlic. Season to taste and spoon the cool yogurt mixture over the warm peppers. Eat while still warm.

Kızarmış biber GRILLED PEPPERS WITH YOGURT

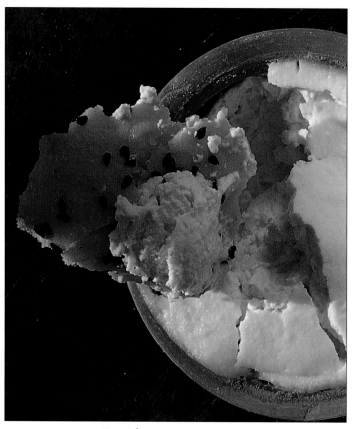

Peynirli güveç BAKED CHEESE

Peynirli güveç
BAKED CHEESE

Earthenware pots filled with a soft, creamy cheese are baked in a hot oven (400F/Mark 6/200C), to lightly brown on top. The hot, spongy cheese is then scooped up in clumps using pide (p. 94), and often eaten with piquant pickled çarliston peppers. This dish can be varied by adding roasted spices, fresh herbs or chopped nuts to the cheese before baking. Any left-over cheese from this dish is often spread on gözleme (p. 96) or rolled in breadcrumbs and deep-fried. Lor or köy peyniri work best, but ricotta is a reasonable substitute.

Humus
CHICKPEA PURÉE

Spiked with cumin and garlic, the Turkish humus is slightly lighter than some of the Middle Eastern versions, which often add tahin *(p. 221) to the purée.*

SERVES 4–6

5oz/150g chickpeas, soaked in water for at least 6 hours, drained

4–6 tablespoons olive oil

juice of 1 lemon

4–5 cloves garlic, crushed with salt

1 teaspoon cumin seeds, crushed

1–2 tablespoons thick yogurt

salt and freshly ground black pepper

TO GARNISH

1 tablespoon olive oil

½ teaspoon *kırmızı biber* (p. 219)

✦ Cook the chickpeas in fresh water until soft. While they are still warm, pound them in a solid bowl with the garlic, cumin, olive oil and lemon juice (or whizz them all together in an electric mixer). Adapt the flavour to your taste by adding more olive oil or lemon juice. Bind with the yogurt and season to taste.

✦ Spoon the *humus* into a bowl, then moisten the surface with a little olive oil. Sprinkle *kırmızı biber* over the top and eat with warm fresh bread or *pide* (p. 94).

Sıcak humus HOT CHICKPEA PURÉE WITH PINE NUTS and *humus* CHICKPEA PURÉE with *pide*

Sıcak humus
HOT CHICKPEA PURÉE WITH PINE NUTS

From central and eastern Anatolia comes this delectable thick humus *that is baked in the oven and served hot. It is filling, nourishing and soothing.*

SERVES 3–4
4oz/120g chickpeas

3 tablespoons *tahin* (p. 221)

4 cloves garlic, crushed with salt

4–5 tablespoons olive oil

juice of 1 lemon

1 teaspoon cumin seeds

salt and freshly ground black pepper

1–2 tablespoons butter

1 tablespoon pine nuts

½ teaspoon *kırmızı biber* (p. 219)

✦ Preheat oven to 400F/Mark 6/200C

✦ Soak and cook the chickpeas as for *humus*. Then pound them with the *tahin*, garlic, cumin, olive oil and lemon juice (or whizz them all together in an electric mixer). Season to taste.

✦ Spoon the mixture into an earthenware pot. Melt the butter in a pan, stir in the pine nuts and *kırmızı biber*, and pour it over the *humus*. Bake it in the oven for about 20 minutes to let it soak up the butter, and serve hot with *pide* (p. 94).

Acı domates ezmesi
CHILLI TOMATO PASTE

This dish can be made with fresh tomatoes chopped to a pulp, or with concentrated tomato purée. Made with tomato purée, it is eaten as a snack on bread in the Anatolian villages. It also goes well with grilled meat.

SERVES 4

3 tablespoons concentrated tomato purée
1 tablespoon olive oil
1 onion, roughly chopped
1–2 hot green chilli peppers, finely chopped
3 cloves garlic, roughly chopped
juice of ½ lemon
rind of ½ lemon, finely chopped
big bunch of parsley (leaves and stalks), roughly chopped
salt and freshly ground black pepper

✧ Mix the tomato purée with the olive oil until smooth. Beat in the onion, garlic, chilli, lemon juice and rind and season to taste. Keep back a little parsley, and stir in the rest. Spoon the mixture on to a plate and garnish with the reserved parsley.

Acı domates ezmesi CHILLI TOMATO PASTE

Haydari MINT YOGURT DIP and
güneşli yoğurt APRICOT YOGURT DIP

Güneşli yoğurt
APRICOT YOGURT DIP

Another delightful dip, brightly speckled with dried apricots, served on its own with bread or as part of a selection of meze. Beat 3–4 tablespoons of süzme (p. 221) with 4–5 chopped dried apricots, 2 cloves of crushed garlic and salt to taste. Mix well, and eat fairly soon after making it as the apricots soon begin to absorb the moisture from the yogurt.

Sarmısaklı mantar
SPICY GARLIC MUSHROOMS

In this tasty dish from central Anatolia the mushrooms are caramelised in the sweetness of their own juice and spiked with garlic, coriander and allspice. The cooked mushrooms are then tossed in whatever pungent fresh herbs are available, usually a mixture of wild oregano, parsley and mint. It is a recipe used for both cultivated and wild mushrooms, but works best with the small round ones.

SERVES 2–3

8oz/225g mushrooms, cleaned and left whole
4 cloves garlic, finely chopped
2 tablespoons olive oil and a little butter
1 teaspoon allspice berries, crushed
1 teaspoon coriander seeds, crushed
pinch of grated nutmeg
salt and freshly ground black pepper
fresh oregano, marjoram, mint, basil or parsley, chopped

Haydari
MINT YOGURT DIP

Thick and creamy, haydari is served on its own with bread to dip in it, or as part of a meze spread. It can be made with strongly flavoured fresh or dried mint, but not spearmint, and it must be made with süzme (p. 221) or a similar thick strained yogurt. Mix 3–4 tablespoons of süzme with 2–3 cloves of crushed garlic, a small bunch of chopped fresh mint (or 1–2 teaspoons dried mint), and salt to taste.

Sarmısaklı mantar SPICY GARLIC MUSHROOMS

✧ Put the mushrooms into a saucepan with the garlic, spices, olive oil and butter. Cook with the lid on over a high heat for about 10 minutes, shaking the pan occasionally, allowing the liquid to froth up. Once the mushrooms begin to caramelize, remove the lid and cook for a further 4–5 minutes until some of the liquid has evaporated. Season to taste.

✧ Spoon the mushrooms into a bowl and toss in a blend of fresh herbs. Serve hot or cold with wedges of lemon.

Anadolu ispanak ezmesi
SPINACH WITH YOGURT AND PINE NUTS

Another dish of which there are endless variations. In Istanbul, Izmir and other parts of western Turkey, chopped spinach is gently softened in butter with chopped onions and then mixed with garlic-flavoured yogurt. Southeast of Ankara you might be lucky to chance upon this version, which is best served warm topped with a cool yogurt dressing.

Anadolu ispanak ezmesi
SPINACH WITH YOGURT AND PINE NUTS with *pide*

<u>*SERVES 2–3*</u>

8oz/225g spinach, washed and steamed

1 small red onion, finely chopped

½ teaspoon sugar

½ teaspoon cumin seeds, crushed

1 tablespoon olive oil

1 teaspoon currants, chopped

1 tablespoon pine nuts

½ teaspoon *kırmızı biber* (p. 219)

salt and freshly ground black pepper

<u>*FOR THE DRESSING*</u>

2 tablespoons thick creamy yogurt

squeeze of lemon juice

2 cloves garlic, crushed with salt

salt

✧ To make the dressing, mix the yogurt with the garlic and lemon juice. Add a little salt to taste and put aside.

✧ Chop the cooked spinach to a pulp. In a small shallow pan soften the onion with the sugar and cumin seeds in the oil. Stir in the currants, pine nuts and *kırmızı biber*. Cook for 2 minutes and then add the spinach. Mix well, season to taste, and cook for 2–3 minutes.

✧ Transfer the spinach to a serving dish. Spoon the yogurt over it and serve with *pide* (p. 94) while the spinach is still warm.

Çılbır
POACHED EGGS WITH YOGURT

This may not sound appealing, but it is surprisingly tasty. The eggs can be poached or fried, served hot with runny yolks, and smothered in garlic-flavoured yogurt. An excellent snack, light lunch or supper.

<u>*SERVES 2*</u>

4 eggs, poached or fried

3 tablespoons thick creamy yogurt

2–3 cloves garlic, crushed with salt

salt and freshly ground black pepper

½ tablespoon butter

½ teaspoon *kırmızı biber* (p. 219)

a few dried sage leaves, crumbled

✧ Mix the yogurt with the garlic and season to taste. Melt the butter with the *kırmızı biber*. Place the hot, freshly poached or fried eggs on a plate. Spoon the yogurt mixture over them and trickle the hot melted butter over the top. Sprinkle with the dried sage leaves and eat while the eggs are still hot.

Çılbır POACHED EGGS WITH YOGURT

Yaprak sarması

CHEESE IN VINE LEAVES

The malty, sour taste of vine leaves lends itself to many dishes (see p. 41 for how to prepare). Here cubes of beyaz peynir (p. 219) or feta are simply wrapped up in vine leaves, threaded on to kebab skewers and grilled over hot charcoal. The crispy-coated vine leaves and melted cheese are then immediately eaten with lemon squeezed over them.

Midye tavası

MUSSELS IN BEER BATTER

A speciality of Istanbul and Izmir, the freshly caught mussels are dipped in a batter made with beer, deep-fried, then served with a garlicky bread-and-walnut sauce, tarator. Hazelnuts and pine nuts can be used instead of walnuts, or the nuts can be completely omitted from the sauce. The smell of fried mussels and garlic wafts along the Bosphorus and the Golden Horn as they sizzle on the boats and in the streets, where they are often skewered on sticks and fried in deep curved pans.

Midye tavası MUSSELS IN BEER BATTER

Equally delicious are the strips of squid, kalamar, *deep-fried in a plain or beer batter, and served with a* tarator *sauce. To soften the squid and draw out its taste, it is first rubbed with lemon juice, sprinkled with a little sugar and bicarbonate of soda, and chilled in the refrigerator for one hour. It must then be well rinsed and drained before being coated in batter and fried.*

Small quantities of midye tavası *and* kalamar tavası *are usually served as hot* meze *in restaurants, but large quantities can be cooked up as a main dish at home.*

<u>*Serves 4–5*</u>
about 40–50 fresh mussels, shelled
sunflower oil for deep frying
<u>*For the batter*</u>
4oz/120g plain flour
½ teaspoon bicarbonate of soda
1 teaspoon salt
2 egg yolks
6–8fl oz /175–250ml beer or lager
<u>*For the sauce*</u>
3oz/90g walnuts
2 slices stale bread, soaked in water
4 cloves garlic, crushed with salt
2 tablespoons white wine vinegar or lemon juice
3–4 tablespoons olive oil
salt and freshly ground black pepper

✧ Rinse the mussels and keep in a bowl of cold water.

✧ To prepare the sauce, pound the walnuts in a mortar. Squeeze the excess water from the bread and add it to the pounded nuts with the crushed garlic. (Or combine the ingredients in an electric mixer.) Slowly add the olive oil and vinegar and beat the mixture to a smooth paste with a little water. Season to taste.

✧ Make the batter. Sift the flour, salt and bicarbonate of soda into a bowl. Make a well and drop in the egg yolks. Gradually pour in the beer, using a wooden spoon to draw in the flour from the sides. Beat until it is thick and smooth.

✧ In a shallow or curved pan, heat enough sunflower oil to deep-fry. Dip each mussel into the batter and drop into the oil. Fry until golden-brown. Serve immediately with the *tarator* sauce.

Kereviz salatası
CELERY AND COCONUT SALAD

This juicy salad originates from the eastern Turkish Mediterranean coast, the home of a number of refreshing fruity salads, devised to calm the palate after the local

Kereviz salatası CELERY AND COCONUT SALAD

spicy food. This one is best made with fresh coconut, but you can substitute desiccated coconut, soaked in water for 30 minutes, drained and squeezed dry.

SERVES 2–3

6–8 firm fresh celery stalks, grated (reserve the leaves for garnish)

4–5 tablespoons freshly grated coconut

FOR THE DRESSING

2 tablespoons thick creamy yogurt

2 cloves garlic, crushed with salt

juice of ¹/₂ lemon

salt and freshly ground black pepper

TO GARNISH

fresh celery and mint leaves

✧ Mix the yogurt with the lemon juice and garlic in a bowl. Add salt to taste. Place the grated celery and coconut in a bowl and pour over the dressing. Toss well and garnish with the celery and mint leaves. Leave to stand a little to let the juices weep and mingle (but if left too long it becomes watery).

Sigara böreği
CHEESE PASTRIES

Large batches of these crispy cigar-shaped pastries are made in every household, as they are so popular. They can be made in advance, stored in a cool place, covered with a damp cloth and fried at the last minute. Made with strips of yufka *(p. 97) filled with cheese, spinach or minced meat, the pastries can also be shaped into triangles (*muska böreği*). See* ıspanaklı gözleme *(p. 96)*

and tepsi böreği *(p. 98) for the spinach and meat fillings. If necessary, substitute* yufka *with filo pastry, which often comes in rectangular sheets. Cut the sheets lengthways into strips at approximately 3in/8cm intervals, and proceed with the recipe.*

Sigara böreği CHEESE PASTRIES

MAKES 30

4 sheets *yufka* (8–10 sheets homemade *yufka*)

4 eggs

1lb/450g *köy peyniri, beyaz peynir* (p. 219) or feta

large bunch of fresh mint, parsley and dill, chopped

sunflower oil for frying

✧ Put the cheese in a bowl with the eggs and the herbs. Mash with a fork and mix to a moist paste.

✧ Lay the rounds of *yufka* on a flat surface, fold them in half, then roll each one into a long, loose cigar. Cut across the cigar at approximately 3in/8cm intervals and unwrap each piece into a long strip.

✧ Take one strip and spoon a little of the cheese mixture on to the end nearest to you. Fold the corners over the mixture to seal it and then roll away from you into a tight cigar. As you reach the end of the strip, dip the end into a cup of cold water and then continue to roll up – this prevents the cigar from unravelling. Always keep the *yufka* moist under a damp cloth while preparing the *böreği*.

✧ Heat enough sunflower oil for deep-frying in a shallow pan. Fry the *böreği* over a medium heat until golden-brown. Serve warm.

Yalancı ıspanak köftesi

SPINACH BALLS WITH YOGURT

A yalancı *dish, literally a 'deceptive' or 'false' dish, is usually a simplified or mock version of a well known one. This* yalancı ıspanak köftesi, *a simple dish of* cooked spinach rolled into balls and served with garlic-flavoured yogurt, acts as an impostor to the more labour-intensive* köfte, *which consist of mashed ingredients, kneaded and moulded into a variety of shapes which are then usually fried or grilled.*

SERVES 4–5

1lb/450g fresh spinach leaves, cleaned and steamed

4 tablespoons thick yogurt

2–3 cloves garlic, crushed with salt

small bunch of fresh dill, chopped

salt and freshly ground black pepper

✧ Drain the steamed spinach well. Pull off small clumps and roll into bite-size balls in the palm of your hand.

✧ Beat the yogurt with the garlic and most of the dill to a smooth, thick consistency. Season to taste.

✧ Place the spinach balls on a plate, spoon the yogurt over them, and sprinkle with the remaining dill.

Nazuktan

AUBERGINE PURÉE WITH MINT AND ALMONDS

From central Anatolia, nazuktan *is a sweet and sour, crunchy dish made from the soft, smoky pulp of charcoal-grilled aubergines, toasted almonds, pekmez (p. 220) and fresh mint. It is delicious served on its own with bread or as part of a meze spread.*

Nazuktan AUBERGINE PURÉE WITH MINT AND ALMONDS

<u>SERVES 2–3</u>
2 aubergines
3 tablespoons thick creamy yogurt
juice of ½ lemon
2–3 cloves garlic, crushed with salt
1 tablespoon *pekmez*
2–3 tablespoons toasted almonds, roughly chopped
small bunch of fresh mint, roughly chopped
salt and freshly ground black pepper
<u>TO GARNISH</u>
a few whole toasted almonds
fresh mint leaves

✧ Place the whole aubergines over a charcoal grill or hold them directly over a high gas flame, turning them until they become very soft. Then slit them open and scoop out the flesh, or place them under a running cold tap and remove the skin. (If you use the tap method, squeeze the flesh dry.)

✧ Chop the flesh to a pulp and put in a bowl. Add the other ingredients and mix well. Season to taste.

Garnish with the almonds and a few mint leaves, and serve while still warm if possible. (Of course, the tap method cools the flesh.)

Şakşuka
FRIED VEGETABLES IN YOGURT

Şakşuka is a dish that has its variants all over Turkey. Along the Aegean and Mediterranean coasts, deep-fried courgettes and aubergines are bound together in a thick, garlicky, yogurt sauce; in Cappadocia, deep-fried aubergines, potatoes and peppers are served with plain yogurt; and in Van, the vegetables are fried with tomato and served hot with yogurt. Deep-fried cauliflower, carrots and pumpkin are also delicious served with a garlicky yogurt sauce. This version is from Bodrum.

<u>SERVES 3–4</u>
2 aubergines, partially peeled in zebra stripes (see p. 25), cut into quarters lengthways and sliced
1 courgette, cut in half lengthways and sliced
sunflower oil for deep-frying
1 red bell pepper, cut into bite-size pieces
1 tomato (optional)
3–4 tablespoons *süzme* (p. 221) (thick strained yogurt)
3–4 cloves garlic, crushed with salt
salt and freshly ground black pepper

✧ Soak the aubergine and courgette slices in salted water for one hour. Drain and squeeze out the excess water.

✧ Heat the oil in a shallow pan and fry the aubergine, courgette and red pepper until golden. Drain on kitchen paper. Grill the tomato, remove the skin, and chop roughly.

✦ Beat the yogurt with the garlic and season to taste. Put the aubergine, courgette and pepper in a bowl and fold in the tomato and yogurt mixture. Serve with *pide* (p. 94) or fresh bread.

Tahinli domates salatası
TOMATO SALAD WITH TAHIN

A delicious salad of fresh ripe tomatoes and spring onions in a piquant dressing. The same dressing is used for a variety of salads using fresh and steamed vegetables such as cucumbers, cauliflowers, celery, potatoes, celery root, Jerusalem artichokes, courgettes and carrots.

SERVES 3–4
4 large ripe tomatoes, skinned, halved and sliced
6 spring onions, roughly chopped
FOR THE DRESSING
2 tablespoons *tahin* (p. 221)
2–4 tablespoons water
juice of ½ lemon
2 cloves garlic, crushed with salt
½ teaspoon cumin seeds, crushed
salt and freshly ground black pepper

✦ Lay the tomato slices on a plate with the spring onions on top. Bind together the ingredients for the dressing until smooth and of pouring consistency. Season to taste, then pour it over the tomatoes and onions and serve.

Çingene pilavı
GYPSY SALAD

Literally translated as 'gypsy pilaf', this salad combines raw vegetables with grated beyaz peynir *(p. 219) instead of rice.*

SERVES 3–4
2 red onions, roughly sliced
6oz/175g *beyaz peynir* or feta cheese, grated
2 long green peppers or 1 bell pepper, roughly sliced
2 tomatoes, skinned and roughly chopped
2–3 cloves garlic, roughly chopped
1 green chilli pepper, roughly chopped
small bunch of parsley, roughly chopped
1 scant teaspoon *kırmızı biber* (p. 219)
2 tablespoons olive oil
salt and freshly ground black pepper

✦ Sprinkle the onions with a little salt to draw out the juices. Add the grated cheese and mix well. Add the other ingredients and toss in the olive oil. Season to taste.

Kıbrıs salatası
GRILLED PEPPER AND FRESH PEACH SALAD

This refreshing salad is often made in the hot summers of southern Turkey and Northern Cyprus.

SERVES 2–3
2 green or 2 red bell peppers
2 large ripe fresh peaches, skinned and stoned

FOR THE DRESSING

2 tablespoons olive oil

2 tablespoons lemon or pomegranate juice

a few mint and dill leaves, chopped

salt and freshly ground black pepper, or a sprinkling of roasted *kırmızı biber* (p. 219)

✧ Grill the peppers over charcoal, directly over a gas flame, or under a conventional grill. Place them in a plastic bag to sweat for 2 minutes, then peel off the skin under a running cold tap. Halve the peppers, remove the stem, seeds and pith, and cut into thick slices. Cut the peaches into similar-sized slices and add them to the peppers. Mix the dressing, season it to taste, and pour over the peppers and peaches. Toss and serve.

Pancar salatası
BEETROOT SALAD WITH YOGURT

For this pretty salad, the beetroot can be grated or chopped finely and folded into the yogurt dressing, or sliced and served with it.

SERVES 3–4

4 whole beetroot, cooked, peeled and sliced

FOR THE MARINADE

2 tablespoons olive oil

1 tablespoon white wine or apple vinegar

1 teaspoon sugar

salt and freshly ground black pepper

FOR THE DRESSING

3–4 tablespoons thick creamy yogurt

2–3 cloves garlic, crushed with salt

salt and freshly ground black pepper

Pancar salatası BEETROOT SALAD WITH YOGURT

✧ To make the marinade, mix together the oil, vinegar and sugar, season with salt and pepper, and pour over the slices of beetroot while still warm. Leave to stand for 2–3 hours.

✧ Lift the beetroot slices out of the marinade (you can add some of this marinade to the yogurt dressing if you like) and arrange on a plate. Beat the yogurt with the garlic, season to taste, and spoon over the slices of beetroot or toss them in it. As the salad sits, the colours will mingle into a pretty shade of purple.

Yalova ezmesi
AUBERGINE WITH CHILLI IN YOGURT

A highly flavoured dish of aubergines softened in olive oil, then mixed with yogurt, garlic, chilli peppers and herbs. It is from Yalova on the Marmara Sea, where it is often made with strong chillies.

Serves 4

1 large aubergine, completely peeled, halved lengthways and
finely sliced
4–5 tablespoons olive oil
2–4 cloves garlic, crushed with salt
juice of ½ lemon
4 spring onions, finely sliced
2 fresh green chilli peppers, finely sliced
large bunch of parsley and dill, chopped
3 tablespoons thick creamy yogurt
salt and freshly ground black pepper

✧ Soak the slices of aubergine in salted water for an hour. Drain well and squeeze out the excess water.

✧ Heat the oil in a shallow pan – enough to cover the base. Lay the aubergine slices in the oil, cover with a lid, and cook gently until softened but not browned. Remove the soft slices from the oil and put them in a bowl. Reserve the oil.

✧ Using a fork, mash the aubergine with the garlic and lemon juice. Add the onions, chilli peppers and herbs. Bind with 2 tablespoons of the warm oil and beat in the yogurt. Moisten with a little more of the oil to taste, and season with salt and pepper. *Yalova ezmesi* should taste of the olive oil. Serve while still warm with bread.

Çoban salatası
SHEPHERDS' SALAD

A salad made from ingredients available in every Turkish home or garden. It contains lots of flat-leaf parsley – the only sort to be found in Turkey – and can be served with practically everything.

Serves 2–3

1 small cucumber, peeled, halved lengthways and chopped
1 big red onion, halved and sliced
2 big tomatoes, skinned and chopped
2 hot green peppers or 1 green chilli, finely sliced
3–4 cloves garlic, roughly chopped
big bunch of fresh parsley, roughly chopped
2 tablespoons olive oil
2 tablespoons lemon juice
salt and freshly ground black pepper

✧ If the cucumber is bitter, sprinkle with a little salt and leave to stand for 5 minutes. Rinse well and drain. Mix the first six ingredients in a bowl, toss in the olive oil and lemon juice and season with the salt and pepper.

Çoban salatası SHEPHERDS' SALAD

Tarama
GARLICKY FISH ROE PURÉE

*A dish from the common Turkish–Greek culinary pool,
tarama is best made fresh using the sticky smoked roe of
grey mullet. Cod's roe works as a good alternative. It is
delicious served with strips of cucumber sprinkled with
salt or chunks of beyaz peynir (p. 219) rubbed in olive oil
and dried oregano and grilled.*

SERVES 4–5

6oz/175g smoked fish roe, skinned
3 slices stale bread, crusts removed
3–4fl oz/100–125ml milk or water
4 cloves garlic, crushed with salt
6–8 tablespoons olive oil
juice of 1–2 lemons
salt and freshly ground black pepper

✧ Soak the bread in the milk or water. Pound the fish
roe to reduce the gritty texture. Squeeze the bread
dry and add to the roe with the garlic. Pound
together to a smooth paste (or blend in an electric
mixer). Gradually beat in the oil and lemon juice,
adding more or less to personal taste, and season with
the salt and pepper. Work the mixture into a pale
creamy paste. Serve with warm or toasted bread.

Portakal salatası
ORANGE AND ONION SALAD

*A piquant salad from Mersin and Antalya on the
Mediterranean. As is so often the case with food from
warm regions, this refreshing salad is delicious when
the sun-ripened oranges are sweet and juicy and the
strong red onions are subtly nippy.*

SERVES 4

3 oranges, peeled and sliced, pith removed
2 red onions, finely sliced
3 cloves garlic, finely sliced
3 tablespoons black olives, stoned
handful of fresh mint and oregano leaves, chopped
FOR THE DRESSING
3 tablespoons olive oil
1 tablespoon lemon juice
½ teaspoon roasted cumin seeds (p. 38), crushed
½ teaspoon roasted *kırmızı biber* (p. 219)
salt

✧ Arrange the orange, onion and garlic slices on a
plate or in a bowl, with the olives and fresh herbs.
Mix together the ingredients for the dressing, add
salt to taste, and pour over the salad. Toss well
and serve.

Hamsi sarması
FRESH ANCHOVIES IN VINE LEAVES

*Small and medium-sized fish are often wrapped in vine
leaves and then poached or grilled. Anchovies and small
red mullet are particularly tasty this way. Sprats or small
sardines could be used instead of anchovies.*

Hamsi sarması FRESH ANCHOVIES IN VINE LEAVES

SERVES 4–6

25–30 fresh or preserved vine leaves, washed and
prepared (see p. 41)

20–30 fresh anchovies, washed and gutted

POACHING LIQUID

2 tablespoons olive oil

juice of 1 lemon

2 cloves garlic, crushed with salt

salt and freshly ground black pepper

TO ACCOMPANY

salt, *sumak* or lemon juice

✧ Wrap the anchovies in the vine leaves, leaving the
heads peeping out. Pack them tightly in the base of a
wide saucepan. Mix the oil and lemon juice with the
garlic, season to taste, and pour over the anchovies.
Place a plate directly on top of them, cover the pan,
and poach gently for 5–8 minutes. Serve hot or leave to
cool, sprinkle with salt, *sumak* (p. 221) or lemon juice,
and pop the whole anchovy package into your mouth.

Çiğ köfte

SPICY TARTARE MEATBALLS

*A speciality from southeastern Turkey, these raw meat-
balls are reputed often to contain 30 different spices.
They are so well kneaded and pounded that the meat
content is almost undetectable. They are usually served
with lots of fresh parsley to cut the spice.*

SERVES 4–6

8oz/225g minced lamb or beef

8oz/225g *bulgur* (p. 219), soaked in boiling water for 30 minutes

2 onions, finely chopped

6 cloves garlic, finely chopped

2 teaspoons concentrated tomato purée

1 teaspoon *kırmızı biber* (p. 219)

½ teaspoon roasted *kırmızı biber* (p. 219)

½ teaspoon ground chilli pepper

½ teaspoon ground coriander

½ teaspoon ground cumin

½ teaspoon ground allspice

½ teaspoon ground cinnamon

¼ teaspoon ground cloves

¼ teaspoon ground fenugreek

1 teaspoon salt

big bunch of fresh parsley

✧ Squeeze the *bulgur* dry, allow it to cool (about 30
minutes), then put it in a bowl with the minced meat.
Knead well, slapping it against the sides of the bowl
until well mixed. Knead in the onions, garlic and
tomato purée, followed by all the spices, a little
chopped parsley and the salt. Knead thoroughly for
20–30 minutes. Shape small portions of the mixture
into balls, indent them with a finger, and arrange
them on a bed of parsley. Serve them with wedges of
lemon to squeeze into the hollows. Eat them with
the remaining parsley leaves.

Fava

BEAN PASTE WITH DILL

*This dish of puréed beans is quite common throughout
Turkey and the Middle East. The thick purée,
moulded into a wedge and cut into slices, is served
with a dill dressing.*

Serves 4–5

8oz/225g dried broad beans, soaked for at least 8 hours

2 onions, chopped

2 tablespoons olive oil

1 teaspoon sugar

1 teaspoon salt

1 pint/600ml water

juice of ½ lemon

For the dressing

2 tablespoons olive oil

juice of ½ lemon

a few sprigs of dill, chopped

salt and freshly ground black pepper

✦ In a saucepan, soften the onions in the oil. Stir in the sugar and salt and pour in the water and lemon juice. Drain the beans and add to the pan. Cook gently, uncovered, for at least 1 hour until the beans are really tender and most of the liquid has evaporated.

✦ Mash the beans to a paste with a fork (or blend in an electric mixer). Spoon the mixture on to a dish and shape into a narrow wedge. Leave for 1–2 hours to dry out and harden.

✦ Mix the ingredients for the dressing and pour over the top. To serve, cut the *fava* into slices. (If you prefer soft *fava*, spoon it into a bowl after mashing and serve with the dressing.)

Taratorlu kabak
COURGETTE AND APPLE IN HAZELNUT SAUCE

A refreshing summer salad in a lemony hazelnut sauce.

Serves 3–4

2 courgettes, cut into thick sticks and soaked in salted water for 30 minutes

1 red apple, cut into segments, peel on

For the dressing

2oz/60g hazelnuts

2–3 cloves garlic, crushed with salt

2 tablespoons olive oil

juice of 1 lemon

2 tablespoons thick creamy yogurt

small bunch of parsley, chopped

salt and black pepper

Taratorlu kabak COURGETTE AND APPLE IN HAZELNUT SAUCE

✧ Drain the courgettes, squeeze dry, and steam with
the apple for 5 minutes. Refresh them under cold
water and drain well. Pound the hazelnuts with the
garlic, and mix in the oil and lemon juice (or blend in
an electric mixer). Bind with the yogurt to the
consistency of double cream, stir in the parsley, and
season to taste. Arrange the courgette and apple on a
plate and pour over the dressing.

Kırmızı soslu patlıcan
AUBERGINE IN TOMATO SAUCE

*A deliciously garlicky cold aubergine dish ideal for a
buffet spread. As many cold aubergine dishes include
yogurt, this one makes a pleasant change.*

SERVES 3–4
2 large aubergines, peeled in zebra stripes (see p. 25), sliced
lengthways and soaked in salted water for one hour
sunflower oil for deep-frying

FOR THE SAUCE
3 big fresh tomatoes, skinned and roughly chopped
8 cloves garlic, crushed with salt
1 teaspoon tomato purée
3 tablespoons olive oil
3 tablespoons white wine vinegar
1 teaspoon sugar
1 teaspoon salt
small bunch of fresh parsley, chopped
salt and freshly ground black pepper

✧ To prepare the sauce, put the tomatoes in a pan with
the rest of the sauce ingredients except the parsley.
Cook gently, uncovered, for 30–40 minutes until
well reduced. Stir in the parsley and season to taste.

Kırmızı soslu patlıcan AUBERGINE IN TOMATO SAUCE

Leave to cool.

✧ Drain the slices of aubergine and squeeze dry. Heat a
thick layer of oil in a shallow pan and fry the
aubergine until golden-brown. Drain on kitchen
paper and arrange on a serving dish. Spread the cold
tomato sauce over the top and serve while the
aubergines are still warm, or when they are cold.

Midyeli pilâki
MUSSELS IN TOMATO SAUCE

This is a cold dish, most often cooked in the summer, and it can be made with any amount of mussels. Bread is always needed to mop up the tasty sauce.

SERVES 4

25–30 mussels, shelled and cleaned
3 tablespoons olive oil
1 onion, chopped
6 cloves garlic, chopped
1 small carrot, diced
1 small potato, diced
1 stick celery, sliced
1 teaspoon white wine vinegar
1 teaspoon sugar
1 teaspoon salt
1 tomato, skinned and chopped
1 tablespoon concentrated tomato purée
bunch of fresh parsley, dill and basil, chopped
½ pint/300ml water
salt and freshly ground black pepper

TO GARNISH
a little extra parsley, chopped

✧ Heat the oil in a pan and soften the onion and garlic in it. Stir in the carrot, potato and celery and cook for 2–3 minutes. Stir in the vinegar, sugar and salt and add the tomato, tomato purée and herbs. Pour over the water, mix well and bring the liquid to the boil. Reduce the heat, cover, and simmer for 25–30 minutes until the vegetables are tender and the liquid has reduced (if the mixture gets too dry, add more water). Add the mussels and cook gently for a further 5–10 minutes. Season to taste and leave to cool in the pan. Garnish with parsley, and serve with wedges of lemon and bread.

Karışık turşu
MIXED PICKLES

Vegetables and fruit are often pickled together, and many vegetables are stuffed before pickling. The pickles themselves are infinite in variety, but the method is the same in each case. Both vegetables and fruit are pickled whole or cut into large chunks, and they are never sweet. This is an introductory recipe to Turkish pickles, but you can vary the quantity and combination to your own taste.

Karışık turşu MIXED PICKLES

6–8 *çarliston* peppers, left whole
2 unripe green tomatoes, halved
6–8 cabbage leaves, torn into pieces
2 carrots, sliced
6–8 unripe apricots
10 cloves garlic, in their skins
PICKLING LIQUID
½ pint/300ml white wine vinegar
1 tablespoon salt

✧ To make the pickling liquid, mix the vinegar with the salt and leave to stand. After washing them, pat the vegetables dry and layer them alternately with the cabbage leaves in a large jar or in several jars. Press them down tightly and pour over the vinegar. Make sure the vinegar rises above the vegetables and reaches the top of the jar (add more if necessary).
Seal the jar and leave to sit for 2–3 weeks at room temperature.

Ispanak kökü salatası
SPINACH ROOT SALAD

A simple salad of tender young spinach roots. Clean the roots and parboil or steam to soften. Drain well and refresh under cold water. Toss them in an olive oil and lemon juice dressing with crushed garlic and roasted poppy seeds (p. 38), sweetened with a teaspoon of honey.

Fasulye piyazı
WHITE BEAN SALAD

Usually made with haricot beans, this salad can also be made with lima, fava or soya beans. For festive occasions, beads of red caviar are folded into the salad.

SERVES 4
8oz/225g haricot beans, soaked for 8 hours
1 large red onion, quartered and finely sliced
1 hot green pepper, finely sliced
4 cloves garlic, finely chopped
small bunch of parsley, roughly chopped
2 tablespoons olive oil
2 tablespoons lemon juice
salt and freshly ground black pepper
TO GARNISH
2 hard-boiled eggs, quartered

✧ Drain the beans, place them in a pan, and cover them in fresh water. Bring to the boil, reduce the heat and simmer the beans for 30–40 minutes until tender but with a bite to them. Drain, and put them in a bowl. Add the onion, hot pepper, garlic and parsley. Mix the oil and lemon juice, season to taste and pour over the salad. Toss well, and garnish with the eggs.

Beyin salatası
BRAIN SALAD

Believed to be the best part of the animal, brains are traditionally served to guests. They are usually fried, grilled or turned into a salad.

SERVES 4

SERVES 4

4 lambs' brains

1 tablespoon white wine vinegar

1 teaspoon salt

FOR THE DRESSING

1 tomato, skinned and chopped to a pulp

2 tablespoons olive oil

2 tablespoons lemon juice

a few sprigs of parsley, chopped

salt and freshly ground black pepper

TO GARNISH

8 black olives, stoned

✧ Soak the brains in cold salted water for 20 minutes. Drain and rinse them. Remove the membranes and place them in a saucepan with the vinegar and salt. Cover with fresh water and bring to the boil. Reduce the heat and simmer for 5–10 minutes. Leave to cool in the pan.

✧ Mix together the ingredients for the dressing and season to taste. Remove the brains from the pan and slice lengthways. Arrange the slices on a plate and spoon the dressing over the top. Garnish with black olives.

Yalancı yaprak dolması

STUFFED VINE LEAVES

Popular throughout the Ottoman Empire, these classic stuffed vine leaves are a familiar sight in Greece, parts of the Middle East and the Balkans. Yalancı, 'false', because they contain no meat, they are stuffed with an aromatic

Yalancı yaprak dolması STUFFED VINE LEAVES

rice mixture, rolled into long, elegant fingers and served cold, whereas the meat-filled vine leaves (p. 167) are rolled into short, stubby logs.

SERVES 6

24–30 fresh or preserved vine leaves, washed and prepared (see p. 41)

FOR THE FILLING

8oz/225g short-grain or pudding rice

2 onions, finely chopped

2 cloves garlic, finely chopped

2 tablespoons olive oil and a little butter

1 scant tablespoon sugar

2 tablespoons currants, soaked in water

2 tablespoons pine nuts

½ teaspoon ground allspice

½ teaspoon ground cinnamon

½ teaspoon ground cloves

salt and freshly ground black pepper

bunch of fresh parsley, dill and mint

<u>COOKING LIQUID</u>

¼ pint/150ml water

2 tablespoons olive oil

2 tablespoons lemon juice

✧ Soak the rice in warm salted water for 10 minutes. Drain and rinse.

✧ Prepare the filling. Soften the onions and garlic in the oil and butter. Stir in the sugar, currants and pine nuts. Cook for 2–3 minutes. Stir in the spices, rice, salt and pepper. Cover with just enough water and bring it to the boil. Reduce the heat and simmer for 10–15 minutes, until the liquid is almost absorbed. Mix in the herbs with a fork, cover the pan and leave for 5 minutes. The rice should still have a bite to it.

✧ Place a few vine leaves in the bottom of a wide pan. Lay the rest of the leaves on a flat surface and place a spoonful of the rice mixture in the middle of each. Fold the near end of each vine leaf over the mixture, then the side flaps to seal it in, and roll it all up into a thin cigar. Arrange the stuffed vine leaves in the pan, tightly packed, and pour over the cooking liquid. Place a plate on top to prevent them from unravelling, and cover with a lid. Bring the liquid to the boil, reduce the heat and cook gently for 1 hour. Leave to cool in the pan, and serve cold with wedges of lemon.

Topik

SPICY CHICKPEA AND POTATO PASTY

This is a surprisingly filling dish of chickpea and potato paste filled with pine nuts, currants and spices and bound with tahin.

<u>SERVES 6</u>

4oz/120g chickpeas, soaked for 8 hours and cooked

4oz/120g potatoes, peeled and boiled

1 tablespoon olive oil

<u>FOR THE FILLING</u>

1 onion, finely chopped

2 cloves garlic, crushed with salt

2 tablespoons olive oil

1 teaspoon pine nuts

Topik SPICY CHICKPEA AND POTATO PASTY

1 teaspoon currants, soaked in water

1 teaspoon sugar

1 teaspoon ground cinnamon

½ teaspoon ground allspice

½ teaspoon ground cumin

½ teaspoon *kırmızı biber* (p. 219)

1 tablespoon *tahin* (p. 221)

salt and freshly ground black pepper

✦ Mash the potatoes and chickpeas and pound to a paste (or purée in an electric mixer). Bind with the oil to make a smooth, pliable paste. Mould it into a ball and put aside.

✦ Now make the filling. Soften the onion with the garlic in the oil. Stir in the pine nuts, currants and sugar and cook for 2–3 minutes. Add the spices and bind with the *tahin*. Season to taste.

✦ Roll the potato and chickpea paste into a rectangle. Spread the filling down the middle and fold over in half, making a large pasty. Pinch the three edges together to seal in the filling. Wrap in a sheet of oiled greaseproof paper and place in the refrigerator for 2– 3 hours. When ready to serve, cut it into slices.

Cacık

CUCUMBER WITH MINT YOGURT

A refreshing and versatile dish, cacık can be served as a salad or as a cold soup. Its most traditional role is as an accompaniment to meat courses, when it is served in small individual bowls and eaten with a spoon in between mouthfuls of meat. The cucumber can be diced or sliced and the yogurt is often flavoured with dried mint instead of fresh.

Cacık CUCUMBER WITH MINT YOGURT

SERVES 2–3

1 cucumber, finely sliced and salted for 5 minutes (to drain the excess water)

½ pint/300ml thick yogurt

2–3 cloves garlic, crushed with salt

small bunch of fresh mint leaves, finely chopped

salt and freshly ground black pepper

a few ice cubes

✦ Beat the yogurt with the garlic. Season with salt and pepper and stir in the mint. Rinse the cucumber and add it to the yogurt. Serve as a salad.

✦ To accompany meat dishes or to serve as a cold soup, thin the yogurt with a little water to get the consistency you require, or chill it with the ice cubes.

SOUPS

Traditionally sheep's heads, trotters and innards were used to flavour thick broths made from pulses and other vegetables. Nowadays strong stocks are made from fish heads and bones, chicken carcasses and the bones of sheep and calves, flavoured with herbs and spices, sometimes coloured with saffron, and sharpened with lemon juice or vinegar. Generally soups are drunk hot, but in the heat of such cities as Adıyaman, Diyarbakır and Gaziantep the usually hot *yoğurt çorbası* (p. 80) is often served cold. It has also become fashionable in Ankara, Istanbul and Izmir to serve *cacık* (p. 77) as a chilled soup.

Hot and nourishing, soups are eaten at any time of the day. In the winter, street vendors sell bowls of soup to the early-morning passing trade and, at the end of the day, to the late-night drinkers. Special soup houses, each known for its particular soup, are open at all hours in every town and village. The *işkembeci*, the seller of tripe soup, is particularly frequented late at night as the soup is reputed to combat the effects of heavy drinking.

Thick soups such as the Anatolian oven-baked *tandır çorbası* are often so rich in pulses, other vegetables and small pieces of meat that they constitute a meal in themselves. Some vegetable soups reveal familiar influences, such as the Black Sea red cabbage soup, *kırmızı lahana çorbası*, which resembles the Russian bortsch; and the thick pumpkin purée, *balkabağı çorbası* (p. 85), variations of which you also find in Greece and the Balkan countries. Festive meals often start with *yoğurt çorbası*, and the wedding feast usually includes a lamb soup flavoured with cinnamon, *düğün çorbası*. The role of the thin soup, which is sometimes thickened with egg yolk and lemon juice, is to whet the appetite. All types of soup can be eaten with yogurt and a squeeze of lemon juice.

Balkabağı çorbası PUMPKIN SOUP

Yoğurt çorbası
HOT YOGURT SOUP

*Probably the most widespread of all the soups.
Variations of it occur throughout Turkey, the most
popular of which is* yayla çorbası, *or 'meadow soup',
which is flavoured with dried mint. Thickened with rice
in Istanbul and with chickpeas,* bulgur *(p. 219) or
barley in Anatolia, it is a nourishing mild-flavoured
soup which can easily be turned into a meal by
floating small* köfte *(p. 219) in it.*

Yoğurt çorbası HOT YOGURT SOUP

<u>SERVES 4</u>

1oz/30g chickpeas, soaked for at least 6 hours or overnight

2oz/60g long-grain rice

1 onion, finely chopped

1 tablespoon clarified or ordinary butter

2 tablespoons plain flour

2 pints/1.2 litres well flavoured lamb stock

¾ pint/450ml thick creamy yogurt

salt and freshly ground black pepper

<u>TO GARNISH</u>

1 teaspoon saffron

✧ Cook the chickpeas in plenty of water for about 40
minutes, until tender. Wash the rice well.

✧ Soften the onion in the butter. Quickly stir in the
flour, gradually pour in the stock, stirring all the
time, and bring the liquid to the boil. Stir in the
chickpeas and the rice, bring the liquid to the boil
again, cover the pan, and simmer gently for about
20 minutes. Season with the salt and pepper.

✧ Beat the yogurt in a bowl and gradually add it to
the soup, stirring all the time. Let it just heat
through and no more – otherwise, it will curdle.
Swirl a little saffron on to the surface and ladle the
soup into bowls. Sprinkle with the rest of the
saffron and serve immediately.

Kırmızı mercimek çorbası
SPICY RED LENTIL SOUP

Lentil and bean soups are usually quite thick and are often flavoured with pieces of lamb. This spicy lentil soup is made in Antakya and Iskenderun, near the Syrian border. Diced potatoes and fresh peas can also be added to the ingredients.

SERVES 4–5

2 onions, roughly chopped

1 carrot, diced

1 tablespoon *kuyrukyağı* (p. 220) (sheep's tail fat), clarified or ordinary butter

3–4 cloves garlic, crushed with salt

8oz/225g lamb or beef scraps, cut into small pieces

1 teaspoon cumin seeds, crushed

1 teaspoon coriander seeds, crushed

1 teaspoon ground fenugreek

2 teaspoons tomato purée

1 teaspoon sugar

3oz/90g small red lentils, washed

2 pints/1.2 litres lamb or beef stock

2 dried chillies

salt and freshly ground black pepper

small bunch of parsley and mint, roughly chopped

✧ Brown the onions and carrot in the fat. Stir in the spices, garlic and meat and cook for 1–2 minutes. Stir in the tomato purée, sugar and lentils and pour in the stock. Stir well and bring the liquid to the boil. Pop in the chillies, cover the pan and simmer gently for about 30–40 minutes, stirring from time to time, until the lentils have pulped up and thickened the soup.

✧ Remove the chillies, and season to taste. Swirl in half the chopped herbs and sprinkle the rest over the top. Serve with yogurt.

İşkembe çorbası
TRIPE SOUP

Renowned for its sobering qualities, işkembe çorbası is often drunk late in the evening. It is also associated with Kurban Bayramı (p. 150), when every part of the sheep, sacrificed for the religious feast, is cooked into specific dishes. The acquired taste of tripe soup is sharpened by spooning garlic-flavoured vinegar over it or by eating it with pickles.

SERVES 4–6

8oz/225g lamb tripe

2 pints/1.2 litres water

1 tablespoon clarified or ordinary butter

2 tablespoons plain flour

1 egg yolk

1 tablespoon lemon juice

salt and freshly ground black pepper

TO GARNISH

1 tablespoon ordinary butter

1 scant teaspoon *kırmızı biber* (p. 219)

TO ACCOMPANY

2–3 tablespoons white wine vinegar

4–6 cloves garlic, crushed with salt

or an assortment of sharp pickles

✧ Wash the tripe, put it in a pan and cover it with the water. Bring to the boil and skim off any froth.

Place a lid at an angle over the pan and continue to boil for 20–25 minutes until tender. Drain the tripe and reserve the cooking liquid. Cut the tripe into fine slices.

✧ Melt the butter in a large saucepan. Take the pan off the heat and stir in the flour to make a roux. Return to the heat and gradually pour in the tripe liquid, stirring until it has thickened slightly. Add the tripe and simmer for 10–15 minutes. In a small bowl, mix the garlic and vinegar together and put aside.

✧ In another bowl, beat the egg yolk with the lemon juice, gradually add a little of the hot soup to it, then pour it into the soup. Stir vigorously and season to taste.

✧ For the garnish, melt the butter in a pan and stir in the *kırmızı biber*. Ladle the soup into individual bowls, trickle the butter over the top, and serve with the garlic-flavoured vinegar or pickles.

Köy çorbası VILLAGE SOUP

Köy çorbası
VILLAGE SOUP

A thick, tasty soup designed to use up old vegetables and bread, which expands in the soup. It is often made with corn bread (see p. 93) and suffices as a meal or snack on its own. Cabbage and peas are often added to this soup.

<u>SERVES 3–4</u>
1 onion, roughly chopped
4–6 cloves garlic, roughly chopped
1 large carrot, peeled and roughly diced
1 stick of celery, roughly diced
1 potato, peeled and roughly diced
2 tablespoons *kuyrukyağı* (p. 220) (sheep's tail fat), clarified or ordinary butter
1 teaspoon caraway seeds, crushed
1 teaspoon coriander seeds, crushed
½ teaspoon sugar
2 ripe tomatoes, skinned and roughly chopped
1 tablespoon tomato purée
2 pints/1.2 litres beef, lamb or chicken stock
salt and freshly ground black pepper
small bunch of fresh parsley, chopped
4 slices corn bread, crusts removed

✧ Heat the fat in a large saucepan and add the onion, garlic, celery, potato and carrot. Cook for 2–3 minutes, then stir in the sugar and seeds. Add the tomatoes and leave to cook for 3–4 minutes. Stir in the tomato purée and pour over the stock. Bring the liquid to the boil, reduce the heat and simmer for 30 minutes.

✧ Check the seasoning and stir in the parsley. Break the bread into the soup, allow it to absorb and expand, and serve.

Tarhana çorbası
ANATOLIAN CURD SOUP

A dish to be planned well in advance (ten days or more), this traditional Anatolian soup is made with a preserved vegetable dough (tarhana) that is dried and then rubbed between the hands, or through a sieve, to create tiny flavoured grains which give the soup a sour, nutty taste. These curds, prepared in the villages weeks or months before the soup is made, are tied up in cotton bags and stored in a cool place for up to a year. This recipe is particular to the Black Sea region, where it is served with melted butter and kırmızı biber (p. 219). The quantities given here make enough tarhana for several occasions.

Tarhana çorbası ANATOLIAN CURD SOUP

FOR THE TARHANA

1 onion, finely chopped

1 pepper, finely chopped

1 tablespoon olive oil

1 tomato, skinned and chopped

small bunch of mint and parsley, finely chopped

4–6oz/120–175g strong white flour

1 teaspoon salt

1 tablespoon *süzme* (p. 221) (thick strained yogurt)

¼ teaspoon dried yeast, dissolved in a little water

FOR THE SOUP

SERVES 4–6

2oz/60g *tarhana*

2 pints/1.2 litres lamb stock

salt and freshly ground black pepper

FOR THE TOP

2 tablespoons butter melted with 1 teaspoon *kırmızı biber*

or 2oz/60g *kaşar peyniri* (p. 219) or Parmesan, grated

✣ To make the *tarhana*, soften the onion and pepper in the oil. Add the tomato, mint and parsley. Cover and cook to a pulp over a low heat for about 20 minutes. Leave to cool.

✣ Sift the flour and salt into a bowl. Make a well in the centre and add the vegetable pulp, *süzme* and yeast. Mix well into a thick dough and knead. Cover with a cloth or foil and leave to sit in a cool place for at least 10 days, kneading it with moistened hands from time to time to prevent it from drying out.

✣ Now pull small lumps off the dough and place them on a cloth sprinkled with flour. Leave them to dry out for a few days, turning them over occasionally. When the pieces of dough are almost dry press them through a wire sieve to produce fine crumbs. Then dry them in the sun, or in a very low oven, before using or storing.

✣ To make the soup, soak 2oz/60g of *tarhana* in a little water for 2 hours. Heat the stock in a pan and stir in the *tarhana*. Bring the liquid to the boil, stirring all the time, cover, and simmer gently for 10 minutes. Season to taste and serve with melted butter and *kırmızı biber* or grated *kaşar peyniri*.

Tahinli karadeniz çorbası
TAHİN SOUP

Made with fresh fish stock, this strong-flavoured garlicky soup is made along the Black Sea and Aegean coasts. It is served in small individual bowls to whet the appetite. Chopped parsley and wedges of lemon to be squeezed into the soup are served separately.

SERVES 6

2 pints/1.2 litres well flavoured fish stock

2oz/60g long-grain rice, soaked in salted water for 30 minutes

salt and freshly ground black pepper

4 tablespoons *tahin* (p. 221)

zest of ½ lemon, grated

4 cloves garlic, crushed with salt

TO GARNISH

small bunch of fresh parsley, finely chopped

✣ Drain the rice. In a large pan, bring the fish stock to the boil, season it, and add the rice. Cook over a high heat for 15–20 minutes.

✧ Beat the *tahin* with the lemon zest and garlic, adding a little water to blend it to a smooth paste.

✧ Gradually add some of the hot stock to the *tahin*, stirring all the time, until it is of pouring consistency. Then pour the *tahin* mixture into the soup, stir well and take off the heat – don't let it boil or it will curdle. Spoon the soup into individual bowls, sprinkle with the parsley, and serve with wedges of lemon.

Balkabağı çorbası
PUMPKIN SOUP

Generally, pumpkins are turned into a nourishing, cinnamon-flavoured winter soup or poached into a popular dessert, balkabağı tatlısı *(p. 185). This recipe is from the villages around Bursa that hug the lower slopes of Uludağ, the ancient Mount Olympus, which is covered in snow in the winter. The soup can be topped with melted butter and* kırmızı biber *(p. 219), or with yogurt and fried leeks.*

Balkabağı çorbası PUMPKIN SOUP

SERVES 4

2 onions, chopped
1 large leek, sliced (reserve a little of it for the garnish)
4 cloves garlic, chopped
2 tablespoons clarified or ordinary butter
1 teaspoon ground allspice
1 teaspoon ground cinnamon
1 teaspoon sugar or honey
2lb/900g pumpkin flesh, cut into small pieces
2 pints/1.2 litres chicken stock
salt and freshly ground black pepper
4 tablespoons thick creamy yogurt
a little extra butter

✧ In a deep pan, soften the onions, garlic and most of the leek in the butter. Stir in the spices, sugar and pumpkin, and pour in the stock. Bring the liquid to the boil, reduce the heat, cover, and simmer for about 30–40 minutes until the pumpkin is soft.

✧ Push the mixture through a sieve (or liquidize in an electric blender), and return to the pan. Heat it through, and season. In a small pan, melt a little butter and soften the remaining leek. Swirl the yogurt into the soup and spoon the leek over the top.

Kuru bamya çorbası
DRIED OKRA SOUP

This traditional Anatolian soup has a distinct sour taste. It is often served at ceremonial feasts, between courses to refresh the palate. Beads of dried okra, most of which are destined for this soup, hang in markets all over Anatolia and in the Egyptian Bazaar in Istanbul.

SERVES 4–6

2oz/60g lamb or mutton scraps, cut into small pieces
2 onions, finely chopped
2 tablespoons *kuyrukyağı* (p. 220) (sheep's tail fat), clarified
or ordinary butter
2 tablespoons tomato purée
2 pints/1.2 litres lamb stock
2oz/60g small dried okra, loose or on strings
juice of ½ lemon
salt and freshly ground black pepper

✧ Brown the onions and the meat in the fat. Stir in the tomato purée and pour in the stock. Bring the liquid to the boil, reduce the heat and simmer for 20 minutes, until the meat is tender.

✧ Rub the strings of okra in a clean towel to remove the dust and hairs. Rinse and place them in a pan with half the lemon juice. Cover with just enough water and boil for 10–15 minutes. Drain and refresh the okra under running cold water and slip them off the strings. Add them to the soup with the rest of the lemon juice and bring to the boil. Season to taste. Cover the pan and simmer for 15–20 minutes. Serve hot on its own, or spoon it over a plain pilaf.

Kuru bamya çorbası DRIED OKRA SOUP

BREADS, SAVOURY DOUGHS AND PASTRIES

Bread, the food of friendship, is the traditional staple of the Turkish diet. Bread is treated with respect, kissed and held to the forehead before being thrown away. Rarely wasted, stale bread is ingeniously used to swell soups – such as *köy çorbası* (p. 82); soaked in water, squeezed dry and pounded with olive oil, vinegar and crushed garlic to make *sarmısaklı sos* to accompany deep-fried seafood; or soaked in syrup like the popular Palace pudding, *ekmek kadayıf*. In the villages of Anatolia bread is often baked in outdoor clay kilns by burying the dough in the ashes or by sticking it to the sides. Both leavened and unleavened breads are eaten with every meal, broken up and used as a scoop, a shovel or a mop to ensure that every juicy morsel of food is devoured. For some, a meal can only be enjoyed and savoured with bread.

Lacking ovens, the pastoral nomads of Central Asia would have made flat breads on some sort of griddle, and it is likely that layered breads, crude forerunners of the more sophisticated *baklava* (p. 192), would gradually have evolved. The most traditional of the flat breads is *yufka* (p. 97), a paper-thin sheet of unleavened dough. In the villages of central and eastern Anatolia the women sit at low round tables, skilfully rolling out fine round sheets of *yufka* using a thin rolling pin, an *oklava*. The sheets of *yufka* are individually toasted on a hot griddle or dried out in the sun, then stacked in a dry place for weeks and reconstituted with water before use. In the cities few people make their own, relying on supplies from the *yufkacı*.

Arguably the most useful of the flat breads is the soft *pide* (p. 94), with its hollow pouch. There are places specializing in plain and savoury versions of *pide*, such as *Karadeniz pidesi* with egg and spicy sausage from the Black Sea; the sweet and melting *helva pide* from Bursa; and the plain sesame seed Ramazan *pide*, eaten to break the fast at sunset. And from central and eastern Anatolia come two similar thin savoury flat breads, *gözleme* (p. 96) and *saç böreği* (p. 96). The *gözleme* is cooked on a flat, griddle and the *saç böreği* in a *saç*, a wide, slightly curved pan. Filled with endless combinations, both of these breads make delicious snacks.

It was probably the migrating Turkic-speaking peoples who brought the noodle dough, *mantu*, from China to Anatolia where it evolved into the Turkish *mantı* (p. 99), variations of which can still be traced eastwards to the Uyghurs of Northern China. As some of the Tartar Turks settled in and around Kayseri, it became famous for its *mantı* makers. In recent years some fashionable resorts and restaurants have ignored their *mantı* heritage, passing it off as a poor man's 'ravioli', perhaps forgetting that what we have come to know as Italian pasta is in fact a descendant of this simple but tasty noodle dish of ancient origins.

There are also numerous dishes made with different types of savoury pastry, collectively known as *börek*. The most traditional of these are made with strips of *yufka*, but an increasing number of recipes have evolved using versions of sophisticated puff and flaky pastries.

Lahmacun ANATOLIAN MEAT SNACK; ASSORTED BREADS; and *ıspanaklı tepsi böreği* BAKED SPINACH PASTRIES

Günlük ekmek
DAILY BREAD

This is a simple bread dough for a standard, everyday loaf. It can be shaped into oblongs, circles, long tubes, plaits or small rolls, glazed with egg yolk or milk, sprinkled with sesame, poppy or nigella seeds, or just left plain. It is usually made with strong white flour, to which a little wholemeal flour is sometimes added. Occasionally mastika *(p. 220) is added to the bread dough to give it an unusual chewy texture.*

<u>*MAKES 1 LOAF*</u>
½oz/15g fresh yeast, or ¼oz/7g dried yeast
½ teaspoon sugar
4fl oz/125ml lukewarm water
1lb/450g strong white flour
1 teaspoon salt
6–8fl oz/175–250ml cold water
scant teaspoon olive or sunflower oil

✧ Preheat oven to 425F/Mark 7/220C

✧ Cream the yeast with the sugar in the lukewarm water until frothy.

✦ Sift the flour with the salt into a bowl. Make a well in the centre and add the yeast and the cold water. Draw in a little of the flour from the sides to make a smooth batter. Sprinkle a dusting of flour over the surface of the batter, cover the bowl with a damp cloth, and leave the batter to sponge for about 20 minutes. Remove the cloth, draw in the rest of the flour, and knead well. Continue to knead the dough on a lightly floured surface until smooth and elastic.

✦ Pour the oil in the bottom of a bowl, flip the bread dough over in it, cover the bowl with a damp towel, and leave the dough to prove for a few hours until doubled in size.

✦ Punch the dough down, knead it again on a lightly floured surface and mould it into the shape you want. Place it on a floured baking tray and leave to prove again under a damp towel. Once it has doubled in size, you can score it with a sharp knife, glaze it, and sprinkle it with a variety of seeds. For a simple plain loaf just brush a little milk over the surface to harden the crust.

✦ Bake it in the oven for 30–40 minutes, then turn it upside down and return to the oven for 5 more minutes. It should sound hollow when the bottom is tapped. Leave to cool a little on a wire rack.

Köy ekmeği
VILLAGE BREAD

Village bread is basically a solid, round or oblong, wholemeal loaf baked in an outdoor clay oven. In southeastern Anatolia it is sometimes spiked with coriander, fennel or caraway seeds.

MAKES 1 LARGE LOAF

½oz/15g fresh yeast, or ¼oz/7g dried yeast

½ teaspoon sugar

3–4fl oz/100–125ml lukewarm water

1lb/450g wholemeal flour

8oz/225g strong unbleached flour

1 teaspoon salt

12–14fl oz/350–400ml cold water

scant teaspoon olive or sunflower oil

✦ Preheat oven to 425F/Mark 7/220C

✦ Cream the yeast with the sugar in the lukewarm water. Leave to froth.

✦ Sift the flours and salt into a bowl. Make a well in the centre and pour in the yeast and most of the water. Draw in some of the flour from the sides to make a loose paste, sprinkle a little of the flour over the surface, cover the bowl with a damp cloth, and leave to sponge for 20–25 minutes. Now knead the mixture together, adding extra water or flour if necessary, into a smooth ball. Continue to knead it on a lightly floured surface until smooth and elastic. Pour the oil into a clean bowl. Roll the dough in it, cover the bowl with a damp towel and leave it to prove until doubled in size.

✦ Punch the dough down and knead again on a lightly floured board. Mould it into a flat circle and place on a floured baking sheet. Cover with a damp towel and leave to double in size. Then place it in the oven for 35–40 minutes. If it doesn't sound hollow when you tap the bottom, return it to the oven, upside down, for 5 more minutes. Leave to cool on a wire rack.

Mısır ekmeği
CORN BREAD

Also a village bread, the yellow corn bread is particularly popular in central and eastern Anatolia. It is often made in the same way as köy ekmeği, *and when stale it is reconstituted in a tasty soup,* köy çorbası *(p. 82). In some villages the corn meal is kneaded with water until elastic, and divided into four or five balls. These are then rolled flat, brushed with melted butter, folded into envelopes, then folded again into small packages and dipped in flour, before being rolled out again into circles or squares. These flat breads are cooked quickly on both sides on a hot* tava *or griddle, spread with melted butter, then browned on both sides until crisp.*

<u>MAKES 1 BIG ROUND LOAF</u>
½oz/15g fresh yeast, or ¼oz/7g dried yeast
3–4fl oz/100–125ml lukewarm water
½ teaspoon sugar
8oz/225g corn meal
1lb/450g strong unbleached flour
1 teaspoon salt
12–14fl oz/350–400ml cold water
scant teaspoon olive or sunflower oil

✥ Follow the method for *köy ekmeği*.

Simit SESAME BREAD RINGS

Simit
SESAME BREAD RINGS

Bread rings rolled in sesame seeds, simit *are sold in every bakery and on every street. The cries of the* simitçi *reverberate in the streets as he makes his way through the crowds with a tray of fresh* simit *on his head. A popular breakfast and snack bread, often eaten on its own,* simit *can be made with a sweetened spongy dough or with this simple bread dough. A teaspoon of* mahlep *(p. 220) is often added to enhance the flavour.*

MAKES 6–8 SİMİT

½oz/15g fresh yeast, or ¼oz/7g dried yeast

½ teaspoon sugar

¼ pint/150ml lukewarm water

1lb/450g strong unbleached flour

1 teaspoon salt

1 tablespoon sugar or honey

1 tablespoon sunflower oil or melted butter

1 egg, beaten

a flat bowl filled with roasted sesame seeds

a few drops olive or sunflower oil

✧ Preheat oven to 400F/Mark 6/200C

✧ Cream the yeast with ½ teaspoon of sugar in a little of the lukewarm water. Leave to froth.

✧ Sift the flour with the salt into a bowl and stir in the tablespoon of sugar. Make a well in the centre and pour in the yeast, oil and the rest of the water, using your hands to draw the flour in from the sides. Add more water if necessary. Knead well on a lightly floured surface until smooth and elastic. Roll the ball of dough in a few drops of oil in a bowl and cover with a damp towel. Leave to prove for a few hours until doubled in size.

✧ Now punch the dough down, knock it back into a ball and divide it into 6–8 pieces. Knead each piece and shape it into a ring, approximately 7in/18cm in diameter, brush it with the beaten egg and dip it into the bowl of sesame seeds. When you have made them all, place them on an oiled baking sheet, cover with a damp towel and leave to relax for 15–20 minutes. Bake for 25–30 minutes or until they are golden-brown and sound hollow when tapped on the bottom.

Pide with mısır ekmeği

Pide
SOFT BREAD POUCHES

Large rounds or ovals of hollowed, knobbly, spongy pide, baked in hot ovens, are served to soak up all kinds of food. They should be soft in texture, with a slightly crispy crust, but can be varied according to personal taste. A swift bake in a high oven produces a crisp crust with a hollow pouch, whereas a longer bake in a lower oven produces a softer bread with a barely discernible pouch – good for mopping up garlicky olive oil and yogurt. Small, thin pouches are filled with grilled köfte and onions and eaten as a snack. To keep them soft and warm, place a dry towel over them when fresh out of the oven, and if they need to be resuscitated before eating sprinkle them with water and place them in a hot oven for a few minutes.

MAKES 2 MEDIUM-SIZED OR 1 LARGE PIDE

½oz/15g fresh yeast, or ¼oz/7g dried yeast

½ teaspoon sugar

4–6fl oz/125–175ml lukewarm water

1lb/450g strong unbleached flour

1 teaspoon salt

2 tablespoons thick yogurt

2 tablespoons olive oil or melted butter

1 egg, beaten

1 tablespoon nigella seeds (p. 220)

a few drops olive or sunflower oil

✧ Preheat oven to 450F/Mark 8/230C

✧ Preheat 2 baking sheets

✧ Cream the yeast with the sugar in a little of the lukewarm water. Leave to froth.

✧ Sift the flour with the salt. Make a well in the middle and pour in the yeast, the tablespoons of oil, the yogurt and the rest of the water, using your hands to draw in the flour from the sides and work the mixture into a sticky dough. Add more water if necessary. Knead until the dough becomes pliable and leaves the sides of the bowl. Continue to knead on a lightly floured surface until the dough is smooth and elastic. Roll it in the few drops of oil in a bowl, cover with a damp towel, and leave to prove until doubled in size.

✧ Punch the dough down, knead it again and divide it into two pieces. Knead each piece well. Flatten them out with the heel of your hand, and stretch them into large uneven rounds or ovals, creating a thick lip around the edges. Indent the dough with your fingertips.

✧ Lightly oil two hot baking sheets and place them in the oven for 2–3 minutes. Place the *pide* on them, brush with a little beaten egg, and sprinkle the nigella seeds over the top. Bake them for 10–15 minutes, until lightly golden with a crisp crust around the edges. Transfer them to a wire rack. If you want them to retain their soft, spongy texture all day, wrap them in foil or in a dry towel while still warm.

Lahmacun
ANATOLIAN MEAT SNACK

This ancient Middle Eastern version of pizza makes a tasty snack. It consists of thin bread dough spread with a layer of piquant minced meat, sprinkled with fresh parsley and lemon juice, then rolled up into a cone.

MAKES 2–3 LARGE LAHMACUN

FOR THE DOUGH

1 scant teaspoon dried yeast

¾ pint/150ml lukewarm water

½ teaspoon sugar

12oz/350g strong white flour

½ teaspoon salt

a few drops sunflower or olive oil

FOR THE FILLING

1 large onion, finely chopped

4 cloves garlic, crushed with salt

knob of butter

8oz/225g minced lamb

1 tomato, skinned and chopped

½ teaspoon sugar

1 green chilli, finely chopped

1 scant teaspoon *kırmızı biber* (p. 219)

1 tablespoon lemon juice

small bunch of parsley and mint, finely chopped

salt and freshly ground black pepper

4–6 teaspoons tomato paste

✧ Preheat oven to 450F/Mark 8/230C

✧ Preheat baking sheets

✧ Cream the yeast with the sugar in a little of the lukewarm water until it froths.

✧ Sift the flour and salt into a bowl. Make a well in the centre and add the yeast and the rest of the water, using your hands to draw in the flour. Add more water, if necessary, to work the mixture into a dough. Knead on a board until the dough becomes pliable. Roll it in a few drops of oil in the base of a bowl. Cover with a damp cloth and leave to prove in a warm place until doubled in size.

✧ Prepare the filling. Soften the onion in the butter and stir in the crushed garlic. Put all the other filling ingredients, except the tomato paste, into a bowl, add the onions and garlic, and knead well.

✧ Now punch down the risen dough and knead on a lightly floured board. Divide the dough into 2–3 equal pieces and roll each one with a thin rolling pin into a flat round, stretching it with your hands. Place each dough base on an oiled baking sheet or flat earthenware dish and spread with a thin layer of tomato paste, follwed by a thin even layer of the meat mixture, spreading it right to the edges.

✧ Bake in the oven for about 12–15 minutes. The dough should still be soft enough to roll up.

✧ Squeeze a little lemon juice over the hot *lahmacun*, sprinkle with roughly chopped parsley and eat flat or rolled up into a cone.

Ispanaklı gözleme
SPINACH-FILLED ANATOLIAN FLAT BREAD

The same idea, but cooked with different utensils – the gözleme on a griddle and the saç böreği in a wide, slightly curved pan (the saç). They can both be filled with an interesting combination of vegetables, cheese, sucuk (p. 221), eggs and pastırma (p. 220). The filling is spread on to the gözleme while it is still cooking, and then it is rolled up into a cone. The saç böreği is prepared by placing the filling in the middle of the uncooked dough; it is then folded in half and the edges are pressed together to seal it like an envelope before cooking it on both sides. Plain gözleme are also eaten for breakfast, spread with honey.

Ispanaklı gözleme SPINACH-FILLED ANATOLIAN FLAT BREAD

MAKES 4 FLAT BREADS
FOR THE DOUGH
4oz/120g strong unbleached flour

½ teaspoon salt

1 tablespoon olive oil or melted butter

2–3fl oz/60–90ml lukewarm water

FOR THE FILLING

1 large onion, chopped

3–4 cloves garlic, crushed with salt

knob of butter

8oz/225g fresh spinach, chopped

½ teaspoon *kırmızı biber* (p. 219)

pinch of grated nutmeg

1 scant tablespoon plain flour

3–4fl oz/100–125ml milk

3 tablespoons grated *kaşar peyniri* (p. 219) or Parmesan

salt and freshly ground black pepper

❖ Sift the flour with the salt into a bowl. Make a hollow in the middle and pour in the oil and water using your hands to draw flour in from the sides. Work the mixture into a dough and knead well. Divide it into 4 pieces and roll them into balls. Place on a floured surface, cover with a damp cloth, and leave them to rest for about 20 minutes.

❖ Prepare the filling. Soften the onion with the garlic in the butter. Add the spinach, nutmeg and *kırmızı biber*, and cook for 2–3 minutes with the lid on. Stir in the flour and pour in the milk, stirring all the time to make a smooth sauce. Beat in the cheese, and season. Keep the mixture warm.

❖ Now roll the balls of dough into flat rounds, 5–6 in/12–15cm in diameter. Whether cooking *gözleme* on the griddle or *saç böreği* in a *saç* or pan, the process is much the same. Heat the griddle or *saç*,

wipe it with a little extra oil or butter, and slap one of the flat rounds on to it. Use your fingers to shift the dough about, making sure it browns and buckles. Brush the upper side with more oil or butter, and flip it over. While this second side is cooking, spread some of the spinach filling evenly over the cooked side. Once the underside is cooked, lift the bread with its filling on to a piece of greaseproof paper and roll it up into a cone. Wrap the paper around it to make it easier to hold, and eat while hot.

Yufka

UNLEAVENED ANATOLIAN BREAD

Yufka has many uses: it can be rolled up with a cold filling and eaten as a snack, dürüm; *it can be cut into strips, rolled up with a filling and fried,* sigara böreği *(p. 62); or sheets of yufka can be layered up with butter, spread with a savoury filling and baked in the oven,* tepsi böreği *(p. 98); or it can be torn into strips and used to scoop up Anatolian food. It can take years of practice to learn how to fan out a perfect round of paper-thin yufka 25in/60cm in diameter. Once quickly cooked on a hot griddle, the yufka can be stacked in a dry place for weeks. Before using it, soften it by sprinkling with a little warm water, folding it over and wrapping it in a cloth for 30 minutes.*

MAKES 12 YUFKA 8–10IN/20–24CM IN DIAMETER
4oz/120g strong white flour

1oz/30g wholemeal flour

½ teaspoon salt

3–4fl oz/100–125ml lukewarm water

Yufka UNLEAVENED ANATOLIAN BREAD
and *sigara böreği* CHEESE PASTRIES

Tepsi böreği
BAKED LAYERED PASTRIES

A tepsi is a deep round baking dish in which a variety of layered savoury pies, using sheets of yufka, are made. Filo can be used instead of yufka. The most common fillings are made with spinach, white cheese and minced meat. Use the spinach filling from ıspanaklı gözleme (p. 96) and the cheese filling from sigara böreği (p. 62). This recipe is made with the minced meat filling that can also be used in gözleme and sigara böreği. Tepsi böreği is delicious hot or cold, ideal for picnics, snacks, lunch and supper. The size of the pie will be determined by the size of the yufka and the oven-proof dish – the dish must be smaller than the sheet of yufka, which should amply fill it and dangle over the sides.

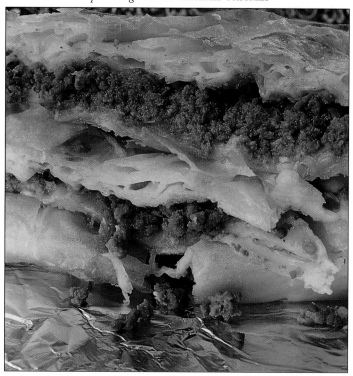

Tepsi böreği BAKED LAYERED PASTRIES

✧ Sift the flours and salt into a bowl. Make a well in the centre, add the water gradually, drawing the flour in from the sides, and knead into a firm dough.

✧ Divide the dough into 12 pieces, roll them into balls, and leave them to rest on a floured surface, covered with a damp cloth, for 30 minutes. Flatten the balls and roll them out into circles, as wide and thin as possible. Keep dusting them with flour if the dough begins to stick.

✧ Heat a griddle until very hot. Shake the excess flour off the *yufka* and cook each side for about 30 seconds, so that they brown in places. These freshly cooked *yufka* can be used straight away or stored, stacked in a dry place.

SERVES 4–6

5 large sheets (10–12 homemade sheets) *yufka*

2 eggs

½ pint/300ml milk

¼ pint/150ml sunflower or olive oil

FOR THE FILLING

1 large onion, finely chopped

2–3 cloves garlic, crushed with salt

knob of butter

8oz/225g lean minced veal, or a mixture of beef and lamb

1 teaspoon cinnamon

small bunch of fresh parsley and dill, finely chopped

salt and freshly ground black pepper

✧ Preheat oven to 400F/Mark 6/200C

✧ Prepare the filling. Soften the onion with the garlic in the butter. Add the meat and cook 3–4 minutes. Stir in the cinnamon and herbs. Season with salt and pepper.

✧ In a bowl, beat the eggs with the milk and the oil. Lightly grease the chosen oven-proof dish. Lay a whole sheet of *yufka* in it, with the sides overlapping the dish. Pour a little of the milk mixture into the centre, and spread it to the sides. Tear 2 *yufka* (or 5–6 homemade ones) into strips and layer most of it in the dish, brushing each layer generously with the milk mixture. Leave the last layer dry, and spread it with the meat filling.

✧ Tear the remaining 2 *yufka* (5–6 homemade ones) into pieces and continue layering and brushing with the milk mixture. Leave a spoonful of the mixture in the bowl and add 1 extra tablespoon of oil. Pull the dangling flaps up over the pie and stick them down, using your hands to smear each fold with the oil and milk. Make sure the top pieces are well oiled.

✧ Put the dish into the oven for about 45 minutes. The pie should puff up and turn golden-brown. (The puff will sink shortly after leaving the oven.) Serve hot or cold.

Mantı
BAKED SAVOURY NOODLES

The squares of noodle dough are filled with pieces of meat or minced meat and shaped into small parcels. Less common, but equally delicious, are the mantı *filled with crushed nuts, chickpeas, spinach or chopped mushrooms. Sealed packages of* mantı *are boiled plain,* klasik mantı; *and the open parcels are baked in stock,* fırında mantı. *Both are smothered in a garlicky yogurt sauce and topped either with melted butter and* kırmızı biber *(p. 219) or a warm garlic-flavoured purée of tomatoes.*

SERVES 6

FOR THE DOUGH

1lb/450g strong unbleached flour

½ teaspoon salt

1 egg

1 egg yolk

1–2fl oz/25–60ml cold water

FOR THE FILLING

8oz/225g minced lamb

1 onion, finely chopped

a few sprigs of fresh parsley, finely chopped

pinch of *köfte* spice (p. 40)

salt and freshly ground black pepper

COOKING LIQUID

1 pint/600ml meat stock

Klasik mantı BOILED SAVOURY NOODLES and *fırında mantı* BAKED SAVOURY NOODLES

FOR THE SAUCE
6 tablespoons thick yogurt
6 cloves garlic, crushed with salt
salt

FOR THE TOP
2oz/60g butter
1 teaspoon *kırmızı biber*

✧ Preheat oven to 400F/Mark 6/200C

✧ Sift the flour and salt into a bowl. Make a well in the centre and drop in the egg and yolk. Using your fingers, draw in the flour and form the mixture into a dough with the water. Knead for 5–10 minutes, cover with a damp cloth and leave to rest for 1 hour.

✧ To prepare the filling, put all the ingredients into a bowl and knead well. To prepare the yogurt sauce, beat the ingredients together and add salt to taste.

✧ Using a thin rolling pin, roll out the dough and cut it into 4 pieces. Roll out each piece as thinly as possible and cut into small squares (about 1in/2.5cm square). Put a little of the meat filling into the middle of each square, then fold the four corners over and bunch them together.

✧ Arrange the *mantı* in a greased oven-proof dish. Place them in the oven, uncovered, for 20 minutes until they turn golden-brown. Bring the stock to the boil. Take the *mantı* out of the oven and pour over the stock. Cover the dish with foil and return it to the oven for a further 15–20 minutes, until the *mantı* have absorbed the liquid.

✧ Quickly transfer the *mantı* to a serving dish and spoon the yogurt sauce over them. Melt the butter, stir in the *kırmızı biber* and spoon it over the top. Eat while the *mantı* are still warm.

Klasik mantı BOILED SAVOURY NOODLES and *fırında mantı* BAKED SAVOURY NOODLES WITH A PURÉE OF TOMATOES

VEGETABLE DISHES

Central Anatolia is the main agricultural base of Turkey. It is here that most of the livestock is raised; and the vast fertile plains, some of which are rich in minerals from underground springs, provide the markets of Turkey with a bounty of ripe fruit and vegetables. The colourful market stalls, arranged with artistic flair, display leeks the size of baseball bats, massive gourd-shaped aubergines, cabbages like giant tortoises and, from Milas and Yatağan, long purple carrots that are coveted for their strong taste – a cross between a sweet orange carrot and a nippy radish.

Huge ripe tomatoes are incorporated in many dishes, and often peeled and eaten like any other fruit. Never are they more welcome than on a long, hot and dusty bus journey through central Anatolia. On one such trip the driver, speeding along with the door open to channel air through the bus, with little room to spare overtook a truck laden with tomatoes, while the reserve driver leaned out of the doorway and deftly skimmed a few tomatoes off the top. With the flick of a knife, the fruit were peeled, halved and offered to those of us sitting at the front of the bus. Tasty, juicy, and thirst-quenching.

One of the cheapest and easiest ways to get around the cities is to leap into a *dolmuş*, a car or boat taxi, crammed with as many people as possible. *Dolmuş* means 'stuffed', and the same word is applied to the endless dishes of leaves, vegetables, fish, chicken or meat tightly packed with stuffing. The most popular vegetable *dolma* are made with vine leaves, aubergines, tomatoes, courgettes and peppers.

Pulse and other vegetable dishes are often eaten on their own as *meze* (p. 47), or as a main course with rice. If they are not stuffed, they are usually cooked with a little meat for flavouring and spooned from a communal pot on to a flat *yufka* (p. 97), *pide* (p. 94) or *gözleme* (p. 96), or gently stewed with olive oil in the ubiquitous *zeytinyağlı* dishes (see pages 116–19). The olive oil, *zeytinyağı*, forms an intrinsic part of these dishes, which are served cold with lemon to cut the oil. At the height of the Ottoman Empire the lavish meals of the nobility, comprising numerous courses, would include at least one cold vegetable dish cooked in olive oil and one hot vegetable dish cooked in butter.

All the dishes in this section are vegetarian.

Kabak mucveri
COURGETTE AND CHEESE PATTIES

These tasty patties, big or small, are popular on every table and in fast-food joints and delicatessen-style shops. They should be flavoured with lots of fresh herbs, particularly dill, and if you can't get beyaz peynir (p. 219) or köy peyniri (p. 219) use a feta cheese. Serve these delicious patties as meze (p. 220), as part of a buffet spread, or as a light lunch with a salad.

<u>SERVES 4–6</u>
3 big firm courgettes, grated with their skins
1 large onion, chopped or sliced
4–5 cloves garlic, crushed with salt
3 tablespoons olive oil
3 eggs
3 tablespoons plain flour
8oz/225g *beyaz peynir*, grated or crumbled
large bunch of dill, parsley and mint, roughly chopped
1 teaspoon *kırmızı biber* (p. 219)
salt and freshly ground black pepper
sunflower oil for frying

Kabak mucveri COURGETTE AND CHEESE PATTIES

✧ Sprinkle the grated courgettes with a little salt. Leave them to weep for 5 minutes (to remove the bitter juices), then squeeze out the excess water. Heat the olive oil in a shallow pan and fry the onion, garlic and courgette until they begin to take on a little colour.

✧ In a large bowl, beat the eggs with the flour to a smooth batter. Add the cheese, herbs and *kırmızı biber*. Season with a little salt and pepper. Beat in the courgette mixture while still warm. Heat a little sunflower oil, just enough to cover the base of a frying pan. Drop a spoonful or two of the courgette mixture into the oil and fry the patties until golden-brown on both sides.

✧ Drain on kitchen paper and serve hot or cold.

estaneli lahana dolması

SPICY CABBAGE LEAVES WITH CHESTNUTS

This is a speciality of Bursa, the first seat of the Ottoman dynasty. The chestnuts grow in the foothill forests of Uludağ, the historic Mount Olympus. It can be made with the leaves of green or red cabbages, and goes well with an egg and lemon sauce (p. 28) or a tahin dressing (p. 65).

<u>SERVES 4–5</u>

20–25 cabbage leaves
8oz/225g chestnuts, cooked and shelled
1 onion, finely chopped
3–4 cloves garlic, finely chopped
1 teaspoon sugar
2 tablespoons olive oil
3oz/90g short-grain rice, washed and drained
1 teaspoon ground allspice
1 teaspoon ground cinnamon
small bunch of dill and parsley, finely chopped
juice of ½ lemon
salt and freshly ground black pepper

✧ Steam the cabbage leaves until soft, then refresh them under running cold water and drain well. Remove the base of the hard central vein of each leaf and put the leaves aside.

✧ Heat 1 tablespoon of the oil in a pan. Brown the onion with the garlic and sugar. Stir in the rice, spices and a little salt, cover with just enough water and bring the liquid to the boil. Reduce the heat and simmer for 15–20 minutes until all the liquid has been absorbed.

✧ Put the chestnuts and herbs in a large bowl and add the rice mixture. Mix well with a fork. Place a cabbage leaf on a flat surface and spoon some of the chestnut and rice mixture into the middle. Fold the sides over and roll it up into a tight parcel. Do the same with the others and pack them snugly in a shallow pan or casserole dish. Mix the remaining tablespoon of oil with the lemon juice and pour it over them. Place a plate directly on top, then cover the dish and cook gently for 20–25 minutes. Serve hot or cold with wedges of lemon.

Kestaneli lahana dolması
SPICY CABBAGE LEAVES WITH CHESTNUTS

Havuç köftesi

CARROT ROLLS WITH APRICOTS AND PINE NUTS

A real treat when you find them, havuç köftesi *rarely make an appearance outside Istanbul and Izmir. Probably the result of experimentation in the Ottoman Palace kitchens, they are delicate in flavour and quite heavenly when served hot with cold garlic-flavoured yogurt.*

SERVES 4

10 medium-sized carrots, peeled and sliced

2 slices bread, rubbed into crumbs

6 dried apricots, finely chopped

3–4 spring onions, finely sliced

2 tablespoons pine nuts

2–3 cloves garlic, crushed with salt

1 teaspoon *kırmızı biber* (p. 219)

1 egg

bunch of parsley, mint and dill, finely chopped

salt and freshly ground black pepper

plain flour for coating

sunflower oil for frying

FOR THE SAUCE

3 tablespoons thick creamy yogurt

juice of ¹/₂ lemon

2 cloves garlic, crushed with salt

salt and freshly ground black pepper

✥ Steam the carrots until soft. Drain well, put them in a large bowl, and mash with a fork. Add the rest of the ingredients and knead well. If there is any liquid in the mixture add more breadcrumbs – but the mixture should be moist and sticky.

✥ Tip a small heap of flour on to a flat surface. Take small portions of the carrot mixture in your hands and mould into oblongs. (This may seem difficult as the mixture is so sticky, but once dipped in flour the *köfte* are easy to handle.) Dip each *köfte* in the flour, and put them aside.

✥ To prepare the sauce, beat the yogurt in a bowl with the garlic and lemon juice. Season to taste.

Havuç köftesi CARROT ROLLS WITH APRICOTS AND PINE NUTS

✥ Heat a thin layer of oil in a large frying pan and place the *köfte* in it. Roll them over to brown on all sides and drain them on kitchen paper. Transfer to a serving dish, and spoon the sauce over the hot *köfte* or serve them separately.

İmam bayıldı AUBERGINES WITH ONION AND TOMATO

İmam bayıldı
AUBERGINES WITH
ONION AND TOMATO

*As the story goes, the imam swooned with sheer
pleasure at the sight of this dish, lavishly dripping in
olive oil. The aubergine, onion and tomato should be
so tender and delicately intertwined that they melt
in the mouth. To achieve the effect enjoyed by the
imam, there is only one way to cook this dish, and
this is it. A green pepper, finely sliced, can be added
to the mixture.*

<u>SERVES 4</u>

2 aubergines

1 large onion, finely sliced

3 large tomatoes, skinned and chopped

6 cloves garlic, finely chopped

bunch of fresh parsley, dill and basil, finely chopped

1 teaspoon salt

¼ pint/150ml olive oil

2fl oz/60ml water

1 tablespoon sugar

✧ Halve the aubergines lengthways. Sprinkle with salt
and leave to weep for 5 minutes. Rinse well and

place the halves side by side, flesh side upwards, in a wide pan.

✧ In a bowl, mix the onion, tomatoes, garlic and herbs with the salt and a little of the oil. Carefully pile the mixture high on top of each aubergine half until all the flesh is covered. Mix the rest of the oil and the water with the sugar and pour it over and around the aubergines.

✧ Cover the pan and cook gently for 1–2 hours. Occasionally baste with the oil, pushing the onion and tomato mixture down into the halves as they cook. The aubergines should end up soft and flat, completely filled with the mixture, sitting in a slightly caramelized flavoured oil.

✧ Leave to cool in the oil. Transfer to a serving dish, spoon the oil over them, and serve with wedges of lemon to squeeze over.

Menemen

VEGETABLE RAGOÛT WITH EGGS

Quick, simple and tasty, menemen *is cooked in bus stations, train stations and ports – anywhere there is passing trade. The eggs can be scrambled into the ragoût or cooked on top, and chunks of* beyaz peynir *(p. 219) or feta can be added to it. Delicious served with garlicky yogurt,* menemen *is the ultimate snack, lunch or light supper.*

SERVES 2

1 onion, roughly sliced

3 *çarliston* peppers or 1 green bell pepper, roughly sliced

1 hot green pepper or chilli pepper, finely sliced

2 tablespoons olive oil and a little butter

3 tomatoes, skinned and chopped, or 1 tin tomatoes

salt and freshly ground black pepper

4 eggs

FOR THE SAUCE (OPTIONAL)

3–4 tablespoons thick yogurt

2 cloves garlic, crushed with salt

½ teaspoon *kırmızı biber* (p. 219)

salt and freshly ground black pepper

✧ Fry the onion, peppers and hot pepper in the oil and butter, until they take on colour. Stir in the tomatoes and cook until most of the liquid has

Menemen VEGETABLE RAGOÛT WITH EGGS

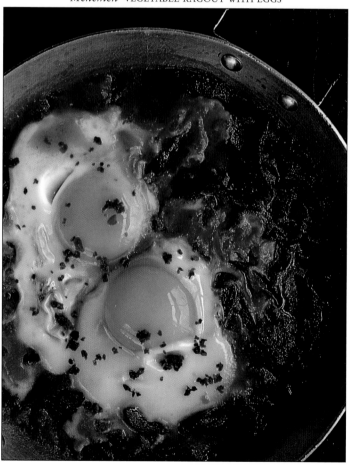

evaporated. Season with the salt and pepper. Crack the eggs over the top, cover with a lid, and cook gently until the eggs are just done.

✧ To prepare the sauce, mix the yogurt in a bowl with the garlic. Stir in the *kırmızı biber* and season to taste. Serve the *menemen* hot, and spoon the yogurt over the top.

Antakya mercimek köftesi
SPICY BEAN AND LENTIL BALLS

These tasty dry balls appear in different forms throughout Turkey and the Middle East. This recipe is from Antakya, where the baked balls are tucked into a pide *pouch (p. 94) with sliced onion, tomato and chopped parsley, and smothered in thick yogurt. They are ideal for a light lunch or supper served with yogurt and* çoban salatası *(p. 67). Broad, lima or fava beans or chickpeas can be used.*

SERVES 4
4oz/120g white broad beans, soaked for 24 hours
4oz/120g large green lentils, soaked for 24 hours
2oz/60g hazelnuts
1 onion, finely chopped
4 cloves garlic, finely chopped
½ teaspoon ground fenugreek
1 teaspoon ground cumin
1 teaspoon ground coriander
1 teaspoon *kırmızı biber* (p. 219)
1 teaspoon salt
small bunch of parsley, finely chopped

✧ Preheat oven to 400F/Mark 6/200C

✧ Drain the beans and lentils, put them into a pan and cover with fresh water. Bring to the boil, reduce the heat and simmer for only 15 minutes. Drain and pound them to a paste (or whizz them in an electric mixer). Add the other ingredients and knead well.

✧ Take portions of the mixture and roll them into small neat balls. Place them on an oiled baking tray and put in the oven for about 25–30 minutes, until browned. Serve hot or cold.

Patlıcan bastısı
AUBERGINE CASSEROLE

This is best with the tiny slim aubergines, but it also works well with chunks. It is often served as part of a meze *(p. 220) spread or on its own with yogurt, or with grilled and roasted meats. A courgette casserole is prepared in the same way.*

SERVES 4–6
12 tiny aubergines, left whole
1 onion, halved and sliced
8 cloves garlic, chopped
1 teaspoon coriander seeds
3–4 tablespoons olive oil
4 large ripe tomatoes, chopped
½ teaspoon ground fenugreek
1 teaspoon brown sugar
bunch of fresh parsley, mint and basil, chopped
salt and freshly ground black pepper

Patates bastısı POTATO CASSEROLE

✧ In a large pan, soften the onion and garlic with the coriander seeds in the oil. Add the aubergines and coat them well in the oil. Cook for 2–3 minutes to soften them. Stir in the tomatoes, sugar, fenugreek and half the herbs. Cover and cook gently for 15 minutes. Add the rest of the herbs, season with salt and pepper and cook, uncovered, for a further 15– 20 minutes until the liquid is reduced. Serve hot or cold.

Patates bastısı
POTATO CASSEROLE

Apart from çips (chips), two of the most popular potato dishes are patates bastısı and patates ezmesi. The latter, which is served as a meze dish, consists of potatoes mashed with crushed garlic, chopped onions and parsley, bound with olive oil and lemon juice. This version of patates bastısı comes from Ayvalik, known for its olives and olive oil factories, on the Aegean coast.

SERVES 4

1½lb/680g new potatoes, peeled and quartered
2 onions, halved and sliced
4 tablespoons olive oil
6 cloves garlic, crushed with salt
1 teaspoon cumin seeds
1 tablespoon wine vinegar
1 teaspoon sugar
2 tablespoons black olives, stoned
4 tomatoes, skinned and roughly chopped
½ teaspoon roasted *kırmızı biber* (p. 219)
2 teaspoons dried oregano
1 tablespoon fresh parsley, chopped

salt
2 tablespoons hazelnuts, chopped

✧ Preheat oven to 400F/Mark 6/200C

✧ In a shallow pan, fry the potatoes and onions in the oil until they take on a little colour. Stir in the garlic and cumin seeds and continue to cook for 2–3 minutes. Stir in the vinegar, olives and sugar. Add the tomatoes, oregano, parsley and *kırmızı biber*. Season with salt.

✧ Spoon the mixture into a shallow oven-proof dish and spread it out evenly. Sprinkle with the chopped hazelnuts and place in the oven for about 30 minutes, until the potatoes are tender and most of the liquid has been absorbed. Serve hot or cold with yogurt.

Kıbrıs böreği
VINE LEAF AND YOGURT PIE

A speciality of Northern Cyprus and the Aegean coast, this is an unusual rich yogurt pie which is best served for lunch on a warm summer's day with a cucumber and tomato salad in a lemon and dill dressing.

SERVES 4–6

12–16 fresh or preserved vine leaves, washed and prepared (p. 41)
4–6 tablespoons thick yogurt
2 shallots, or 3–4 spring onions, finely sliced
bunch of fresh parsley, dill and mint, finely chopped
4 tablespoons rice flour
salt and freshly ground black pepper
3–4 tablespoons olive oil and a little melted butter

FOR THE TOP

2 tablespoons coarse breadcrumbs or roasted sesame seeds

Kıbrıs böreği VINE LEAF AND YOGURT PIE

- ❖ Preheat oven to 350F/Mark 4/180C

- ❖ Brown the shallots in a little of the olive oil and butter. Put aside to cool.

- ❖ Brush a shallow oven-proof dish with some of the oil and butter mixture. Line the bottom and sides with half the vine leaves, letting them hang over the sides and brushing each one with oil and butter.

- ❖ In a bowl, mix the yogurt with the herbs and shallots. Season to taste. Beat in the rice flour and spoon the mixture on to the vine leaves, spreading it out evenly. Place the remaining leaves over the top, brushing them with oil and butter, and pull the dangling leaves up over the top to create a tight package. Brush generously with the rest of the oil and butter, and sprinkle the breadcrumbs or sesame seeds over the top, or leave plain.

- ❖ Bake in the oven for about 45 minutes, until it is firm to touch and the top leaves are crisp. Leave to cool for a few minutes. Eat hot or cold.

Yaz türlüsü
SUMMER VEGETABLE STEW

Türlü is made in the summer and in the winter, using seasonal vegetables. Sometimes small pieces of meat are added for flavouring. It can be cooked in the oven (350F/Mark4/180C) or on top of the stove and usually constitutes a meal in itself, served with a plain pilaf and yogurt.

SERVES 5–6
1 tablespoon tomato purée
½ pint/300ml water
1 tablespoon white wine or apple vinegar
1 teaspoon ground cinnamon
1 teaspoon ground fenugreek
1 teaspoon sugar
3–4 bay leaves
bunch of fresh parsley, dill and mint, roughly chopped
3 onions, quartered
10 cloves garlic, roughly chopped
1 tablespoon coriander seeds
4 tablespoons olive oil
1 large aubergine, thickly sliced
2 courgettes, thickly sliced
3 artichoke hearts, quartered
6 *çarliston* peppers or 2 bell peppers, thickly sliced
4 tomatoes, skinned and quartered
handful of fresh green beans
salt and freshly ground black pepper

- ❖ Mix the tomato purée with the water, vinegar, cinnamon, fenugreek and sugar. Stir in the bay leaves and chopped herbs.

✧ Heat the oil in a large pan and soften the onions and garlic with the coriander seeds. Toss in all the other vegetables, mix well, and pour over the herb and tomato liquid. Season with salt and pepper, cover the pan, and cook gently for about 1 hour until the vegetables are tender. Add more water if necessary. Serve hot with yogurt.

Nohut yahnisi
CHICKPEA STEW

This is a simple mildly spiced dish from Edirne, an early capital of the Ottoman Empire. It is best served with wedges of lemon to squeeze over it and is eaten with spoonfuls of thick yogurt. It can also be served with pickles.

SERVES 4

8oz/225g chickpeas, soaked overnight

2 onions, halved and sliced

4 cloves garlic, chopped

2 tablespoons olive oil and a little butter

1 teaspoon cumin seeds, crushed

1 teaspoon fennel seeds, crushed

1–2 teaspoons brown sugar or *pekmez* (p. 220)

1 tablespoon white wine vinegar or lemon juice

½ teaspoon roasted *kırmızı biber* (p. 219)

3–4 tomatoes, skinned and chopped

4oz/120g fresh spinach leaves

small bunch of fresh parsley, dill and mint, chopped

salt

✧ Drain the chickpeas, put them in a pan, cover with fresh water and bring to the boil. Reduce the heat and simmer for 30–40 minutes. Drain well.

✧ Brown the onions and garlic, cumin and fennel seeds in the oil and butter. Stir in the sugar and cook for a minute. Stir in the vinegar and add the tomatoes and *kırmızı biber*. Cook over a high heat until the tomatoes begin to pulp up. Stir in the spinach and chickpeas and add a little water to increase the cooking liquid. Cook over a medium heat for 20–25 minutes. Season with salt and stir in the fresh herbs. Serve hot with wedges of lemon and thick yogurt.

Kabak çiçeği dolması
STUFFED COURGETTE FLOWERS

Late spring heralds the arrival of the young courgettes with their pretty pale-green and yellow flowers, both of which Turkish cooks are always eager to stuff. In Istanbul the flowers are often stuffed with a rice and meat mixture, and in parts of Anatolia they are filled with bulgur *(p. 219). This delicately flavoured recipe from Bolu omits meat.*

SERVES 3–4

8–10 fresh courgette flowers

6 shallots, finely chopped

4 cloves garlic, finely chopped

1 tablespoon pine nuts

1 tablespoon olive oil and a little butter

2 courgettes, grated and sprinkled with a little salt

4oz/120g *bulgur*

1 tablespoon currants, soaked in water

1 teaspoon *kırmızı biber* (p. 219) or 1 small red chilli pepper, finely chopped

small bunch of parsley, dill and mint, chopped

salt and freshly ground black pepper

COOKING LIQUID

2 tablespoons olive oil

2 tablespoons water

juice of ½ lemon

2 cloves garlic, crushed with salt

✦ Preheat oven to 350F/Mark 4/180C

✦ Rinse the flowers and leave to drain on a few layers of absorbent kitchen paper.

✦ In a deep pan, soften the shallots and garlic with the pine nuts in the oil and butter. Squeeze the courgette to drain the excess water, and add to the pan. Mix well and cook for 2–3 minutes. Stir in the *bulgur* with the currants and *kırmızı biber*. Add the salt and pour over enough water to just cover. Bring the water to the boil, reduce the heat and simmer for 15–20 minutes until the liquid has been absorbed. Mix in the fresh herbs with a fork. Season to taste.

✦ Carefully spoon the mixture into each flower, folding the tops over to encase the filling, and pack them tightly into an oven-proof dish.

✦ To make the cooking liquid, mix the lemon juice, oil and water together with the crushed garlic, and pour it over the stuffed flowers. Cover the dish and place it in the oven for about 40 minutes, until the liquid has been absorbed. Serve hot or cold, with wedges of lemon to squeeze over them.

Yalancı patlıcan dolması STUFFED AUBERGINES IN OLIVE OIL

Yalancı patlıcan dolması
STUFFED AUBERGINES IN OLIVE OIL

A delicious, succulent addition to a buffet spread. The aubergine is stuffed whole with a delicately spiced rice mixture, and cooked in olive oil. In southern Anatolia, where aubergine skins are dried just for this dish, tomatoes and hot peppers are added to the rice mixture. In other parts of Turkey fresh aubergines are used. To loosen the flesh from the skin, the aubergine is

rolled, massaged and pummelled in the same manner as for the mackerel in uskumru dolması *(p. 138). Carefully cut around the stalk base with a sharp knife. Get a good grip of the stalk and pull – the insides should come out with it, leaving a long hollow ready to fill. Put the flesh aside for another dish. Courgettes, bell peppers and tomatoes can also be stuffed with rice and cooked in olive oil.*

<u>SERVES 5–6</u>

3 long thin aubergines, hollowed as described above

2 onions, chopped

4 cloves garlic, chopped

1 tablespoon olive oil and a little butter

2 tablespoons pine nuts

2 tablespoons currants, soaked in water

1 teaspoon ground cinnamon

1 teaspoon ground allspice

1 teaspoon sugar

1 pint/600ml water

8oz/225g short-grain or pudding rice, washed and drained

salt and freshly ground black pepper

bunch of parsley and dill, chopped

1 tomato, sliced

<u>COOKING LIQUID</u>

3–4fl oz/100–125ml water

2 tablespoons olive oil

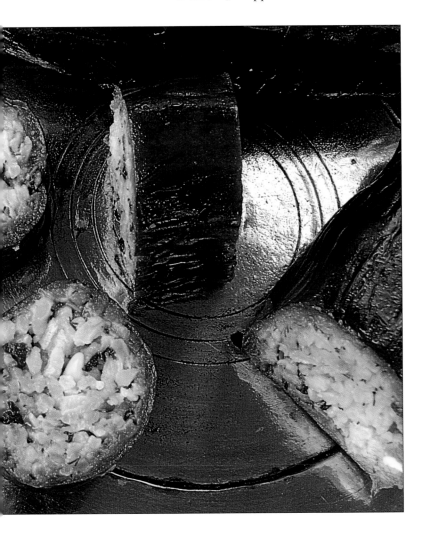

✧ Soften the onions and garlic with the pine nuts in the oil and butter. As they begin to brown, stir in the currants and spices with the sugar. Pour in a little of the water and cook for 10 minutes, until most of the liquid is reduced. Stir in the rice, pour over the rest of the water, season with salt and pepper, and bring to the boil. Reduce the heat and simmer until the liquid is absorbed. Mix in the fresh herbs with a fork.

✧ Stuff the aubergine cavities with the rice mixture until they resemble their former selves. Seal the hole with a slice of tomato. Lay the aubergines in a pan. Mix up the cooking liquid and pour over them. Cover the pan and cook gently for 30–40 minutes, until all the water has evaporated and only oil remains. Leave the aubergines to cool in the pan.

✧ Place them on a serving dish. Slice each one into 4 or 5, and serve with wedges of lemon to squeeze over them.

Zeytinyağlı havuç

CARROTS AND LENTILS IN OLIVE OIL

A refreshing zeytinyağlı *dish that is particularly good served with garlic-flavoured yogurt. The carrots should be slightly undercooked, so that they retain their crunchiness.*

SERVES 4

3–4 carrots, peeled and finely sliced
2oz/60g small green lentils, soaked for 2–3 hours
1 onion, halved and finely sliced
3 cloves garlic, chopped
1 teaspoon coriander seeds
4 tablespoons olive oil
1 tablespoon tomato purée
1 teaspoon sugar
8fl oz/250ml water
bunch of fresh dill, parsley and mint, chopped
salt and freshly ground black pepper

✧ Drain the lentils and put them in a pan, cover with fresh water and bring to the boil. Simmer for 10–15 minutes. Drain well.

✧ Soften the onion and garlic in the oil with the coriander seeds. Add the carrots and cook for 2–3minutes. Stir in the tomato purée, sugar and lentils. Pour over the water and bring to the boil. Reduce the heat, cover, and simmer for 30 minutes. Stir in most of the fresh herbs, season with the salt and pepper, and continue to simmer, uncovered, for 10 minutes until most of the liquid has evaporated. Leave to cool in the dish.

✧ Garnish with the rest of the chopped mint, dill and parsley and serve cold with wedges of lemon.

Zeytinyağlı havuç CARROTS AND LENTILS IN OLIVE OIL
and *zeytinyağlı barbunya* BARLOTTI BEANS IN OLIVE OIL

Zeytinyağlı barbunya

BARLOTTI BEANS IN OLIVE OIL

The pink and meaty barlotti or pinto beans are used for this garlicky, oily dish, which is served with yogurt and lots of bread to soak up the oil. If using fresh beans, shell them and boil them in water for 15 minutes to get rid of the gas, before proceeding with the recipe.

SERVES 4–6

6oz/175g dried barlotti beans, soaked for 8 hours or overnight
2 onions, halved and roughly sliced
8–10 cloves garlic, roughly chopped
6 tablespoons olive oil
1 teaspoon sugar
3 large ripe tomatoes, peeled and roughly chopped
bunch of fresh dill and parsley, roughly chopped
½pint/300ml water
salt and freshly ground black pepper

✧ Drain the beans, put them in a pan of water and bring to the boil. Cover and simmer for 30 minutes. Drain well.

✧ Brown the onions and garlic in the olive oil. Stir in the sugar and add half the tomatoes and herbs. Cook together gently for 15 minutes. Add the beans, pour over the water, and bring it to the boil. Reduce the heat and simmer for 20 minutes. Stir in the remaining tomatoes and herbs, season to taste, and simmer for a further 20–25 minutes until most of the liquid has evaporated. Leave to cool in the pan.

✦ Tip the beans on to a dish and serve with wedges of lemon, yogurt and bread, or as an accompaniment to grilled meat and *köfte* (p. 219).

Zeytinyağlı enginar ARTICHOKES IN OLIVE OIL

Zeytinyağlı enginar
ARTICHOKES IN OLIVE OIL

In this king of the zeytinyağlı dishes, the artichoke hearts are gently cooked in olive oil and eaten cold. Variations can include diced potatoes, carrots and peas; in this version the spring onions and dill complement the taste of the artichokes. A dish of celery root in olive oil, zeytinyağlı kereviz, is cooked in a similar way and often served with an egg and lemon sauce (p. 28).

SERVES 4

4 globe artichokes, trimmed down to the hearts, and retaining part of the stalk

6–8 spring onions

4fl oz/125ml olive oil

juice of ½ lemon

2fl oz/60ml water

salt

small bunch of dill, chopped

✦ Place the artichokes in a pan with the spring onions, oil, lemon juice and water. Cover and cook gently for 35–40 minutes. Add salt to taste and most of the dill, baste the artichokes, and continue to cook for 15–20 minutes until they are tender. Leave to cool, then garnish with the rest of the dill. Eat cold and serve with wedges of lemon to squeeze over them.

Zeytinyağlı pırasa
LEEKS IN OLIVE OIL

Particularly popular in Istanbul, Ankara and Izmir, this dish is often served as a salad to accompany meat. According to personal preference, carrots are sometimes cooked with the leeks.

SERVES 4

1lb/450g fresh leeks, washed and trimmed
into 1in/2.5cm cubes
1 onion, chopped
4 cloves garlic, chopped
6 tablespoons olive oil
juice of ½ lemon
1 teaspoon sugar
1 tablespoon long-grain rice, washed and drained
½ pint/300ml water or chicken stock
small bunch of dill, chopped
salt and freshly ground black pepper

✧ Soften the onion and garlic in the oil. Add the leeks and cook for 2–3 minutes. Stir in the lemon juice, sugar, rice and water. Bring the liquid to the boil, reduce the heat, cover, and simmer for 20 minutes. Stir in most of the dill, season to taste and continue to simmer, uncovered, for 15 minutes, until the leeks are tender and most of the water has evaporated. Leave to cool in the pan.

✧ Garnish with the rest of the dill and serve with lemon wedges.

Zeytinyağlı fasulye
GREEN BEANS IN OLIVE OIL

There are many variations of this dish, using fresh green or broad beans. It is popular as a salad served with a meat or fish dish, or on its own with lemon and yogurt.

SERVES 4

1lb/450g green beans, trimmed
1 onion, sliced
4 cloves garlic, chopped
4 tablespoons olive oil
2 tomatoes, skinned and roughly chopped
1 teaspoon sugar
½ pint/300ml water
juice of ½ lemon
salt and freshly ground black pepper

✧ Soften the onion and garlic in the oil. Add the tomatoes and sugar and cook for 2–3 minutes. Stir in the beans and pour over the water. Bring the liquid to the boil, reduce the heat, cover, and simmer for 30 minutes. Add the lemon juice, season to taste, and simmer uncovered for 10–15 minutes until most of the liquid has evaporated. Leave to cool in the pan and serve with wedges of lemon.

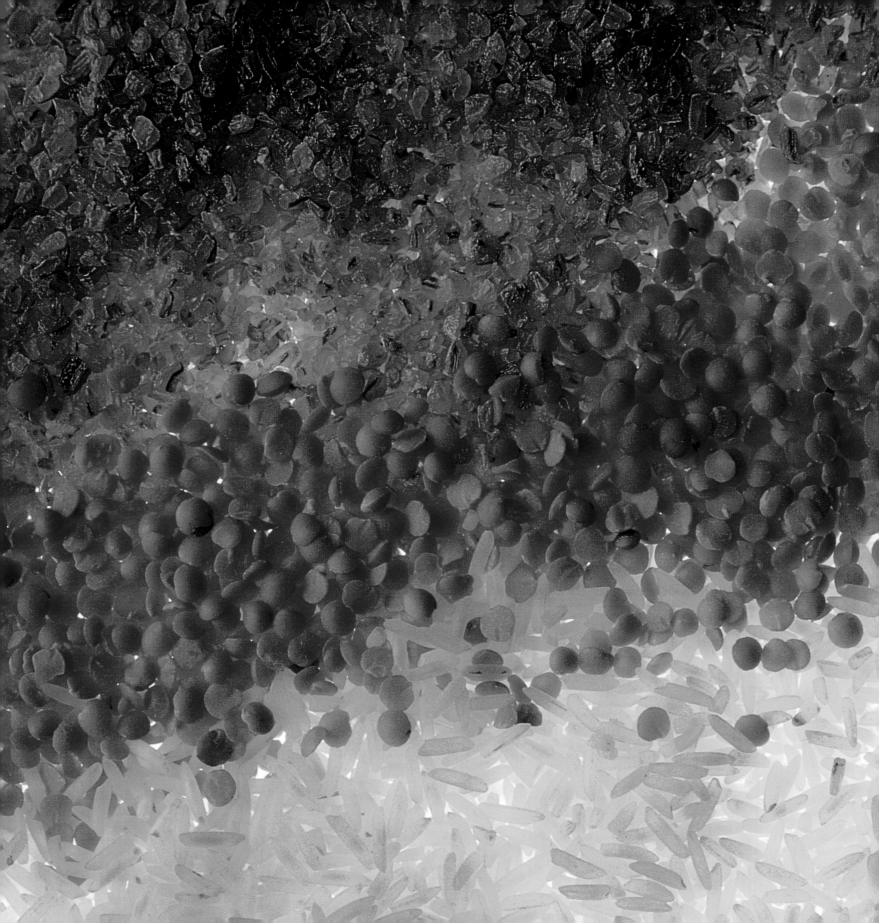

PILAFS

Rice would have been brought to Turkey from China, via India and Persia, by the migrating Turkic-speaking tribes. Although rice can now be found on every table it was not initially a staple of the Turkish diet, as the price was prohibitive. For centuries it was only eaten by the wealthy, who transformed it into a celebratory dish while the poor continued to live off wheat.

During the Ottoman period elaborate rice dishes were served at banquets and feasts, which often ended with a large platter of plain rice served with a bowl of stewed dried fruits, *hoşaf* (p. 200), to clean the palate. Inferior rice was flavoured with spices, currants and pine nuts, and stuffed into vegetables; cooked with milk and sugar; baked into a heavy, moist bread; or soaked in water and ground to a pulp to form *sübye*, the basis of all traditional milk puddings. And the black slaves of the Ottoman courts were given the task of cooking *aside*, a mound of boiled rice which was lightly compressed and hollowed out to create a well in which a stew of meat, peppers and okra was served.

Eastern Anatolia is the main grain- and cereal-producing region. The lush valleys around Erzurum, once the home of the *Gürcü* (Georgians), flourish with rice paddies. Each area claims to have its own nourishing *pilav*, cooked in sheep's tail fat, *kuyrukyağı* (p. 220), or a slightly rancid-tasting clarified butter, both of which lend their distinct flavours to the dish. In eastern Anatolia *pilav* is often eaten with the rich, creamy yogurt and strong cheeses that are in constant supply from the high grazing pastures around Van and Kars. And the arrival of spring is celebrated in the villages of central and eastern Anatolia by the gathering of crocus bulbs which are then cooked into a special *pilav* over open fires.

A high-quality long-grain rice (which can be replaced with Basmati) is used for *pilav*, and a short round grain is used for stuffing vegetables. The Turkish word *pilav*, which is simply a dish of cooked grains and pulses, probably originates from the Persian methods, *cilow* and *pilow*. When a Persian method of cooking rice is used in eastern Anatolia, the word *çilav* is used to describe the dish. In many parts of central and eastern Anatolia the Turks still favour *bulgur*, cracked wheat, which is less expensive and just as flexible. Long-grain rice and *bulgur* are often married with lentils, beans, barley or vermicelli to make a more substantial *pilav*.

The Turks have their own methods of cooking rice and *bulgur*: *salma* – in which the rice is boiled in water or stock, simmered until almost all the liquid is absorbed, and then covered and left to steam; *kavurma* – in which the ingredients are fried in butter, oil or meat fat before the uncooked rice is added, followed by the liquid, and then cooked as above; and *buryani* – in which the cooked rice is combined with cooked meat, fish or vegetables and tossed over the heat to allow the flavours to mingle. The sturdy uncooked grains of rice are usually soaked in tepid salted water for about half an hour to remove the excess starch (know your rice before doing this, as an inferior grain will become too soft if soaked before cooking). To ensure light, fluffy results the rice is never stirred while cooking. The exception to the rule is *lapa*, which is stirred with salt until soggy and offered with lemon juice as a remedy for upset stomachs.

Çerkez pilavı
CIRCASSIAN RICE

In Turkey fresh coriander is used only in the cuisine of the Çerkez (Circassians). With the addition of coconut, called hindustan cevizi *(meaning 'Indian walnut'), the flavours evoke tastes associated with India. This dish can be made with rice or* bulgur *(p. 219), and makes a refreshing accompaniment to the numerous* köfte *(p. 219), kebab and grilled fish dishes.*

SERVES 4
8oz/225g long-grain rice
2 tablespoons clarified or ordinary butter
1 onion, chopped
4 cloves garlic, chopped
1 teaspoon sugar
2 tablespoons desiccated coconut
small bunch of fresh coriander leaves, chopped
1 pint/600ml stock or water
salt and freshly ground black pepper

✧ Wash the rice and soak if necessary. Drain well.

✧ Brown the onion and garlic with the sugar in the butter. Stir in the coconut, rice and most of the coriander. Pour over the stock, season with salt, and bring the liquid to the boil for 1–2 minutes. Reduce the heat and simmer until almost all the liquid has been absorbed. Remove the pan from the heat, cover with a dry dish-towel, and press the lid on tightly. Leave to steam for 15–20 minutes. Using a fork, toss the remaining fresh coriander in the rice and serve.

Vişneli pilav CHERRY PILAF

Melt the butter in a deep pan. Add the cherries and the sugar, and cook for 2–3 minutes, stirring them carefully. Stir in the caraway seeds and rice, and cover with the water. Add the salt and bring the liquid to the boil for 1–2 minutes. Reduce the heat and simmer, uncovered, until almost all of the water has been absorbed. Remove the pan from the heat, cover with a clean dish-towel, press the lid down firmly on top and let it steam for about 15–20 minutes.

Fluff it up with a fork, and serve with grilled or roasted chicken or meat.

Vişneli pilav
CHERRY PILAF

A lovely summer pilaf, tinged a slight shade of pink, and served hot or cold. Usually fresh sour cherries are used, but it can be made with dried cherries, reconstituted in water for an hour.

SERVES 4–5
8oz/225g long-grain rice
2 tablespoons clarified or ordinary butter
6oz/175g fresh cherries, washed and stoned
1 teaspoon sugar
1 teaspoon caraway or fennel seeds
1 pint/600ml water
½ teaspoon salt

Wash the rice and, if it is sturdy and starchy, soak it in warm salted water for about half an hour. Rinse and drain well.

Kürt bulgur pilavı
KURDISH CRACKED WHEAT PILAF

As bulgur is a versatile grain, it can be cooked and eaten with almost anything. Cooked plain with water or stock, it is tasty and healthy. This recipe is common in eastern Anatolia, where it is claimed by both the Turks and the Kurds, and it is eaten with spoons from a communal pot. A well is made in the hot cooked bulgur into which cool creamy yogurt is spooned, and melted butter is poured over the top. Traditionally the fat used to cook the bulgur would come from the sheep's tail.

SERVES 4–6
12oz/350g *bulgur*
1 tablespoon *kuyrukyağı* (p. 220) (sheep's tail fat), clarified or ordinary butter
1 onion, finely chopped
1 pint/600ml water or lamb stock
salt and freshly ground black pepper

Kürt bulgur pilavı KURDISH CRACKED WHEAT PILAF

6 tablespoons thick creamy yogurt
1 oz/30g clarified or ordinary butter

✧   Wash the *bulgur* and drain. Soften the onion in the fat, add the *bulgur* and cook for 1–2 minutes. Pour in the water or stock, season with salt and pepper, and bring the liquid to the boil. Cook vigorously for 3–4 minutes, then reduce the heat and simmer until almost all the liquid is absorbed. Remove the pan from the heat, place a dry dish-towel over it and press the lid down tightly on top. Leave to steam for a further 15–20 minutes. The cloth will absorb all the moisture.

✧   Fluff up with a fork and tip out on to a serving dish. Make a well in the centre and spoon the yogurt into it. Melt the butter and pour over the yogurt. Eat while the rice is still hot, cooled by the yogurt.

Nohutlu pilav
CHICKPEA PILAF

Every Friday when Mahmut Pasha, the famous Grand Vizier of Mehmet the Conqueror, invited his ministers to lunch he would serve an intriguing mound of rice and chickpea pilaf as the climax to the meal. Intriguing, because dispersed amongst the chickpeas would be solid gold balls, moulded by his goldsmiths to resemble chickpeas, which would bring good fortune to the guests lucky enough to procure them in their spoons. Finely chopped leek or spinach can be added to this pilaf.

<u>SERVES 4</u>

2oz/60g chickpeas, soaked for 6 hours or overnight

6oz/175g long-grain rice

1 onion, chopped

2 tablespoons *kuyrukyağı* (p. 220) (sheep's tail fat), clarified or ordinary butter

1 pint/600ml water or chicken or beef stock

salt and freshly ground black pepper

✧ Drain the chickpeas and cook in fresh water for about 45 minutes, until tender. Drain well. Wash the rice and soak if necessary.

✧ Soften the onion in the fat. Stir in the chickpeas and the drained rice. Pour in the stock, season with the

Nohutlu pilav CHICKPEA PILAF

Kıbrıslı üzümlü pilav LAMB AND SULTANA PILAF

salt and pepper and bring the liquid to the boil. Reduce the heat and cook until almost all the liquid has been absorbed. Remove the pan from the heat, cover with a dry dish-towel, and press the lid down tightly on top. Leave to steam for 15–20 minutes.

✧ Fluff gently with a fork and serve.

Kıbrıslı üzümlü pilav
LAMB AND SULTANA PILAF

There are many rice dishes that include meat, usually sweet or spicy. This version, sweetened with sultanas, is favoured in Northern Cyprus and western Turkey. It is often made, or served, with peppers and eaten with yogurt. Peppers accompanying this dish should be grilled, roasted or pickled.

<u>*SERVES 3–4*</u>

8 oz/225g long-grain rice

1 onion, chopped

1 red or green pepper, chopped (optional)

2 tablespoons *kuyrukyağı* (p. 220) (sheep's tail fat), clarified
or ordinary butter

2 tablespoons sultanas

2 tablespoons sunflower seeds

1 teaspoon ground cinnamon

½ teaspoon ground allspice

1 teaspoon cumin seeds, crushed

1 teaspoon *kırmızı biber* (p. 219)

1 pint/600ml water or lamb stock

1lb/450g minced lamb

salt and freshly ground black pepper

extra ground cinnamon

or chopped fresh parsley to sprinkle over the top

✧ Wash the rice and soak if necessary. Soften the onion and pepper in the fat. Stir in the sultanas, sunflower seeds and spices. Add the drained rice and pour over the stock. Season with the salt and pepper and bring the liquid to the boil for 1–2 minutes. Simmer gently until almost all the liquid has been absorbed. Remove the pan from the heat, cover with a dish-towel, then put the lid on tightly. Leave to steam for 15–20 minutes.

✧ Fry the lamb in its own fat in a shallow pan. Cook for 2–3 minutes until most of the liquid has evaporated. Season to taste.

✧ Layer the rice mixture with the minced lamb on a serving dish, starting with rice and ending with meat. Sprinkle the extra ground cinnamon or parsley over the top. Cover with foil and keep warm in the oven if not eating immediately. Serve hot.

Hamsili pilav
ANCHOVY PILAF

The one pilaf you can guarantee to find in the Black Sea region is hamsili pilav. *Long famous for its anchovies, the Black Sea is also well known for this rice dish made with them. It is often served on its own with lemon wedges to squeeze over it, or with other fish dishes. Sprats or small sardines could be used in place of fresh anchovies. Similar pilafs include prawns, mussels, scallops and octopus – these are sautéed in butter before being added to the rice,* buryani *style (p. 122).*

<u>*SERVES 6*</u>

1lb/450g fresh anchovies, cleaned and boned

12oz/350g long-grain rice

1 onion, finely chopped

2 tablespoons clarified or ordinary butter

1 teaspoon sugar

2 tablespoons pine nuts

2 tablespoons hazelnuts, roughly chopped

1 tablespoon currants

½ teaspoon ground allspice

1 teaspoon cinnamon

1½ pints/900ml water

salt and freshly ground black pepper

<u>*TO GARNISH*</u>

ground *sumak* (p. 221)

✧ Preheat oven to 375F/Mark 5/190C

✧ Sprinkle the anchovies with salt and put aside.

✧ Wash the rice and soak if necessary. Drain well.

✧ Soften the onion in 1 tablespoon of the butter. Stir in the nuts, currants, sugar and spices. Stir in the rice and pour over the water. Season with salt and pepper and bring the liquid to the boil. Reduce the heat and simmer until all the liquid has been absorbed.

✦ Grease a casserole dish generously with butter. Rinse the anchovies and line the dish with half of them. Tip the rice mixture on top, level it out, and arrange the remaining anchovies on top. Melt the other tablespoon of butter and pour it over them, cover the dish with foil, and place in the oven for 20 minutes until the fish are cooked.

✦ Sprinkle with *sumak* and serve hot with wedges of lemon.

Patlıcanlı pilav
AUBERGINE PILAF

Also known as Sultan Reşat pilavı, *this is a magnificent rice dish made extra delectable with meaty morsels of fried aubergine. Variations include mixtures of rice and* vermicelli, *rice and* kuskus (couscous), *or rice and* bulgur *(p. 219). Some of the best* patlıcanlı pilav *is to be found in a handful of restaurants in Istanbul.*

SERVES 4–6
2 aubergines, peeled in zebra stripes (see p. 25), cut in
quarters lengthways and sliced
sunflower oil for deep-frying
12oz/350g long-grain rice
1 onion, chopped
4 cloves garlic, chopped
2 tablespoons clarified butter or olive oil
1 teaspoon sugar
1 teaspoon cumin seeds

1 teaspoon coriander seeds
2 tomatoes, skinned and chopped
1 teaspoon tomato purée
1½ pints/900ml water
salt and freshly ground black pepper

✦ Soak the aubergine slices in salted water for 1 hour.

✦ Wash the rice and soak if necessary. Drain well.

✦ Soften the onion and garlic in the butter or olive oil. Stir in the sugar, coriander and cumin seeds and cook for 1–2 minutes. Stir in the tomato purée and tomatoes, and cook for a further 3–4 minutes. Add the rice and pour in the water, season with salt and pepper and bring the liquid to the boil for 1–2 minutes. Simmer gently until almost all the liquid has been absorbed. Remove the pan from the heat, cover with a dish-towel, then press the lid down tightly on top. Leave to steam for 15–20 minutes.

✦ Heat a thick layer of sunflower oil in a shallow pan. Drain the aubergines, squeeze them dry, and fry in the oil until golden-brown. Drain on absorbent kitchen paper.

✦ Turn the rice mixture on to a serving dish. Fluff up with a fork, tossing the aubergine in it. Serve hot or cold.

Ermeni pilavı
ARMENIAN RICE WITH PUMPKIN

This unusual sweet and fruity caramelized rice dish, of Armenian origin, is particularly good served in the winter with grilled or roasted meat. Melted honey can be used instead of sugar.

Patlıcanlı pilav AUBERGINE PILAF

SERVES 4–5

8oz/225g long-grain rice

1½lb/675g peeled pumpkin flesh, finely sliced and parboiled

1 tablespoon sultanas, chopped

1 onion, chopped

3–4 cloves

1 tablespoon clarified butter

1 pint/600ml water

2–3oz/60–90g sugar

1 teaspoon cardamom seeds, crushed

1 teaspoon ground cinnamon

1 teaspoon ground allspice

3oz/90g ordinary butter

salt and freshly ground black pepper

✧ Preheat oven to 400F/Mark 6/200C

✧ Wash the rice and drain. Melt the clarified butter in a deep pan, soften the onion and stir in the rice, cloves and sultanas. Pour over the water, season with salt and pepper, and bring the liquid to the boil. Reduce the heat and simmer until it has been absorbed.

✧ Generously grease an oven-proof dish, sprinkle it with a little of the sugar, and line it with half the pumpkin slices. Mix the cardamom seeds with the cinnamon, cloves and the rest of the sugar. Melt the ordinary butter in a pan and pour half of it over the bottom layer of pumpkin. Sprinkle half the spiced sugar over the top. Spoon the rice mixture on top of that, spread it evenly, and sprinkle with a little of the spiced sugar. Arrange the remaining slices of pumpkin over the top and press them down firmly. Pour over the remaining butter and sprinkle with the rest of the spiced sugar.

✧ Place in the oven for about 25–30 minutes, until the pumpkin is tender and caramelized on top. Serve hot.

İç pilavı

CHICKEN LIVER PILAF
WITH PINE NUTS AND ALMONDS

Made with chicken livers in Istanbul and Izmir and with lambs' liver in parts of Anatolia, iç pilavı is a delightful aromatic rice dish. It is often eaten on its own with yogurt, although it goes well with a plain kebab or with meat cooked in the kavurma *style (see p. 150).*

SERVES 6

8oz/225g chicken livers, trimmed and cut into small pieces

12oz/350g long-grain rice

2 tablespoons clarified or ordinary butter

1 onion, chopped

4 cloves garlic, chopped

2 tablespoons pine nuts

2 tablespoons almonds, quartered lengthways

1 tablespoon currants, soaked in water

½ teaspoon ground allspice

1 teaspoon dried basil

small bunch of fresh parsley and dill, chopped

salt and freshly ground black pepper

1½ pints/900ml chicken stock or water

TO GARNISH

Turkish saffron or chopped fresh parsley

✧ Wash the rice and soak if necessary.

✧ In a wide saucepan, soften the onion and garlic in the butter. Stir in the nuts and cook for 2 minutes. Stir in the currants, allspice and basil and add the chicken livers. Cook until lightly browned. Season with salt and pepper and toss in the fresh herbs. Remove the mixture from the pan and put aside.

◆ Put the drained rice in the pan and toss it for 1–2 minutes in the butter. Pour over the stock, and bring the liquid to the boil for 1–2 minutes. Simmer gently until it has been absorbed. Carefully fold the chicken liver mixture into the rice, then remove the pan from the heat. Cover with a dish-towel, press the lid down tightly on top, and leave to steam for 15–20 minutes.

◆ Tip it all on to a serving dish. Fluff up with a fork and sprinkle with the saffron or parsley.

Kuzulu bulgur pilavı
CRACKED WHEAT WITH SPICY LAMB

This spicy dish from central and eastern Anatolia is delicious on its own or as part of a meat course. This particular recipe from Kayseri also works well with kuskus *(couscous). Chopped spinach is sometimes added to the pan with the meat at the end of the recipe.*

SERVES 3–4
12oz/350g *bulgur* (p. 219)
8oz/225g shoulder of lamb, cubed
1 onion, chopped
2 tablespoons *kuyrukyağı* (p. 220) (sheep's tail fat), clarified or ordinary butter
1 teaspoon tomato purée
1 pint/600ml lamb stock or water
1 teaspoon ground cumin
1 teaspoon ground coriander
1 teaspoon *kırmızı biber* (p. 219)
salt

◆ Wash and drain the *bulgur*. Soften the onion in the fat and stir in the *bulgur* with the tomato purée. Pour over the stock or water, season with a little salt and bring the liquid to the boil for 1–2 minutes. Reduce the heat and simmer until almost all the liquid has been absorbed. Remove from the heat, cover with a dry dish-towel, place the lid down tightly, and leave to steam for 15–20 minutes.

◆ Toss the chunks of lamb in the spices. Heat a wide, shallow pan and fry the meat quickly in its own juices until almost done. Tip the *bulgur* into the pan with the meat and cook them together for a few minutes. Serve hot with yogurt.

Kuzulu bulgur pilavı CRACKED WHEAT WITH SPICY LAMB

FISH AND SEAFOOD

In Islam fish and bread symbolize fertility, and Turkey appears to be resplendent in both. With shores on five seas, it certainly should be fish-rich. The markets still display catches of red and grey mullet, shark, swordfish, sea perch, sea bass, mackerel, tuna, turbot, sardines and many others but, regrettably, the numbers are dwindling, the result of serious overfishing.

The Black Sea is still famed for its anchovies and the infinite variety of dishes prepared with them. Anchovies are salted and dried, pickled, baked in roof tiles, baked into bread and pastries, cooked into rice and soup and even made into puddings. Celebrated in song and parable, the Black Sea anchovy has become almost immortal. But although Izmir and Istanbul still do good trade in the seafood drawn from their waters, the days when people could lean out of their *yalı* windows along the Bosphorus to buy fish from the passing boats are gone.

To anyone visiting Turkey briefly it might seem that a certain imagination is lacking in the cooking of fish, as it invariably arrives at the table either grilled or fried. Yet speak to anyone who is involved in fishing or indeed in boats or the sea in general, and he will enthusiastically share with you the joys of wrapping fish in vine leaves, spicing it with caraway and wild basil, stuffing it with nuts or casseroling it with tomato and cinnamon. Following ancient rules for preservation, small mackerel are cleaned, split open and salted before being hung up on lines to dry in the sun. Raw sardines and anchovies are marinaded in vinegar, and some fish are fried whole with their roe.

Fresh-water fish such as carp are popular in some areas. The people of Cappadocia eat a fat yellow fish that is reputed to be tasty. And a number of trout and salmon fisheries have sprouted up near Istanbul and Ankara, producing a palatable farmed fish which is gradually working its way into the cuisine of those cities. Although not native to Turkey, the salmon has featured in old records describing Ottoman feasts.

Fish, whole or in portions, is usually marinaded in lemon or onion juice with local dried herbs before frying, baking or grilling; and deep-fried seafood is served with a traditional *tarator* sauce (p. 221) made from walnuts, pine nuts, almonds or hazelnuts or with a garlicky bread sauce, *sarmısaklı sos* (p. 89).

Balık kebabı

FISH KEBABS IN VINE LEAVES

As long as the flesh is firm enough to cut into chunks most fish, from trout to swordfish and shark, lend themselves to kebabs. A simple kebab is made by alternating chunks of marinaded fish with pieces of tomato, onion or pepper on a kebab stick or spear, and grilling them over hot charcoal. Wrapping the chunks in vine leaves is more time-consuming, but you'll find it's worth it when you pop each juicy parcel into your mouth. Scallops and prawns also work well wrapped in vine leaves.

SERVES 2–3

12 large-bite-size chunks of firm-fleshed fish, skinned and boned

12 fresh or preserved vine leaves, washed and prepared (see p. 41)

FOR THE MARINADE

2 onions

juice of ½ lemon

2 tablespoons olive oil

4 cloves garlic, crushed

1 tablespoon dried oregano

1 teaspoon nigella seeds (p. 220)

salt and freshly ground black pepper

✧ Prepare the marinade. Grate the onions into a bowl, crush the onion pulp with a teaspoon of salt and leave to weep for about half an hour. Push the pulp through a sieve to extract the juice. Add the lemon juice, oil, garlic, oregano and nigella seeds. Season with a little salt and pepper.

✧ Soak the chunks of fish in the marinade and leave to sit for at least an hour, basting from time to time. Meanwhile, prepare the charcoal grill.

Balık kebabı FISH KEBABS IN VINE LEAVES

✧ Lay the vine leaves on a flat surface and place a piece of fish in the middle of each one, fold the edges over the fish and wrap up into a small parcel. Push the parcels on to a sharp kebab spear and brush with any remaining marinade. Place on a rack over the hot charcoal and cook for 2–3 minutes each side.

✧ Serve immediately with lemon wedges.

Midye dolması
MUSSELS STUFFED WITH PINE NUTS

Throughout the summer, families chug their way up and down the Bosphorus in their old wooden boats, diving in the shallows and amongst the foundations of the houses for mussels that they will later fry or stuff. Both Izmir and Istanbul are prized for their delectably aromatic stuffed mussels. They can be served as meze *or as a main course.*

SERVES 5–6
30 large fresh mussels, cleaned
2 onions, finely chopped
2 cloves garlic, finely chopped
2 tablespoons pine nuts
1 teaspoon sugar
3–4 tablespoons olive oil
1 tomato, finely chopped
1 teaspoon ground allspice
1 teaspoon ground cinnamon
½ teaspoon ground cloves
bunch of fresh dill and parsley, finely chopped
5oz/150g short-grain rice, soaked in warm salted water for 15 minutes
2 tablespoons currants, soaked in water for 30 minutes
salt and freshly ground black pepper

✧ Put the mussels into a bowl of cold water.

✧ Heat the oil in a pan and soften the onions, garlic and pine nuts with the sugar until they take on a little colour. Stir in the tomato, spices and herbs. Drain the rice and currants and add them to the pan. Season with salt and pepper and pour over just enough water to cover the rice. Simmer for 10–15 minutes, until the liquid is absorbed. Leave the rice mixture to cool.

✧ Place a colander or steamer in a pan with a little water. Using a sharp knife carefully prise each mussel shell open wide enough to spoon some of the rice mixture into it. Close the shells and pack them tightly into the steamer. Place a plate, weighed down with a stone, directly on top of them, to prevent them from opening, or tie a piece of thread around each shell. Cover the pan and steam the mussels for 20–25 minutes.

✧ Leave to cool, and serve cold with wedges of lemon.

Lüfer yahnisi CLASSIC BLUE FISH STEW

Lüfer yahnisi
CLASSIC BLUE FISH STEW

A way of cooking fish using the traditional flavourings – cinnamon to spice, currants to sweeten and vinegar to sharpen. Often made with blue fish (sea perch), it works well with the fillets or steaks of any firm-fleshed fish.

SERVES 3–4

4 blue fish fillets, cut into large pieces
2 red onions, halved and sliced
3–4 cloves garlic, chopped
2–3 tablespoons olive oil
6 plum tomatoes, peeled and left whole
1 tablespoon white wine vinegar
2 tablespoons currants, soaked in water for 30 minutes
1 teaspoon ground cinnamon
6–8fl oz/175–250ml water
salt and freshly ground black pepper
TO GARNISH
small bunch of chopped fresh parsley or Turkish saffron

✧ Heat the olive oil and soften the onions with the garlic. Lightly flour the fish pieces and add them to the pan. Quickly brown them on both sides, then remove from the pan. Stir in the vinegar, cinnamon, currants and tomatoes with a little of the water, and cook for 10–15 minutes. Pour in the rest of the water, adjust the seasoning and carefully place the pieces of fish in the sauce. Cook gently for a further 10 minutes.

✧ Serve hot, sprinkled with the saffron or parsley, and accompanied by a plain rice and lentil, or rice and vermicelli, pilaf.

Fırında kalamar dolması

SQUID STUFFED WITH HERBS

Another Ottoman dish, another cavity to stuff. This surprisingly rich dish requires young, tender squid and a lot of patience, but it is well worth while.

The squid are trimmed and cleaned by holding the body in one hand and tugging the head firmly with the other, so that the head and innards are released in one go. Whip out the transparent backbone and rinse the body sac inside and out. Sever the tentacles just above the eyes and trim the extra-long ones. Once rinsed, pat it dry.

<u>SERVES 4–6</u>
10–12 small young squid
2oz/60g *bulgur* (p. 219), soaked in boiling water for 30 minutes, drained and squeezed
big bunch of fresh mint, parsley and dill, finely chopped

Fırında kalamar dolması SQUID STUFFED WITH HERBS

2 cloves garlic, finely chopped

2 tablespoons tomato purée

2 tablespoons olive oil

juice of 1 lemon

salt and freshly ground black pepper

❖ Preheat oven to 400F/Mark 6/200C

❖ To prepare the filling, mix the *bulgur* with the herbs, garlic and tomato purée in a bowl. Bind with a little of the olive oil and lemon juice and season to taste.

❖ Using a teaspoon or your fingers, carefully stuff each squid with the mixture and seal up the hole with the tentacle plate. Lay them flat in a shallow oven-proof dish, pour over the rest of the oil and lemon juice, and bake in the oven for 15 minutes.

❖ Serve immediately.

SERVES 4

1 large whole mackerel

2 onions

2–3 cloves garlic, crushed with salt

2–3 tablespoons olive oil

1 tablespoon pine nuts

2oz/60g almonds, finely chopped

2oz/60g hazelnuts, finely chopped

2oz/60g walnuts, finely chopped

6 dried apricots, finely chopped

1 tablespoon currants, soaked in water

1 teaspoon ground cinnamon

1 teaspoon ground cloves

1 teaspoon ground allspice

1 teaspoon ground ginger

1 teaspoon *kırmızı biber* (p. 219)

small bunch of fresh parsley and dill, chopped

juice of ½ lemon

salt and black pepper

Uskumru dolması

MACKEREL STUFFED WITH NUTS AND SPICES

An impressive legacy of the lavish feasts produced in the Ottoman kitchens, uskumru dolması *is still one of Istanbul's most inspired dishes. The whole mackerel is emptied of its flesh, which is cooked with nuts and spices and then stuffed back into its skin. The end result is quite magnificent, and incredibly satisfying. It is fairly rich, and the addition of ginger to the spice mix, although not traditionally Turkish, gives it an interesting kick.*

Uskumru dolması MACKEREL STUFFED WITH NUTS AND SPICES

- Take the mackerel and, using a sharp knife, cut into the flesh just below the gills on the underside, as if to sever the head. Make sure the head remains attached to the backbone. Push your fingers down into the body and remove the guts. Rinse the fish inside and out under running cold water.

- Take a heavy mallet and gently bash the fish up and down the body on both sides, to soften the flesh and smash the backbone. Then massage and pummel the skin with your hands, loosening the flesh all the time. Be careful not to rip the skin.

- Squeeze from the tail end, gradually working your way up the fish as if you were trying to force the last out of an empty tube of toothpaste, to spew the mashed flesh out of the opening. Reach inside to extract the bits of backbone, and remove any small bones from the (surprisingly small) pile of flesh. After you have made sure that there is nothing left to squeeze out, once more rinse the empty mackerel inside and out. Put aside.

- Soften the onions and garlic in the oil. Add the nuts and cook for 2–3 minutes. Add the currants, apricots and spices and toss the fish flesh in the mixture until it is cooked. Stir in the fresh herbs, moisten with the lemon juice and season with salt and pepper. Leave to cool.

- Now hold the empty mackerel upright in one hand and pack the stuffing through the opening, shaking the mackerel to sink the mixture into the tail. As the cavity fills squeeze downwards, toothpaste-tube style, to ensure the stuffing is compact. Use your finger to keep pushing and stuffing, until the mackerel resembles its former self. (If there is any stuffing left over, stir in a little beaten egg and

mould into mini-*köfte*. Toss them in flour and fry them up to serve with the mackerel.)

- The stuffed mackerel can be either rolled in flour and fried, or grilled. As few pans are big enough to fit the whole fish, a hot charcoal grill is preferable. Cook for 2–3 minutes each side to buckle and brown the skin.

- Cut into thick slices and serve with wedges of lemon.

Balık köftesi
FISH BALLS WITH SUNFLOWER SEEDS AND CURRANTS

Fish köfte *(p. 219) are particularly popular in Istanbul and Izmir. They can be prepared with fresh or cooked fish flavoured with a variety of herbs and spices. They even work well with canned tuna.*

SERVES 4
1lb/450g fresh fish fillets
2 slices stale bread, rubbed into crumbs, or soaked in water and squeezed dry
4–5 spring onions, finely chopped
2–3 cloves garlic, crushed with salt
1 tablespoon sunflower seeds
1 tablespoon currants, soaked in water
2 teaspoons tomato purée (optional)
1 teaspoon ground cinnamon
small bunch of parsley and dill, finely chopped
1 egg
salt and freshly ground black pepper
a little plain flour for coating the *köfte*
sunflower oil for frying

✤ In a bowl, break up the fish with a fork. Add all the other ingredients and knead well with your hand. Form the mixture into small balls, flatten them, and coat them in the flour.

✤ Heat the oil in a shallow pan and brown the *köfte* on both sides. Then reduce the heat and continue to cook for 10–15 minutes, occasionally turning them until they are golden-brown all over.

✤ Serve hot with wedges of lemon and a salad version of *cacık* (p. 77).

Kırmızı biberli ahtapot
FRIED OCTOPUS

A simple light dish that takes seconds to cook. It makes a delicious meze, *light lunch or supper – just alter the quantities accordingly. To tenderize the fresh octopus, throw it repeatedly against a rock, on to the ground or against some other hard surface. Then remove the innards, eyes and beak and pound a few more times.*

SERVES 2–3
1 medium-sized octopus, prepared as described above
2 tablespoons olive oil with a little butter
1 tablespoon *kırmızı biber* (p. 219)
1 tablespoon green olives, stoned and finely chopped
2 tablespoons fresh parsley, finely chopped
juice of ½ lemon
salt and freshly ground black pepper

✤ Prepare the octopus as described above, and rinse well. Cut it up into bite-size pieces. Heat the oil

Kiremitte alabalık TILE-BAKED TROUT IN CABBAGE LEAVES

and butter in a shallow pan until very hot. Stir in the *kırmızı biber* and add the octopus, flipping it over and over, as it turns pink. Take the pan off the heat, and quickly toss in the olives, parsley and lemon juice. Season to taste, and serve immediately with bread and a salad.

Kiremitte alabalık

TILE-BAKED TROUT
IN CABBAGE LEAVES

In some parts of Anatolia whole fish are baked in the curve of a concave earthenware roof tile, the kiremit, *and placed in the hot* tandır *oven (p. 221), a method still in practice on the Black Sea coast. Further inland, too, in Cappadocia, fish is baked in a* kiremit – *this one a flat earthenware dish with a slight lip which can be placed in the* tandır *or directly over a flame. Reasonable-sized fish like trout, sea bass and mackerel are basted with olive oil and lemon juice and wrapped in cabbage leaves with a sprinkling of fish spice.*

SERVES 2–3

1 trout, cleaned and gutted
6–8 cabbage leaves, parboiled and refreshed
1 teaspoon fish spice (p. 40), crushed
1 tablespoon butter, melted
salt

FOR THE MARINADE

2 onions
1 tablespoon olive oil
1 tablespoon lemon juice

✧ Preheat oven to 325F/Mark 3/170C

✧ Grate the onions, pound the pulp with a little salt and leave to weep for half an hour. Push the pulp through a sieve to extract the juice and stir in the oil and lemon juice. Place the fish in a flat dish and pour over the marinade. Leave for at least one hour, turning the fish in the marinade from time to time.

✧ Lay a bed of cabbage leaves in the hollow of the tile, and place the fish in it. Pour over the remaining marinade, sprinkle with the spice and a little salt, and fold the leaves over the fish. Brush the leaves generously with the melted butter and bake for 30–35 minutes.

✧ Serve straight out of the oven with wedges of lemon.

Taratorlu sardalya dolması STUFFED SARDINES WITH PINE NUT SAUCE

Taratorlu sardalya dolması

STUFFED SARDINES WITH PINE NUT SAUCE

Large fleshy sardines are boned, filled and trussed for this delicious dish with its soothing sauce. Use a sharp knife to slit the underside of each sardine from head to tail. Remove the guts and carefully smooth the area around the backbone with your fingers to gently prise it out. Once released, snap it off at each end, keeping the rest of the fish intact. Rinse well under cold water.

As with all fish, these sardines are tastiest when cooked over a charcoal grill, but a conventional grill can be used.

SERVES 4–6

12 large sardines, prepared as described above

FOR THE STUFFING

6–7 spring onions, finely chopped

2–3 cloves garlic, crushed with salt

1 tablespoon olive oil

1 teaspoon cumin seeds, crushed

2 teaspoons ground *sumak* (p. 221)

small bunch of fresh parsley, finely chopped

1 egg, beaten

salt and freshly ground black pepper

FOR THE SAUCE

3oz/90g pine nuts, crushed

2 cloves garlic, crushed with salt

1 slice stale bread, soaked in water

juice of ½ lemon or pomegranate

2 tablespoons olive oil

salt and freshly ground black pepper

———

12 thin sharp sticks for trussing

✧ Preheat the charcoal grill

✧ Brown the onions with the garlic in the oil. Stir in the cumin seeds, *sumak* and parsley. Season to taste and put aside to cool.

✧ Prepare the sauce. Squeeze the bread to get rid of the excess water, and pound it with the nuts and garlic in a bowl (or whizz together in an electric mixer). Slowly trickle in the oil and lemon juice, beating all the time to form a smooth paste. Add extra oil or lemon to taste, and season with salt and pepper. Put aside, with a piece of damp greaseproof paper pressed down on top to keep it moist.

✧ Now moisten the stuffing with a little of the beaten egg, and spread a thin layer of stuffing down the middle of each sardine. Seal the flaps by threading the sticks in and out of the flesh. Sprinkle with a little extra *sumak*, and grill over hot charcoal for 2–3 minutes each side. Serve immediately with the pine nut sauce.

Karides güveç
BAKED PRAWNS

A dish with Mediterranean tones, karides güveç is usually cooked in small individual earthenware pots which were traditionally buried in the ashes of a hot open fire or kiln to slowly bake the contents. In Istanbul it is often made with fresh dill and parsley; along the Aegean, the principal flavouring comes from dried oregano; and the south Aegean and Mediterranean produce a spicier version using the local wild basil, caraway and coriander seeds. You can substitute

Karides güveç BAKED PRAWNS

Parmesan cheese for the kaşar peyniri *(p. 219) and, if you cannot find the pungent wild basil, use a greater amount of fresh Continental basil leaves.*

SERVES 4
1lb/450g fresh prawns, shelled and cleaned
2 tablespoons olive oil with a little butter

1 onion, finely sliced

2 çarliston peppers or 1 green bell pepper, finely sliced

1 green hot pepper or 1 mild chilli pepper, finely sliced

1 teaspoon sugar

3–4 cloves garlic, crushed with salt

1 teaspoon caraway seeds

1 teaspoon coriander seeds

handful of fresh wild basil leaves, ripped into pieces

3–4 large juicy tomatoes, chopped to a pulp

1 heaped teaspoon tomato purée

2oz/60g *kaşar peyniri*, coarsely grated

salt and freshly ground black pepper

❖ Preheat oven to 400F/Mark 6/200C

❖ Soften the onion and peppers in the oil and butter. Stir in the garlic, sugar, coriander and caraway seeds and cook for 1–2 minutes. Add the prawns and let them take on a little colour, then stir in the basil, tomato purée and tomatoes. Mix well, and cook gently for 5–10 minutes. Season to taste, spoon the mixture into individual pots, and sprinkle the cheese over the top.

❖ Bake in the oven for 15–20 minutes, or until the cheese browns on top. Serve straight from the oven.

Izgara balık
GRILLED FISH WITH DILL YOGURT

For many Turks there is only one way to cook fresh fish: grill it over charcoal. It is an easy way to cook shark, swordfish, tuna, sea bass and the sweet red mullet. Large fish are occasionally gutted before grilling, but small fish are left intact. Grilled fish are most often served with wedges of lemon on a bed of rocket leaves, but they also taste good with a light tahin *dressing (p. 221), a mild* tarator *sauce (p. 221), or simply with dill-flavoured yogurt.*

SERVES 2–3

4 medium-sized red mullet, cleaned

FOR THE MARINADE

4 onions

2 teaspoons salt

juice of ½ lemon or 4 tablespoons *sumak* juice (p. 221)

2 tablespoons olive oil

6–8 bay leaves, crushed between your fingers

FOR THE SAUCE

5 tablespoons thick yogurt

juice of ½ lemon

3 cloves garlic, crushed with salt

handful of fresh dill, finely chopped

salt and freshly ground black pepper

❖ Preheat the charcoal grill.

❖ Grate the onions, pound the pulp with the salt and leave to weep for 10–15 minutes. Push the pulp through a sieve, or squeeze it through a piece of muslin, to extract the juice. Mix it with the lemon juice, oil and bay leaves. Pour the mixture over the

FRESH RED MULLET WITH DILL

fish in a flat dish. Leave to marinade for 1–2 hours, basting from time to time.

✧ To prepare the sauce, beat the yogurt with the garlic and lemon juice. Season to taste, and stir in as much dill as you like – the sauce should have a lemony dill flavour. Put aside.

✧ Place the fish over the hot charcoal grill, brush them with the marinade and cook each side for 3–4 minutes. Serve immediately with the dill yogurt.

Sarhoş kalamar
SQUID WITH OLIVES IN RED WINE

It is rare to find wine or spirits used in classic Turkish cooking, but the wine in this dish gives it a gutsy flavour. It conjures up the essential taste of the Mediterranean and is known around the coast from Kuşadası to Marmaris as sarhoş kalamar, *drunken squid.*

SERVES 4–6
2lb/900g large fresh squid
2 red onions, sliced
4–6 cloves garlic, crushed with salt
3 tablespoons olive oil
4 tablespoons black olives, stoned
1 teaspoon ground cinnamon
1 teaspoon sugar
½ pint/300ml red wine
large bunch of fresh parsley, coarsely chopped
salt and freshly ground black pepper

✧ Rinse the squid, sever the head, trim the tentacles by cutting off the particularly long strands and gooey parts, pull out the bone, rinse again, and slice the tube into thick rings. Put aside.

✧ Brown the onions and garlic in the oil. Stir in the squid head and rings, and cook for 1–2 minutes. Add the olives, cinnamon and sugar, and pour in the wine. Cover and cook over a gentle heat for about 40 minutes, until most of the liquid is absorbed. The squid should be tender.

✧ Toss in the parsley, season to taste, and serve hot with lots of bread to soak up the sauce.

Tuzlanmış balık
SALT-BAKED FISH

This is a popular way of cooking fish in the cooling tandır *ovens (p. 221), once all the bread has been baked. Any large thick-skinned fish, such as sea bass, can be used. You immerse it in sea salt, which bleaches the flesh and enhances the taste of the sea.*

SERVES 4
1 fish (2–3lb/900g–1.4kg)
sea salt

✧ Preheat oven to 375F/Mark 5/190C

✧ Wash the fish and leave intact. Cover the bottom of an oven-proof dish with a thick layer of salt, and press down hard with the heel of your hand. Lay the fish on top of the salt and cover completely with another thick layer of salt. Again press down on the salt until it is compact.

✧ Place the dish in the oven for about an hour. Crack the salt with a hard object and carefully remove the top layer of the salt, taking the skin of the fish with it. Serve the whitened fish immediately, with wedges of lemon.

MEAT DISHES

The early Turks of Central Asia first bred horses for eating and riding, which were in turn used for herding sheep to new pastures. Since then every part of the sheep has been used for cooking in interesting ways: for instance, the popular *kokoreç*, grilled sheep's intestines stuffed with offal and spices; *kelle paça çorbası*, a soup made with the head and trotters of sheep; and in parts of Anatolia the flabby tails are burnt to release the fat, *kuyrukyağı* (p. 220), which has already figured in several recipes in this book and is used for cooking meat and grains. In addition to mutton and lamb, the early pastoral nomads lived off the animals they hunted, such as deer and hare. The meat was fried or grilled in its own fat over a high heat – the *kavurma* method – which enabled it to be stored for months underground in earthenware pots, protected in the congealed fat.

Later, cattle were domesticated, introducing beef and veal into the diet. As the calves are still reared naturally and slaughtered when one or two years old, the meat is pinkish-red in colour, lean and tasty. It is so well hung that even cuts of veal and beef used for mincing resemble fillet steak. Beef, veal and lamb are passed through the mincer twice, pounded, and then kneaded into all shapes and sizes of *köfte*. Minced meat is also stuffed with rice into vegetables, as in *etli dolma* (p. 168), or added to some rice, bean and other vegetable dishes to enhance the flavour. A special Anatolian circumcision dish, *keşkek*, which consists of *bulgur* (p. 219) and diced lamb, is prepared by the women, who take it in turns to stir the mixture until it is the consistency of porridge.

The *et mangal*, a portable outdoor meat grill, is popular in the spring and summer. Families leave the cities behind at the weekends to eat grilled meats in shaded country locations. A whole day may be spent around the *et mangal*, eating, drinking, playing games and dancing. Slices of lambs' liver, beaten lamb chops, chicken and *sucuk* (p. 221) are grilled over charcoal, sprinkled with oregano and *kırmızı biber* (p. 219), and served with yogurt.

Şiş kebabı LAMB KEBABS WITH TOMATO, PEPPERS AND ONIONS

And in eastern Anatolia *çöp şiş*, literally 'rubbish kebab', is made from scraps of meat marinaded in onion juice, threaded on to a skewer, charcoal-grilled, and then wrapped up in strips of *yufka* (p. 97) with slices of red onion, a sprinkling of dried oregano and a squeeze of lemon juice.

Islam imposes certain rules of fasting and feasting on holy days, as well as restrictions concerning meat and alcohol. The Koran forbids the consumption of animals slaughtered in any other manner than by having the throat cut; the consumption of an animal slaughtered for any other God; and the eating and drinking of an animal's blood, which it regards as a pollutant; and it prohibits any form of pork. This latter restriction is curiously overlooked by some airlines flying in and out of Turkey and its neighbouring countries.

At Kurban Bayramı, the festival to mark the near-sacrifice of Isaac, sheep are paraded for sale through the streets and markets of Turkey. Each family that buys a sheep sacrifices it, reserves a little meat for themselves, and distributes the rest to the poor. With the meat they have reserved the family will prepare *tatlı yahni*, a lamb stew with apples, apricots and onions; or *sarmısaklı yahni*, a garlicky stew with onions; or simply *kavurma*, by frying the meat in its own fat. The podgy tail is boiled and eaten with thick bread in a delicacy called *kıkırdak poğaçası*; and the intestines are boiled up into soup, *işkembe çorbası* (p. 81), or grilled, stuffed with spices, currants, pine nuts, onions and liver – a dish called *bumbar dolması*, which is similar to *kokoreç* (p. 149).

Patlıcan musakkası
SULTAN'S MOUSSAKA

Moussaka tends to be associated with Greece, yet it is as much part of Turkish cuisine as it is of Greek. In Turkish the word musakka *simply denotes a dish of fried vegetables with minced meat. Although the cuisines of the two countries share a history of imaginative dishes using aubergines and minced lamb, the white sauce was probably invented by the chefs of the Palace kitchens in Istanbul, who would have devised milk-based sauces to lend an air of sophistication to certain dishes. Today a sauceless version seems popular, but it does not match up to the classic cinnamon-spiced* musakka, *which is particularly good made with* keçup *(p. 41), instead of currants, to bind and sweeten the meat, then capped with its soothing white sauce. It should melt in the mouth.*

<u>SERVES 4–5</u>

4 aubergines, sliced crossways and soaked in salted water for 1 hour
sunflower oil for frying
2 tablespoons clarified butter, or olive oil with a little butter
2 onions, chopped
6 cloves garlic, chopped
2 tablespoons *keçup*, or 2 tablespoons currants, soaked in water
1lb/450g lean minced lamb
1–2 tablespoons ground cinnamon
1–2 teaspoons dried basil or oregano

Patlıcan musakkası SULTAN'S MOUSSAKA

salt and freshly ground black pepper

FOR THE SAUCE

1 tablespoon butter

2–3 tablespoons plain flour

10–12fl oz/300–350ml milk

pinch of salt and freshly grated or ground nutmeg

✧ Preheat oven to 400F/Mark 6/200C

✧ Drain the aubergines and squeeze dry. Heat a thick layer of sunflower oil in a frying pan and fry the

aubergines until golden-brown. Drain them on kitchen paper and put aside.

✧ Soften the onions and garlic in the butter or olive oil. Stir in the lamb, and cook for 3–4 minutes. Add the *keçup*, cinnamon and basil and cook for 4–5 minutes, until the liquid has been absorbed. Season the mixture with salt and pepper. Layer the aubergines and meat tightly in an oven-proof dish, starting and ending with the aubergines.

✧ Prepare the sauce. In a saucepan, melt the butter, remove from the heat and stir in enough flour to make a thick roux. Add the milk and stir continuously over a medium heat until the sauce is thick and smooth. (To make a richer sauce you can add 1–2 beaten egg yolks at this stage – first beat a little of the hot sauce into the egg yolks, then add them to the pan and beat vigorously.) Season with the salt and nutmeg. Spoon the sauce evenly over the top layer of aubergines, and place the dish in the oven for 25–30 minutes to brown the top and let the flavours mingle. Serve straight from the oven.

Arnavut ciğeri
LIVER SPICED WITH CUMIN

Directly translated as 'Albanian liver', this tender dish consists of liver cut into small cubes or long strips, spiced with cumin and kırmızı biber *(p. 219), and served hot or cold on a bed of sliced red onion. This method of cooking liver can be traced all the way up to Venice and Vienna. It is a popular* meze *(p. 220) and main-course dish in Istanbul, Izmir and Ankara, and a particularly spicy version is served in Adana.*

Arnavut ciğeri LIVER SPICED WITH CUMIN

Serves 3–4

1lb/450g lambs' liver

1 tablespoon plain flour

1 teaspoon _kırmızı biber_, ground or crushed

2 red onions, finely sliced

4 cloves garlic, chopped

2 teaspoons cumin seeds

2 tablespoons olive oil

salt

small bunch of fresh parsley and dill, chopped

✦ Using a sharp knife, remove the skin and ducts of the liver and cut it into thin strips or small cubes. Sprinkle the flour and _kırmızı biber_ over it, and toss well.

✦ Lay the onions on a serving dish. Sauté the garlic and cumin seeds lightly in the oil. Add the liver and fry quickly, turning it over and over. At the last minute, sprinkle with salt, toss in the herbs, then spoon the liver on to the bed of onions.

✦ Serve with thick yogurt and wedges of lemon.

Adana kebabı HOT ADANA KEBAB

Adana kebabı

HOT ADANA KEBAB

From Adana in the south of Turkey, this never fails to live up to its reputation for being the hottest of the Turkish kebabs. Spiced primarily with hot kırmızı biber (p. 219), it is grilled in one long piece as the sheath to the sword on which it is cooked. When presented at the table, the sword is ceremoniously pulled out of its sheath, which is then divided up.

Serves 4

1lb/450g minced beef (or beef and lamb mixed)

2 teaspoons _köfte_ spice mix (p. 40)

2 teaspoons _kırmızı biber_

1 egg white

salt

2 long kebab swords

✦ Preheat the charcoal grill or barbecue

✦ Pound and knead the meat with the spices in a bowl. Pick it up and slap it down into the bowl. Add the egg white and a little salt, and continue to knead until the mixture resembles a dough more than minced meat.

✦ Wipe the kebab swords with oil. Divide the meat mixture in two and roll into two thick sausage shapes. Push a sword through the middle of one, lengthways, and squeeze the mixture up and down the sword, spreading it evenly. Repeat with the other. Make sure the meat is firmly attached to the swords. Grill the kebabs for 3–4 minutes so that they are just cooked.

✦ Serve immediately with yogurt.

Şiş kebabı
LAMB KEBABS WITH TOMATO, PEPPERS AND ONIONS

Şiş kebabı and other kebabs are traditionally cooked over open fires and eaten outdoors. Marinaded cubes of meat are usually threaded on to skewers alternating with tomatoes, hot peppers and small pieces of sheep's tail fat, kuyrukyağı *(p. 220), for flavour. Pieces of aubergine, onion and mushrooms are sometimes added to the line-up, which can also include lambs' kidneys – as in* kuzu böbreği şişte. *Invariably, kebabs are served with* pide *(p. 94) and yogurt.*

Serves 4
1lb/450g shoulder of lamb, cubed
3 small tomatoes, cut into eighths
8 hot or sweet green peppers, cut into bite-size pieces
For the marinade
juice of 2 onions
4 cloves garlic, crushed with salt

1 teaspoon cumin seeds, crushed
1 tablespoon olive oil

✦ Preheat the charcoal grill

✦ Mix up the marinade ingredients, then marinade the lamb for at least 6 hours to absorb the flavour. Thread the marinaded lamb pieces, tomatoes and peppers alternately on to skewers.

✦ Cook over a hot charcoal grill for 3–4 minutes, until the lamb is just cooked. Serve with yogurt and *pide*.

Kadınbudu köfte
LADIES' THIGHS

*There's no mistaking the origin of this one. A spasm of humour, passion or debauchery took over the Ottoman Palace kitchens, resulting in colourful names for certain dishes. In contrast to the meaty ladies' thighs, images of ladies' navels (*kadın göbeği*, p. 196), young*

Kadınbudu köfte LADIES' THIGHS

*girls' breasts (*kız memesi, *p. 183) and sweetheart's lips (*dilber dudağı, *p. 196) were also conjured up in specific syrupy desserts.*

<u>SERVES 4–6</u>
1lb/450g minced lamb
4oz/120g short-grain rice, cooked
1 tablespoon clarified or ordinary butter
1 onion, chopped
½ teaspoon *köfte* spice (p. 40)
½ teaspoon ground cinnamon
2 eggs
big bunch of fresh parsley, finely chopped
salt and freshly ground black pepper
plain flour for coating
2 eggs, beaten, for dipping
sunflower oil for frying

✧ In a shallow pan, brown the onion in the butter. Add half of the meat and cook until all the liquid is absorbed. Stir in the rice and mix well.

✧ Put the remaining half of the meat in a bowl with the parsley, the 2 eggs, the cinnamon and *köfte* spice, a little salt and pepper. Add the cooked meat and rice and knead well. Mould small portions of the mixture into oval shapes, flatten them and dip them in the flour.

✧ Heat a thick layer of oil in a frying pan. Dip each *köfte* into the beaten egg and drop into the oil. Cook until firm and golden-brown on both sides. Drain on kitchen paper and serve hot.

Klasik köfte CLASSIC MEATBALLS

Klasik köfte
CLASSIC MEATBALLS

Splendidly simple and tasty, these classic köfte *evoke all the flavours of the Ottoman Palace kitchens. They are best served with a salad version of* cacık *(p. 77).*

<u>SERVES 4–6</u>
8oz/225g minced lamb
1 red onion, finely chopped
4 cloves garlic, crushed with salt

Kiremitte kebab TILE-BAKED KEBAB

1 tablespoon *keçup* (p. 41)

1 tablespoon pine nuts or sunflower seeds

1 tablespoon currants, soaked in water

1–2 teaspoons ground cinnamon

½ teaspoon *kırmızı biber* (p. 219)

2 slices bread, rubbed into crumbs

1 egg

big bunch of fresh parsley and dill, chopped

salt and freshly ground black pepper

plain flour for coating

sunflower oil for frying

✧ In a bowl, pound the meat with the onion and garlic. Add all the other ingredients and knead well, slapping the mixture against the sides and base of the bowl. Shape the mixture into small round balls, flatten them and roll them in the flour.

✧ Heat a deep layer of oil in a frying pan and brown the *köfte* on all sides. Drain on kitchen paper and serve with lemon wedges, yogurt or *cacık*.

Kiremitte kebab
TILE-BAKED KEBAB

In Cappadocia one restaurant has invented its own version of this dish – testi kebab, which is cooked in an earthenware pot shaped like a vase. The meat is pushed down the neck into the belly of the pot with peppers, tomato and spices, and is then left standing near the ovens all day to cook slowly, sealed with a thin piece of dough. To serve, the neck is whacked off with a heavy blade, and the contents are spilled from the belly. In the rest of central Anatolia, the meat is simply cooked gently in a flat earthenware dish or on a roof tile. Diced potatoes can also be added to the following recipe.

1lb/450g shoulder of lamb, diced into small pieces

1 tablespoon sheep's tail fat (*kuyrukyağı*, p. 220), clarified or ordinary butter

1 large onion, sliced

1 large green pepper, sliced

4–6 cloves garlic, chopped

2 large juicy tomatoes, skinned and chopped

1 scant teaspoon ground fenugreek

1 teaspoon dried oregano

1 teaspoon cumin seeds

salt and freshly ground black pepper

✧ Preheat oven to 300F/Mark 2/150C

✧ Melt the fat in an earthenware dish and spread it to the sides. When the dish is hot, brown the meat in the fat. Stir in the rest of the ingredients except the salt and pepper, and mix well. Cover the dish with foil, place it in the oven and cook for about 2 hours, until the meat is very tender and well flavoured. Season to taste, and serve.

Kavurma dana pirzola
VEAL CHOPS WITH LEMON AND OREGANO

Using the ancient kavurma *method (p. 149), this is the simplest way of preparing meat. The veal chops are trimmed and flattened with a heavy object before frying quickly in their juice and fat. If the meat is well hung and tender, it is extremely tasty.*

6–8 veal chops, trimmed and flattened

juice of ½ lemon

1 teaspoon dried oregano

½ teaspoon salt

✤ Heat a griddle or heavy-based shallow pan. When hot, place the chops on it and cook for 1–2 minutes until lightly browned. Flip them over and start to brown the other side. Squeeze the lemon over them, allow the juices to sizzle, and sprinkle with the oregano and salt. They should be lightly browned and only just done.

✤ Serve immediately with wedges of lemon and *çingene pilavı* (p. 65), or any salad, vegetable dish or *pilav*.

Kavurma dana pirzola
VEAL CHOPS WITH LEMON AND OREGANO

Izgarada boğa yumurtası GRILLED BULLS' TESTES

Izgarada boğa yumurtası
GRILLED BULLS' TESTES

The testes of bulls and rams, koç yumurtası, *are particularly popular in eastern Anatolia. They are invariably grilled and served with* rakı, *often enjoyed by groups of men huddled around the* et mangal, *the outdoor meat grill. This version is from Amasya in central Anatolia.*

SERVES 4

4 fresh individual testes, washed, with outer membrane removed

2 tablespoons butter

2 cloves garlic, crushed with salt

kırmızı biber (p. 219) (optional)

✤ Preheat the chargoal grill

✤ Grill the whole testes over hot charcoal for 25–30 minutes. When cooked they should be lightly browned on the outside, with clear juices running inside.

✧ Melt the butter with the garlic. Slice each testis finely and pour over the melted butter. Sprinkle with *kırmızı biber*, if you like, and eat while still hot.

Karnıyarık
AUBERGINE STUFFED WITH LAMB

Literally, karnıyarık *means 'split stomach', which describes the way the dish is prepared. Although versions of it are made throughout Anatolia, this classic dish owes its origins to the inventiveness of the Palace kitchens. It can be made with any size of aubergine but, as it is quite filling, it is best made with smallish thin ones. The stuffed aubergines can be cooked on top of the stove or in the oven.*

SERVES 4

4 thin aubergines, peeled into zebra stripes (see p. 25) and soaked in salted water for 1 hour
sunflower oil for frying

FOR THE FILLING

8oz/225g minced lamb or beef, or both mixed together
1 large onion, finely chopped
2 tomatoes, skinned and chopped
3–4 cloves garlic, crushed with salt
1 tablespoon tomato purée

Karnıyarık AUBERGINE STUFFED WITH LAMB

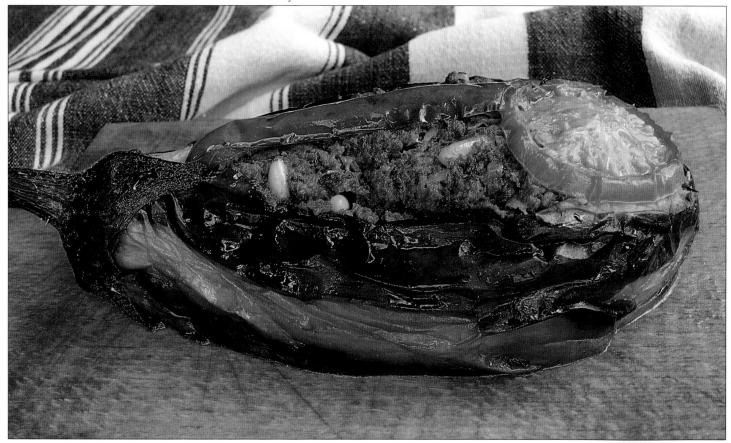

1 tablespoon pine nuts

1 teaspoon ground cinnamon

1 teaspoon ground allspice

bunch of fresh parsley, dill and mint, chopped

1 tablespoon olive oil

salt and freshly ground black pepper

FOR THE TOP

½ green bell pepper (halved lengthways)

1 tomato, sliced

COOKING LIQUID

4 tablespoons olive oil

4 tablespoons water

juice of ½ lemon

1 teaspoon sugar

❖ Preheat oven to 400F/Mark 6/200C

❖ In a large bowl, mix together all the ingredients for the filling. Knead well, lifting the mixture up into the air and slapping it back down into the bowl. Continue to knead until it resembles a paste.

❖ Drain the aubergines. Heat enough sunflower oil to deep-fry them in a shallow pan. Roll the aubergines in the oil, and cook until lightly browned and soft. Transfer them to a shallow oven-proof dish. Slit them down the middle lengthways, not quite reaching either end and taking care not to cut what is now the bottom of each aubergine; then prise open with tongs. Carefully stuff some of the meat mixture into each one, swelling them out until all the meat is used up and the aubergines look like canoes.

❖ Cut the half-pepper into 4 slices and place a slice of pepper and a slice of tomato over the stuffing of each aubergine.

❖ Mix together the ingredients for the cooking liquid and pour it over the aubergines. Cover with foil and place in the oven for 25–30 minutes. Remove the foil and put back in the oven for a further 40 minutes, until the meat and aubergines are very tender and almost all the liquid has evaporated. Serve hot or cold.

İçli köfte
MOTHER-IN-LAW'S MEATBALLS

A traditional Anatolian dish prepared by the mother-in-law of a new bride. She hollows out the köfte, *fills them with a spicy mixture, seals them, and presents them to her new daughter-in-law. This signifies that the bride's lips must now be sealed with discretion.*

İçli köfte MOTHER-IN-LAW'S MEATBALLS

SERVES 4–6

FOR THE KÖFTE

8oz/225g minced lamb

8oz/225g *bulgur* (p. 219)

1 teaspoon *kırmızı biber* (p. 219)

1 teaspoon salt

2 tablespoons plain flour for coating

sunflower oil for deep-frying

FOR THE FILLING

1 onion, finely chopped

4 cloves garlic, crushed with salt

1 tablespoon clarified butter, or olive oil and a little butter

1oz/30g walnuts, finely chopped

1 teaspoon coriander seeds, crushed

4–5 allspice berries, crushed

½ teaspoon cumin seeds, crushed

4oz/120g minced lamb

½ teaspoon dried thyme

½ teaspoon dried oregano

small bunch of fresh parsley, chopped

salt and freshly ground black pepper

✧ Put the *bulgur* in a bowl, cover with boiling water and soak for 30 minutes. Squeeze it dry and add the minced lamb, *kırmızı biber* and salt. Knead well and pound to a thick paste. Take small portions of the mixture and mould into egg-shaped *köfte*. Using a finger, hollow out an opening in each one and put them aside.

✧ Prepare the filling. Soften the onion and garlic in the butter or oil, then stir in the spices and walnuts and add the second lot of minced lamb. Cook for 3–4 minutes. Stir in the herbs and season to taste.

✧ Stuff some of the filling into each hollowed-out *köfte* and pinch the top edges together to seal it.

Roll the sealed *köfte* in a little flour and fry in plenty of oil until golden-brown. Serve hot with yogurt and *çoban salatası* (p. 67), *portakal salatası* (p. 68), or *kereviz salatası* (p. 61).

Ekşili köfte

MEATBALLS IN EGG AND LEMON SAUCE

These 'sour meatballs' are also known as terbiyeli *('well behaved')* köfte. *The dish dates back to a period of experimentation with sauces in the Palace cooking during the Ottoman Empire. It is usually served with a plain* pilav.

SERVES 4–6

FOR THE KÖFTE

1lb/450g minced lamb

1 onion, grated

1 tablespoon rice, washed and drained

Ekşili köfte MEATBALLS IN EGG AND LEMON SAUCE

bunch of fresh dill and parsley, chopped
1 teaspoon salt
1–2 tablespoons plain flour for rolling
FOR THE COOKING LIQUID
2 carrots, peeled and diced
1½ pints/900ml water
2 potatoes, peeled and diced
FOR THE SAUCE
2 egg yolks
juice of 2 lemons
salt and freshly ground black pepper

❖ Knead the *köfte* ingredients together and pound to a paste. Take small portions of the mixture and shape them into small balls. Roll them in the flour and put aside.

❖ Put the carrots in a pan and add the water. Bring to the boil and cook for 10 minutes. Drop the *köfte* into the water with the carrots, cover the pan and bring the liquid to the boil again. Reduce the heat and simmer for 15–20 minutes. Add the potatoes and extra water if necessary, and simmer for a further 15–20 minutes until the rice has cooked in the *köfte* and the vegetables are tender but not soft. At this stage the dish will resemble a thin meatball soup.

❖ At the last minute, in a bowl beat the egg yolks until light. Beat in the lemon juice, add a little of the hot liquid from the pan to the mixture, and pour it all into the pan to make the cooking liquid into a sauce. Stir well and heat through, but be careful not to boil the liquid. Season and serve.

Kuru köfte
PICNIC MEATBALLS

Although translated as 'dry meatballs', these köfte *are beautifully moist, light and tasty. They are called 'dry' because, unlike most other* köfte *which are often combined with currants, pine nuts, vegetables, batters and sauces, these are simply flavoured with onion and herbs. When cooked they retain their moistness and keep for days. Ever since they were packed into the* sefer tası, *a stack of tin dishes once used by soldiers, merchants and traders and carried on journeys, they have become associated with travelling and picnics.*

SERVES 4–6
1lb/450g minced veal or lamb
1 onion, grated
1 slice stale bread, soaked in water and squeezed dry
1 egg, beaten
1 teaspoon dried thyme or oregano
small bunch of fresh parsley, finely chopped
salt and freshly ground black pepper
sunflower oil for frying

❖ Mix and knead all the ingredients together. Punch the mixture with your knuckles to knock out the air, lift it into the air and slap it down into the bowl. Repeat until the smooth surface of the pasty mixture begins to crack. Roll and shape small portions of it into logs, and gently flatten them.

❖ Heat a thick layer of oil in a shallow pan. Brown the flattened *köfte* in the oil and watch them puff out, back to the original log shape. Serve hot or cold.

Kuru köfte PICNIC MEATBALLS

Kuzu ve ayva yahnisi
LAMB AND QUINCE STEW

The early Mevlani texts refer to lamb cooked with apples, plums, grapes, apricots, quinces and figs. Lamb and fruit casseroles are particularly popular in Bursa and Konya, two Islamic strongholds. This dish works equally well with veal.

SERVES 4–6

2lb/900g shoulder of lamb, cut into bite-size chunks

3 tablespoons *kuyrukyağı* (p. 220) (sheep's tail fat), clarified butter, or oil with a little butter

8–10 shallots, peeled and left whole

4 cloves garlic, roughly chopped

2 quinces, peeled, cored and each cut into 8 segments

1 teaspoon cloves, crushed

1 teaspoon ground cinnamon

1 tablespoon tomato purée

¼ pint/150ml water

bunch of fresh parsley, chopped

salt and freshly ground black pepper

1 tablespoon sugar or honey

✧ Preheat oven to 400F/Mark 6/200C

✧ Heat the fat in a pan. Brown the meat and remove from the pan. Add the shallots, garlic, quince and spices to the fat in the pan and cook for 3–4 minutes. Remove the quince from the pan and stir in the tomato purée. Return the meat to the pan and pour over the water. Bring the liquid to the boil, reduce the heat, and simmer for 15–20 minutes. Stir in the parsley and season to taste.

✧ Tip the mixture into an oven-proof dish. Lay the slices of quince over the top and sprinkle with the sugar. Place in the oven for 20–25 minutes until the quince segments have caramelized on top. Serve hot with *nohutlu pilav* (p. 125).

Yoğurtlu paça
SHEEP'S TROTTERS IN YOGURT

This earthy dish is particularly popular in southeast Anatolia, where it is one of the many designed to use up spare parts of the sheep cooked at the Islamic festival Kurban Bayramı.

SERVES 4

8 sheep's trotters, scrubbed, blanched in boiling water and drained

6–8 slices stale bread, crusts removed

2–3 tablespoons sheep's tail fat (*kuyrukyağı*, p. 220) or butter

STOCK

juice and rind of 1 lemon

4 cloves garlic, bruised

4 bay leaves, crushed

1 teaspoon coriander seeds, crushed

1 hot red chilli

salt and freshly ground black pepper

FOR THE SAUCE

½ pint/300ml thick yogurt

4 cloves garlic, crushed with salt

FOR THE TOP

2 tablespoons butter

1 teaspoon *kırmızı biber* (p. 219)

✧ Preheat oven to 350F/Mark 4/180C

✧ Place the trotters in a saucepan, and cover with water and all the stock ingredients except for the salt and pepper. Bring to the boil, reduce the heat, cover, and simmer for about 4 hours. Drain the trotters, reduce the stock and season with the salt and pepper. Bone the trotters and put the meat aside.

✧ Fry the bread in the fat until crisp. Lay the slices flat in a shallow oven-proof dish and arrange the meat on top. Moisten with a little of the reduced stock, cover with foil and place in the oven for 5–10 minutes, to heat through.

✧ Prepare the sauce. Beat the yogurt with the garlic and bind with a little of the stock. Melt the butter and stir in the *kırmızı biber*. Take the dish out of the oven, spoon the yogurt over the top and garnish with the melted butter. Serve immediately with *pide* (p. 94) to soak up the sauce.

Ermeni köftesi
MINCED MEAT LOAF

Variations of this dish can be found in central and eastern Anatolia – this recipe is Armenian. Instead of the minced meat being shaped into small balls, it is spread flat in an oven-proof dish or baking tin and cut like a loaf. It is delicious served with yogurt or beğendi *(p. 166).*

SERVES 3–4
1lb/450g minced lamb or veal
1 onion, chopped
4 cloves garlic, crushed with salt
1 tablespoon clarified butter, or olive oil with a little butter

1 teaspoon cumin seeds, crushed
1 teaspoon coriander seeds, crushed
1 egg, beaten
salt and freshly ground black pepper
butter for greasing
FOR THE SAUCE
1 tablespoon tomato purée
2 tablespoons *tahin* (p. 221)
2 cloves garlic, crushed with salt
1 teaspoon cumin seeds, crushed
½ teaspoon coriander seeds, crushed
small bunch of fresh parsley, chopped
4–6fl oz/175–250ml water
salt and freshly ground black pepper
TO GARNISH
2 teaspoons ground *sumak* (p. 221)

✧ Preheat oven to 350F/Mark 4/180C

✧ Soften the onion and garlic in the butter or olive oil, with the cumin and coriander seeds. Leave to cool.

✧ Pound the meat in a bowl. Add the onion mixture, the egg and the seasoning. Knead well, lifting it up and slapping it down into the bowl until it resembles a paste. Grease a baking tin or shallow oven-proof dish with the butter, and spread the meat evenly in it. Bake in the oven for about 30–40 minutes, until it is firm and browned on top.

✧ Prepare the sauce. Mix together the tomato purée, the water, *tahin*, cumin and coriander seeds, parsley and garlic. Beat to a smooth consistency. Season with salt and pepper. Turn the meat loaf out of its tin on to an oven-proof serving dish or plate. Stir a little of the excess oil into the sauce and pour it evenly over the meat. Return it to the oven for

10–15 minutes, until the meat has absorbed some of the sauce. Cut the meat loaf into squares or wedges, sprinkle with *sumak* and serve while hot, with yogurt or *beğendi*.

Hünkâr beğendili köfte

MEATBALLS IN TOMATO SAUCE WITH AUBERGINE PURÉE

A classic Istanbul dish, a relic of the Ottoman Empire; literally translated as köfte *with 'Sultan's Delight'. The* beğendi *component is the aubergine purée, which can also be served with a number of other grilled meat and* köfte *dishes (p. 219). The meatballs and sauce can be prepared ahead of time, but the* beğendi *is best served fresh. You can replace* kaşar peyniri *(p. 219) with Parmesan.*

Hünkâr beğendili köfte
MEATBALLS IN TOMATO SAUCE WITH AUBERGINE PURÉE

SERVES 4–6

FOR THE KÖFTE

1lb/450g minced beef

2 onions, grated

4 cloves garlic, crushed with salt

small bunch of parsley, chopped

1 teaspoon *kırmızı biber* (p. 219)

½ teaspoon salt

2 tablespoons plain flour for rolling

sunflower oil for frying

FOR THE SAUCE

1 onion, finely chopped

5 cloves garlic, crushed with salt

2 tablespoons olive oil

5 tomatoes, skinned and chopped

2 hot green peppers or 1 green chilli, kept whole

1 tablespoon white wine vinegar

1 teaspoon sugar

salt and freshly ground black pepper

FOR THE PURÉE (BEĞENDİ)

4 aubergines

1 tablespoon butter

2 tablespoons plain flour

½ pint/300ml milk

4oz/120g *kaşar peyniri*, grated

salt and freshly ground pepper

✧ Mix all the *köfte* ingredients in a bowl and knead well. Shape the mixture into tiny balls, roll them in the flour, and put aside in the refrigerator or a cool place.

✧ To make the sauce, soften the onion and garlic in the olive oil. As they begin to colour add the tomatoes and peppers. Stir in the sugar and vinegar, and cook for 20–25 minutes. Add a little water if the tomatoes are not juicy, and season to taste.

✧ Prepare the purée. Cook the aubergines over a gas flame or charcoal grill until soft. Remove the flesh and chop to a pulp. Melt the butter in a saucepan, and stir in the flour to make a roux. Then pour in the milk, stirring all the time. Add the cheese, and stir until the sauce is smooth. Beat in the aubergine pulp and season to taste.

✧ Heat a thick layer of sunflower oil in a pan and fry the *köfte* until brown. Drain on kitchen paper, then drop them into the tomato sauce. Cook together for 5–10 minutes. Serve hot with the warmed-up *beğendi*.

Etli yaprak dolması
VINE LEAVES STUFFED WITH MEAT

These stuffed vine leaves are often spiked with a little hot pepper and tomato in parts of central and south-east Anatolia. This is the Istanbul version, served hot with yogurt.

SERVES 4
25–30 fresh or preserved vine leaves, washed and prepared (p. 41)

Etli yaprak dolması VINE LEAVES STUFFED WITH MEAT

FOR THE FILLING

12oz/350g minced lamb

2 onions, finely chopped

4oz/120g long-grain rice, washed and drained

bunch of dill, parsley and mint, finely chopped

1 tablespoon olive oil

salt and freshly ground pepper

COOKING LIQUID

¼ pint/150ml water

juice of ½ lemon

2 tablespoons olive oil

❖ Pound and knead the ingredients for the filling in a bowl. Lay the leaves on a flat surface and place a little of the meat mixture at the top of each leaf. Fold the sides over and roll the leaf up into a tight package. Arrange them in the base of a wide saucepan, jammed together so that they don't open while cooking. Mix together the cooking liquid ingredients and pour the liquid over the vine leaves. Place a plate on top, cover with a lid, and cook gently for 40–45 minutes. Serve hot with yogurt.

Karışık et dolması
VEGETABLES STUFFED WITH MEAT

Any vegetable that can be hollowed out is ideal for stuffing. The most common are large tomatoes, peppers, large onions, marrows and courgettes, aubergines and artichokes. It is more interesting and attractive to prepare a selection of stuffed vegetables. You cook the vegetables, decapitated and hollowed out before stuffing, in exactly the same way as the etli yaprak dolması *(p. 167) and serve hot with plain yogurt, garlic-flavoured yogurt or an egg and lemon sauce (p. 28).*

Karışık et dolması VEGETABLES STUFFED WITH MEAT

Kıymalı yumurta
SPICY MINCED LAMB WITH EGGS

In addition to köfte *(p. 219), minced lamb is cooked into many simple, tasty dishes, such as* kıymalı semiz otu, *a stew of minced lamb and lamb's lettuce, and* lahana kapaması, *cabbage leaves layered with minced lamb and baked. More than any of these dishes,* kıymalı yumurta *evokes the tastes of southern Anatolia and parts of the Middle East. It is ideal for a simple supper.*

SERVES 2

8oz/225g minced lamb

2 tablespoons sheep's tail fat (*kuyrukyağı*) (p. 220), clarified or ordinary butter

2 onions, halved and sliced

4 cloves garlic, crushed with salt

2oz/60g walnuts, chopped

1 teaspoon coriander seeds

1 teaspoon cumin seeds

1 teaspoon *kırmızı biber* (p. 219)

½ teaspoon dried oregano or thyme

small bunch of fresh parsley, chopped

salt and freshly ground black pepper

4 eggs

✧ Soften the onions with the garlic in the fat. Stir in the walnuts and spices. Cook for 2–3 minutes. Add the meat and cook for 3–4 minutes. Stir in the herbs and season with salt and pepper. Crack the eggs over the top, cover, and cook gently until the eggs are just done. Serve hot with yogurt.

Çebiç
ROASTED KID OR LAMB

Lambs and young goats are roasted whole on spits for special celebrations and ceremonies in Anatolia. The feasts will include courses of yogurt or okra soup, stuffed vine leaves, pilaf, yogurt, pickles and baklava. *Traditionally, the lamb or kid is roasted on a spit over a* tandır *(p. 221) oven. The slaughtered animal is dehorned, skinned, gutted and wiped clean before being spiked with pieces of garlic, inserted into holes pierced by a sharp knife point. The flesh is then rubbed with a marinade of yogurt, tomato purée, onion juice, crushed garlic, ground coriander and cumin, and whole onions are stuffed into the body cavity along with the liver, heart and kidneys. The flavours are left to penetrate the flesh for at least two hours.*

The feet of the animal are then tied with string and attached to an iron spit, which is lowered over the tandır. *A pan is placed at the bottom of the pit to catch the roasting juices, which will later be used to moisten the meat. As the fire dies down, the spit is gradually lowered until the animal is fully inside the pit oven. Wire mesh is placed over the opening and caked with mud to seal the heat inside. Depending on the age and weight of the kid or lamb, it can take 2–4 hours for the meat to cook. In the meantime, a huge* bulgur *(p. 219) pilaf is prepared and spread out on a platter. When the meat is done, it is placed on this bed of* bulgur *and basted in the roasting juices – then it's ready to eat.*

POULTRY AND GAME

The most common sort of poultry is chicken. Lean and tasty, it is most often used in soups and rice dishes, roasted with almonds and honey, stuffed with fresh figs and apricots, casseroled, or sliced and layered with peppers and sheep's tail fat (*kuyrukyağı*, p. 220) in *piliç döner*; and the breasts are used to make the famous milk pudding, *tavuk göğsü* (p. 198). The name for turkey is *hindi tavuk*, 'Indian chicken', which denotes the origins of the bird – not from India but from the New World. Reaching the Ottoman Empire all the way from Mexico in the sixteenth century, it is now mainly used for soup and rice dishes. Quails and their eggs are also popular, but perhaps these birds reached their celebratory heights during the lavish banquets of the Empire, when they were ingeniously stuffed whole into aubergines.

Although game is abundant in Turkey, many Turks of today have never eaten it. Early hunters and rulers, depicted in ferocious hunts on ceramic and silk, once ate deer and hare. But apart from a few exceptions like Mehmet IV (sultan, 1648–87), who led large hunting groups into the forests around Bolu, the Ottoman period saw a change of focus in the hunt as it ceased to be a quest for food and became more an activity designed to train young men for war. Hunting has now claimed a niche in the tourist industry, with brown bear, wolves and jackal in the forests of Artvin, Hakkari and Antalya, and wild boar in the Aegean, but outside the hunting areas it is rare to see even rabbit, hare or wild duck on a plate.

Patlıcan sarması CHICKEN THIGHS IN AUBERGINE

Çerkez tavuğu
SHREDDED CHICKEN WITH WALNUT AND CORIANDER

This is an Anatolian dish of Circassian origin, although the Armenians also claim it as their own. Its pale colour is believed to reflect the complexions of the Circassian women who, famed for their fair features and beauty, were captured to serve the Ottoman sultans in the harems, as concubines and wives. A true çerkez tavuğu is made with fresh coriander leaves, used liberally in traditional Circassian cooking but omitted by the tamer palates of the Istanbul chefs. If you prefer the Istanbul version, without coriander, finish the dish by spooning a little melted butter and kırmızı biber (p. 219) over the top. A less common dish, prepared in the same way, is çerkez fasulye, which is made with broad beans. Both are ideal for lunch and buffets.

SERVES 6
1 whole medium-sized chicken
3 slices dry white bread, crusts removed
¼ pint/150ml milk
6oz/175g walnuts, shelled
6 cloves garlic, crushed
small bunch of fresh coriander leaves, roughly chopped
salt and freshly ground black pepper

Çerkez tavuğu SHREDDED CHICKEN WITH WALNUT AND CORIANDER

STOCK
1 onion, roughly chopped

4 cloves

4 allspice berries

4 red or black peppercorns

3–4 bay leaves

1 teaspoon coriander seeds

salt

TO GARNISH

1 teaspoon olive oil

1 teaspoon *kırmızı biber*

3–4 walnuts, finely chopped

6–8 fresh coriander leaves, finely chopped

✧ Remove the excess fat from the chicken, and put it into a large pan with all the stock ingredients and enough water to almost cover the chicken. Bring the water to the boil, cover the pan and lower the heat, and leave to simmer for about an hour. When cooked, remove the chicken from the pan and leave it to cool a little before taking the meat off the bone – discard the skin. Tear the meat into thin strips and put them into a large bowl. Boil up the stock for a further 15–20 minutes to reduce it. Check the seasoning and strain.

✧ Soak the bread in the milk, grind the walnuts and garlic to a paste and beat into the soaked bread (or blend them all together in an electric mixer). Add the mixture to the strips of chicken and bind together with spoonfuls of the warm seasoned stock. Keep adding small quantities of stock until the consistency is light and creamy. Fold in the fresh coriander and season it to your taste. (If not serving immediately, trickle a little extra stock over the surface to keep it moist, and reserve some fresh coriander to fold in at the last minute.)

✧ When ready to eat, spoon the mixture on to a serving dish, combine the ingredients for the garnish and sprinkle them over the top.

Patlıcan sarması
CHICKEN THIGHS IN AUBERGINE

The sophistication of this dish suggests Ottoman origins, as each marinaded chicken thigh is carefully wrapped in strips of fried aubergine. It also works well with chicken breasts or pieces of veal fillet, and strips of courgette can be used as an alternative to aubergine. The deliciously lemony taste is best appreciated straight out of the oven.

SERVES 4

8 chicken thighs, boned and skinned

4–5 long thin aubergines

2 tablespoons toasted almonds, chopped

sunflower oil for frying

FOR THE MARINADE

juice of 3 lemons

4 cloves garlic, crushed with salt

4–6 allspice berries, crushed

✧ Preheat oven to 350F/Mark 4/180C

✧ Combine the ingredients for the marinade in a large bowl. Carefully roll the chicken thighs in the marinade and leave to soak up the flavour for at least 2 hours, turning them occasionally. Partially peel the aubergines in zebra stripes (p. 25) and slice finely, lengthways. Soak the slices in cold salted water for one hour to remove the bitter taste of the indigestible juices. Then drain them and squeeze out the excess water.

✧ In a shallow pan heat a thick layer of sunflower oil and fry the aubergines, a few at a time, until they take on a golden colour (be careful not to fry them harshly, or they will become too crisp for the purposes of this dish). Drain the slices on absorbent paper. Select 16 of them for wrapping and line the base of an oven-proof dish with those that are left over.

✧ Lay two slices of aubergine, one over the other, in a cross and place a marinaded chicken thigh in the centre. Tuck the thigh into a neat bundle, wrap the slices of aubergine tightly around it and place it, seam down, in the dish. Do the same with the other thighs, pour the remaining marinade over the top and sprinkle with the toasted almonds. Cover the dish with a lid or foil, and cook for 25–30 minutes. Serve the chicken straight from the oven.

Güveçte piliçli bamya
CHICKEN AND OKRA CASSEROLE

Okra is nearly always combined with tomatoes in a vegetable ragoût, or in a casserole with lamb or chicken. This chicken and okra casserole is popular all over Turkey, and is usually served with a plain pilav *or plenty of bread to mop up the sauce.*

<u>SERVES 4</u>
1 small chicken, cut into quarters
1lb/450g fresh okra
1 tablespoon olive oil and a little butter
2 onions, finely sliced
2 teaspoons coriander seeds
1 teaspoon roasted *kırmızı biber* (p. 219)
4–5 cloves garlic, crushed with salt
½ teaspoon sugar
1 tablespoon dried oregano
1 tablespoon tomato purée
3 large tomatoes, skinned and chopped
¼ pint/150ml water
juice of 1 lemon
salt and freshly ground black pepper

✧ First, prepare the okra: wash them, cut off the stalks and place them in a bowl. Sprinkle 2–3 tablespoons of white wine or apple vinegar and 1 tablespoon of salt over them. Mix thoroughly and leave to sit for at least one hour. (This enables them to retain their colour and removes most of the sliminess associated with cooked okra.)

✧ In a large pan or casserole dish, brown the chicken pieces in the olive oil and butter. Remove them and put aside. Add the onions, coriander seeds and *kırmızı biber* to the hot oil and cook for 2–3 minutes. Stir in the crushed garlic, sugar and oregano followed by the tomato purée, tomatoes and water. Mix well and bubble the sauce up for a few minutes before adding the chicken pieces. Cover the pan and cook gently for 25–30 minutes.

✧ Rinse the okra thoroughly and arrange them on top of the chicken. Pour the lemon juice over them, cover the pan again and cook gently for a further 20 minutes, shaking the pan from time to time. The okra should be slightly crunchy, not mushy.

✧ Place the chicken pieces on a serving dish, stir the okra into the tomato sauce, season it and spoon it over the chicken. Serve hot with yogurt and *nohutlu pilav* (p. 125), or a plain *bulgur* (p. 123) or *kuskus* (couscous) *pilavı.*

Güveçte piliçli bamya CHICKEN AND OKRA CASSEROLE

Patlıcanlı bıldırcın

AUBERGINES STUFFED WITH QUAILS

Quails are often boned and flattened, trussed up and grilled, then eaten in the hollow of a pide (p. 94). As they are so small, they can be wrapped in vine leaves, stuffed with fresh cherries and gently roasted or, as in this Palace creation, they can be fitted snugly into whole aubergines.

SERVES 2

2 plump aubergines, partially peeled in zebra stripes (p. 25)
and soaked in salted water for 1 hour
sunflower oil for deep-frying
2 quails, cleaned
2 bay leaves
2 tablespoons olive oil

FOR THE SAUCE

1 onion, finely sliced
2–3 cloves garlic, crushed with salt
1 tablespoon sunflower seeds
3 tomatoes, chopped
½ teaspoon ground aniseed
1 teaspoon sugar
small bunch of fresh parsley and mint, chopped
salt and freshly ground black pepper

✧ Preheat oven to 325F/Mark 3/170C

✧ Heat the olive oil in a shallow pan and brown the quails on all sides. Take them out, place a bay leaf in the cavity of each, and put them aside.

✧ Now make the sauce. Add the onion, garlic and sunflower seeds to the olive oil in the pan. Sauté for

2–3 minutes, then stir in the tomatoes, aniseed and sugar. Cook gently for about 10 minutes and then stir in the mint and parsley. Season with salt and pepper to taste.

✧ Rinse and drain the aubergines. Heat a thick layer of sunflower oil in a frying pan and roll the aubergines in the oil to brown them all over. Drain them on kitchen paper and slit down the middle lengthways without quite reaching the ends, taking care not to cut the bottoms of the aubergines. Prise the slit wide open with tongs and carefully fit a quail snugly into each one.

✧ Place the stuffed aubergines in an oven-proof dish and spoon the tomato sauce over them. Cover with a lid or foil, and place them in the oven for 1 hour. Then remove the lid, baste with the sauce, and cook for 25–30 minutes.

✧ Serve straight from the oven with wedges of lemon.

Tahinli piliç

CHICKEN IN SESAME SAUCE

This simple dish is most often found in the Aegean region and in Northern Cyprus, although there is a Black Sea version made with fish. Garlicky with a crunchy topping, it is quite rich and is best served hot with a light herb and lettuce salad.

SERVES 4–6

4 chicken breasts, cut into thin strips
4 tablespoons *tahin* (p. 221)
1–2 teaspoons *pekmez* (p. 220)

Tahinli piliç CHICKEN IN SESAME SAUCE

juice of 1 lemon
4–6 cloves garlic, crushed with salt
salt and freshly ground black pepper
FOR THE TOP
1–2 tablespoons breadcrumbs
1 tablespoon pistachios, finely chopped,
or roasted sesame seeds

✦ Preheat oven to 400F/Mark 6/200C

✦ In a bowl, beat the *tahin* with the *pekmez*, lemon juice and garlic. Bind to a smooth, creamy consistency with a little water. Season with the salt and pepper and add the strips of chicken. Mix well and leave to marinade for 1 hour.

Tavşan yahnisi SPICED RABBIT CASSEROLE

✧ Spoon the mixture into a shallow oven-proof dish. Sprinkle the breadcrumbs and pistachios over the top and place in the oven for 25–30 minutes. Serve hot.

Tavşan yahnisi
SPICED RABBIT CASSEROLE

Although hares were once hunted for food, neither furry game nor alcohol feature much in the classic Turkish dishes. This recipe, though, contains both. The wine enhances the richness of the sauce.

SERVES 3–4

1 rabbit, jointed into 4 or 6 portions
2 tablespoons clarified butter, or olive oil with a little butter
10–12 shallots, peeled and left whole
8–10 cloves garlic, peeled and left whole
6 allspice berries, crushed
6 cloves, crushed
1 teaspoon coriander seeds, crushed
1 teaspoon roasted *kırmızı biber* (p. 219)
1 strong-smelling cinnamon stick
2 tablespoons raisins
1 tablespoon *pekmez* (p. 220)
¼ pint/150ml water
small bunch of fresh parsley, roughly chopped
salt and freshly ground black pepper
FOR THE MARINADE
1 tablespoon olive oil
2 tablespoons red wine vinegar
¼ pint/150ml red wine
2–3 bay leaves, crushed

✧ Mix together the marinade ingredients, and marinade the rabbit for at least 8 hours.

✧ Drain the rabbit joints and reserve the marinade. Heat the butter in a large pan or casserole dish and brown the joints. Transfer them to a plate and put aside.

✧ Brown the shallots with the garlic and spices in the same butter. Stir in the raisins and *pekmez* and return the rabbit joints to the pan. Pour over the marinade, add the water, and bring the liquid to the boil. Reduce the heat, cover, and cook gently for about 1 hour, until the rabbit is tender.

✧ Once cooked, transfer the joints to a serving dish. Bubble up the sauce, season it to taste, and remove the cinnamon stick. Spoon the sauce over the rabbit, sprinkle with the parsley, and serve with a spinach or plain *pilav*.

Portakalı piliç
CHICKEN IN SPICY ORANGE SAUCE

This dish comes from the area around Mersin in the south of Turkey where sweet, thin-skinned juicy oranges grow. The combination of oranges and spices gives it a tangy taste and, depending on the strength of the chilli peppers, it can be quite hot. It is delicious cooled with mint-flavoured yogurt and works well with the legs, thighs or breasts of chicken and turkey.

SERVES 4

6 chicken thighs
2 tablespoons clarified butter, or olive oil with a little butter
2 red onions, sliced
4–5 cloves garlic, crushed with salt
2 small thin-skinned oranges, each cut into
8 segments with the peel on

1 teaspoon nigella seeds

2 teaspoons coriander seeds

2 tablespoons currants, soaked in water for 30 minutes

1 tablespoon dark honey

1 strong-smelling cinnamon stick

1 teaspoon ground cinnamon

2–3 chilli peppers

a few fresh mint leaves

juice of 1 orange

¼ pint/150ml water

salt and freshly ground black pepper

To accompany

3–4 tablespoons yogurt

1 tablespoon fresh mint, roughly chopped

✧ Heat the butter or oil in a shallow pan or casserole dish, and lightly brown the thighs. Lift them out and put aside. Add the onions, garlic, orange segments, nigella and coriander seeds to the pan, and cook for 2–3 minutes. Stir in the currants, honey, ground cinnamon, cinnamon stick, mint leaves and chilli peppers and pour in the orange juice and water. Bring the liquid to the boil, reduce the heat and simmer for about 10 minutes. Return the thighs to the pan, cover with a lid, and cook gently for 20–25 minutes.

✧ Remove the cinnamon stick and chilli peppers and check the seasoning. Mix the yogurt with the chopped mint. Serve it with the chicken, or swirl it into the dish just before serving.

Tahir amcanın ördeği
UNCLE TAHİR'S WILD DUCK

A hunter's recipe for roasted duck, stuffed with chestnuts and herbs. Once shot, the bird is hung for 1–3 days and then cleaned, stuffed and roasted over an open fire. It is also good roasted in a conventional oven with honey and almonds.

Serves 2

1 wild duck, with giblets

salt

For the stuffing

1 red onion, or 2–3 shallots, roughly chopped

2–3 tablespoons clarified or ordinary butter

6–8oz/175–225g cooked chestnuts, roughly chopped

4–6oz/120–175g breadcrumbs

bunch of fresh dill, parsley and sage, roughly chopped

salt and freshly ground black pepper

To glaze

2 tablespoons golden runny honey

2 tablespoons whole almonds

✧ Preheat oven to 400F/Mark 6/200C

✧ Prepare the stuffing. Melt the butter and fry the onion until golden. Stir in the chestnuts and herbs and cook for 2 minutes. Bind with the breadcrumbs and season to taste. Put aside to cool.

Tahir amcanın ördeği UNCLE TAHİR'S WILD DUCK

✧ Clean the duck and trim the giblets. Rub the inside
and outside of the duck with salt, and spoon the
stuffing into the cavity. Skewer the legs with a stick
and place the duck on an oven tray or earthenware
dish, and scatter the giblets and almonds around it.
Spoon the honey over the duck and roast for
approximately 35 minutes.

✧ Serve straight from the oven with cherry pilaf (p. 123).

DESSERTS

Turkey is a nation of sweet tooths. Milk puddings and pastries are eaten at any time of the day. Every town boasts a maker of milk puddings (a *muhallebici*). On opposite sides of the country, Istanbul is famous for its *baklava*, Artvin for its milk puddings. Business is brisk, as people pop in and out of the specialist shops to drool over large portions of their favourite desserts and wash them down with a sherbet drink, before going on their way again.

Early records of layered pastries can be found in Turkish culinary history. Sheets of *yufka* (p. 97) would have been baked dry with chopped nuts and sugar, a forerunner of the more sophisticated *baklava* (p. 192). During the Ottoman period, a classic *baklava* created by the inventive Palace chefs consisted of fifteen layers, eight of them pastry dough and seven filling. During the reign of Mehmet the Conqueror, the Topkapı kitchens witnessed the industrious activity of specialist pastry makers, milk pudding makers, yogurt makers and *helva* (p. 203) makers. Amongst the special skills was the creation of the complex shredded *kadayıf* pastry, which is made by throwing the liquid batter through a sieve on to a sheet of metal suspended over a fire. As the dough sets it is scraped off the sheet and then stretched over cheese and baked, as *künefe*, or filled with nuts and moulded into syrupy desserts such as *kız memesi kadayıf*, 'young girls' breasts'.

According to Islamic custom, milk should have ceased flowing before it is consumed. It is rarely drunk neat, but turned into comforting milk puddings and ice-cream instead. The sweet and nourishing puddings are as varied and as popular as the syrupy pastries. Traditionally, all milk puddings are made from *sübye*, a milky substance extracted from rice that has been soaked in water and then ground to a pulp – the secrets of which few are willing to reveal. *Sübye* helps to set the puddings with a smooth texture, but a mixture of cornflour and ground rice, or rice flour, serves as a practical alternative. The *muhallebici* is

Baklava and *şöbiyet* (p. 192)

also the creator of the thick rolls and logs of *kaymak*, a clotted cream made from the milk of cows or water buffalo, which gleam like pieces of milky marble. Piled on top of puddings and pastries, or stuffed into them, *kaymak* can be replaced by any clotted cream.

Several desserts are linked to specific religious feasts: *güllaç*, paper-thin sheets of pastry layered with chopped nuts and soaked in milk and rose-water, is eaten throughout the month of Ramazan; *aşure* (p. 197) is eaten on the 10th day of Muharrem, the first month of the Muslim calendar, to commemorate the martyrdom of the Prophet's grandson, Hüseyin, as well as being associated with Noah's salvation from the Flood; and *lokma* (p. 199), small crispy pastries soaked in syrup, believed to represent the Prophet's seal, are eaten during the celebrations of Kandil when the minarets of the mosques are illuminated throughout Turkey.

Kaymak

Balkabağı tatlısı PUMPKIN IN SYRUP

Balkabağı tatlısı
PUMPKIN IN SYRUP

A nourishing winter dessert which turns a warm shade of golden orange when cooked. From November to the end of March the markets are full of large pumpkins, expertly cut into cubes and rectangles ready to be made into this popular dessert. Invariably, chopped walnuts are the preferred topping in Istanbul, while the contrasting green pistachios are favoured in parts of Anatolia.

SERVES 4
2lb/900g pumpkin flesh
8oz/225g sugar
¼ pint/150ml water
juice of ½ lemon

FOR THE TOP
2 tablespoons walnuts or pistachios, finely chopped or ground

✧ Cut the pumpkin into rectangular or square blocks. Place the pieces in a wide, thick-based pan, sprinkle with the sugar and pour over the water and lemon juice. Cover the pan and poach gently for at least one hour, basting from time to time until the pumpkin is tender. Leave it to cool in the pan, then place the pumpkin pieces on a dish and spoon the syrup over them. Sprinkle with the nuts and serve plain or with *kaymak* (p. 219).

Ayva tatlısı
QUINCES IN SYRUP

When the large pale-yellow quinces are in season, their sweet floral perfume wafts through the kitchens of Turkey. Sliced into fine segments as meze *(p. 220), cooked into jam, casseroled with meat or made into this pretty pink dessert, quinces are wonderfully versatile. The natural pectin in the fruit and seeds transforms the poaching liquid into a light jelly. The chefs of Istanbul pick out the seeds and cloves from the jelly before serving, but elsewhere the crunchiness of the sweetened seeds and cloves is enjoyed.*

SERVES 6
3–4 quinces, peeled, halved from stalk to head, and cored
(keep the seeds)
4 tablespoons sugar
juice of ½ lemon
½ pint/300ml water
8–10 cloves

✧ Place the quince halves in the bottom of a wide, thick-based pan. Sprinkle them with the sugar and pour over the water and lemon juice. Add the quince seeds and cloves to the pan and poach the fruit gently for about an hour, basting from time to time, until the fruit is tender and has turned pink. Leave to cool in the pan.

✧ Transfer the quinces, with or without the cloves and seeds, to a serving dish and spoon the jelly over and around them. Serve with a dollop of *kaymak* (p. 219).

Ayva tatlısı QUINCES IN SYRUP

Gül dondurması
ROSE-PETAL SORBET

The ancient tastes of fragrant roses and pomegranates are deliciously captured in exotic water-ices. Cool and refreshing, this delicate crystal sorbet is traditionally made with the fresh petals, but two tablespoons of rose-water can be used instead. The sorbet is often served in frosted-glass bowls or glasses,

and decorated with crystallized rose petals – which are easily made by brushing the petals with whisked egg white, dipping them in sugar, and then leaving them to dry until crisp.

SERVES 3–4
petals of 2 scented red or pink roses
1 pint/600ml water
8oz/225g caster sugar
2 tablespoons lemon juice
2 teaspoons rose-water

✧ Wash the rose petals and cut off the white bases. Place them in a pan with the water, bring to the boil, cover, and simmer for 10 minutes. Strain the liquid and reserve the petals.

✧ Put the strained liquid and the sugar into a pan and bring to the boil, stirring all the time. Reduce the heat and simmer for 5–10 minutes. Stir in the lemon juice and rose-water, followed by the petals, and leave to cool in the pan.

✧ Pour the mixture into a bowl or ice-tray and place in the freezer. As it sets, whisk the sorbet from time to time to disperse the ice crystals. Let it sit at room temperature for a few minutes before serving.

Revani
SEMOLINA SPONGE IN SYRUP

Named after a sixteenth-century Turkish poet who wrote reams extolling the delights of food, revani is an old favourite. It is light and delicately flavoured.

Revani SEMOLINA SPONGE IN SYRUP

<u>SERVES 8</u>
4oz/120g semolina or cream of wheat
2oz/60g plain flour
4oz/120g sugar
6 eggs, separated
zest of 1 orange, grated
<u>FOR THE SYRUP</u>
juice and zest of 2 lemons
6oz/175g caster sugar
½ pint/300ml water
<u>TO GARNISH</u>
desiccated coconut

✧ Preheat oven to 350F/Mark 4/180C

✧ Grease and line with greaseproof paper a cake tin approximately 10in/25cm in diameter, 2–3in/6–8cm deep.

✧ Sift the flour into a bowl and stir in the semolina. In a large bowl, beat the egg yolks with the sugar until light and creamy. Beat in the orange zest, then gradually beat in the flour and semolina. Whisk the egg whites to stiff peaks and fold them into the

batter. Spoon the mixture into the prepared tin, smooth it out, and bake for about 30 minutes until golden-brown on top.

✧ Prepare the syrup: put all the ingredients into a pan and bring to the boil, stirring all the time. Reduce the heat and simmer for 5–10 minutes.

✧ Take the *revani* out of the oven and cut into squares. Pour warm syrup over them and return to the oven for 2 minutes. Leave to cool and absorb the syrup in the tin.

✧ Transfer to a dish, sprinkle with the coconut, and serve at room temperature on their own or with chilled *kaymak* (p. 219).

Peynir tatlısı
CHEESE SPONGES IN SYRUP

These delectable sweet sponges should be made with unsalted beyaz peynir *(p. 219) or* köy peyniri *(p. 219), which could be replaced with feta or ricotta. If you use a salty cheese, omit the teaspoon of salt in the recipe. There is no rule as to the shape or size.*

<u>SERVES 4–6</u>
4oz/120g plain flour
1oz/30g icing sugar
¼ teaspoon bicarbonate of soda
1 teaspoon salt
2oz/60g butter
3oz/90g white cheese, crumbled or mashed
1 egg
<u>FOR THE SYRUP</u>
8oz/225g sugar

Peynir tatlısı CHEESE SPONGES IN SYRUP

8fl oz/250ml water
1 tablespoon lemon juice
2 teaspoons lemon rind, finely shredded

✧ Preheat oven to 400F/Mark 6/200C

✧ Make the syrup: put the ingredients in a pan and bring to the boil, stirring all the time. Reduce the heat and simmer for 5–10 minutes. Put aside.

✧ Grease a medium-sized baking tin. Sift the flour, icing sugar, bicarbonate of soda and salt into a bowl. Rub the butter into the flour until it resembles breadcrumbs. Make a hollow in the centre and drop in the cheese and the egg. Draw the flour over the cheese and egg and knead into a sticky dough.

✧ Rinse the sticky dough off your hands but keep them damp to mould small portions of the dough into balls or other shapes, and place them at intervals in the prepared baking tin. Put in the oven for 20 minutes.

✧ Heat up the syrup and pour it over the sponges. Return them to the oven for 2–3 minutes, take them out once more and baste with the syrup, then return them to the oven for a final 2–3 minutes. Leave them to cool in the baking tin. (The syrup vanishes rapidly as the sponges soak it up.)

✧ These cheese sponges are best eaten fresh and moist, with or without *kaymak* (p. 219). If you make masses of them to a last a few days, they can easily be re-moistened with a little extra syrup and put in the oven for 5 minutes.

Vişneli ekmek tatlısı
SUMMER CHERRY PUDDING

A delicious way of using up bread, this summer pudding can be made with fresh strawberries, mulberries, apricots or peaches, but when made with cherries it turns a lovely shade of purple. A slightly richer version can be made by frying the bread in butter until crisp, instead of baking it.

SERVES 4
8oz/225g fresh sour cherries

8fl oz/250ml cold water

6oz/175g sugar

1 tablespoon icing sugar

8–10 slices stale white bread, crusts removed

✧ Preheat oven to 400F/Mark 6/200C

✧ Put the cherries, sugar and water in a pan and bring to the boil, stirring all the time. Reduce the heat and simmer gently for 10 minutes. Drain the cherries over another pan to collect the syrup and put it aside. Squeeze the cherries between thumb and finger and pop out the stones. Set them aside.

✧ Heat the syrup in the pan and sift in the icing sugar. Stir until the liquid begins to thicken. Leave to cool.

✧ Bake the slices of bread lightly in the oven. Place a few in the bottom of a flan dish, and pour over some of the syrup followed by a layer of cherries. Layer it up in this way, finishing with cherries on the top. Cook the pudding in the oven for 15–20 minutes, then leave it to cool. Chill and serve with cream.

Sakızlı dondurma
CLASSIC CHEWY ICE-CREAM

A distinct feature of Turkish ice-cream is its chewy texture, deriving from the mastika *(p. 220) which is added to almost every sort. The most popular are flavoured with rose petals, cherries, white mulberries, pistachios, chocolate, orange blossom and orchid root. This recipe combines the mild flowery taste of orchid root,* salep *(p. 220), with the gummy, bark-scented* mastika. *Cornflour or arrowroot can be used in place of the orchid root, but neither emits its subtle flavour.*

SERVES 4
1½ pints/900ml full-fat milk

½ pint/300ml double cream

8oz/225g sugar

3 tablespoons ground *salep*

1 piece of *mastika*, crushed with a little sugar

Sakızlı dondurma CLASSIC CHEWY ICE-CREAM

- In a bowl, slake the *salep* with a little of the milk. Put the rest of the milk into a saucepan with the cream and sugar. Bring it to the boil, stirring all the time. Reduce the heat, stir a few spoonfuls of the hot liquid into the slaked *salep*, then add it slowly to the pan, stirring all the time until smooth. Beat in the *mastika* and simmer gently for 10–15 minutes.

- Pour the liquid into a bowl or freezer tray, cover with a dry towel and leave to cool. Remove the towel, cover the bowl with foil and place in the freezer. Leave to set, beating at intervals to disperse the ice crystals. Before serving, place it in the fridge for 10–15 minutes. Beware – this ice-cream melts quickly.

İncir tatlısı
STUFFED FIGS WITH BAY LEAVES

This dessert was devised in the eastern pocket of the Black Sea coast – the lush, wet tea-growing region. The dried figs are first soaked in tea to soften them, then stuffed with chopped nuts and baked in a syrup flavoured with the tea, honey, lemon and bay leaves or rosemary. The dish is served hot or cold, and it can also be made with milky tea or a mild aromatic tea and served with cream. In other parts of Turkey incir tatlısı is usually made with a sweetened milk syrup flavoured with rose-water.

SERVES 3–4
8oz/225g dried figs
½ pint/300ml boiling water
1 teaspoon strong or mild scented tea-leaves
FOR THE FILLING
2oz/60g walnuts, coarsely chopped
1oz/30g almonds, coarsely chopped
FOR THE SYRUP
8fl oz/250ml tea
2–3 tablespoons honey or sugar
zest of 1 lemon, grated
2–3 bay leaves

- Preheat oven to 350F/Mark 4/180C

- Leave the tea-leaves to infuse in the boiling water for a few minutes, then strain the tea into a bowl. Add the figs to the hot tea and soak for at least 6 hours.

- Drain them and reserve 8fl oz/250ml of the tea. Hold the figs by their stalks and make a small incision in the soft end of each one. Mix the nuts, then stuff them through this hole to fill out the figs and place them, stalk upwards, in an oven-proof dish.

- Now make the syrup. In a pan, bring the tea to the boil with the lemon zest, honey and bay leaves. Reduce the heat and simmer for about 10 minutes. Sweeten the syrup to your taste with more honey. Pour the syrup over the figs and bake in the oven for 20 minutes.

- Serve hot or cold.

İncir tatlısı STUFFED FIGS WITH BAY LEAVES

Kaymaklı kayısı
CREAM-FILLED APRICOTS

A popular sweet fix or a delicious finale to any meal, here dried apricots are simply soaked in water, poached in syrup, filled with kaymak *(p. 219) and chilled. Trays of these gleaming fruit enticingly decorate Turkish sweet shops in winter and early spring.*

SERVES 4

8oz/225g dried apricots, soaked in water for at least 6 hours

FOR THE SYRUP

8fl oz/250ml soaking water

6oz/175g sugar

1 tablespoon lemon juice

zest of 1 lemon, grated

1 tablespoon orange-blossom water

FOR THE FILLING

4 tablespoons *kaymak*, or clotted cream

1 tablespoon blanched almonds, finely chopped (optional)

TO GARNISH

a few blanched almonds, pistachios
or walnuts, finely chopped

✧ Drain the apricots well and reserve 8fl oz/250ml of the apricot water. For the syrup, put the sugar and apricot water in a pan and bring to the boil, stirring all the time. Reduce the heat and stir in the lemon juice, lemon zest and orange-blossom water. Add the apricots to the syrup, and poach gently for 15–20 minutes. Leave them to cool in the syrup.

✧ In a bowl, fold the almonds into the *kaymak*. Take the apricots out of the syrup and fill each one with some of the *kaymak* mixture. Place them on a serving

dish and spoon the syrup over them. Serve chilled, sprinkled with the chopped nuts.

Keşkül
ALMOND CREAM

This delicately flavoured milk pudding is a speciality of the muhallebici, *the maker of milk puddings. It is particularly popular in Istanbul and Bursa, and is best served chilled in individual bowls.*

SERVES 4

4oz/120g blanched almonds

1 pint/600ml milk

1oz/30g ground rice or rice flour

4oz/120g sugar

TO GARNISH

1 tablespoon desiccated or freshly grated coconut
or finely ground pistachios

Keşkül ALMOND CREAM

✧ Pound the almonds and work to a smooth paste with a little of the milk (or blend in an electric mixer). In a bowl, slake the ground rice with a little of the milk.

✧ Put the sugar into a saucepan with the rest of the milk and bring it to the boil, stirring all the time. Reduce the heat. Mix 2–3 tablespoons of the hot milk into the slaked ground rice, and then stir it into the milk in the pan. Add the almond paste, stirring all the time. Simmer gently for 25–30 minutes, stirring it at intervals, until the mixture thickens.

✧ Pour it into individual bowls, sprinkle the garnish over the top and leave to cool. Chill and serve.

Baklava

Perhaps the most famous of the Turkish sweets, baklava is surprisingly difficult to make well. It is possible to cheat by using ready-prepared filo pastry but, if you have the patience, it is worth while attempting to make the real thing. Once mastered, it opens doors to a variety of other delectable sticky pastries: balkabağı baklavası, *sheets of pastry layered with sliced pumpkin and soaked in syrup;* dürüm, *a roll of paper-thin pastry filled with chopped pistachios;* bülbül yuvası, *'nightingale's nest', created by spreading chopped nuts over a sheet of pastry, rolling it into a wrinkled tube, then winding it into a spiral like a nest;* şöbiyet,

Baklava

diamond-shaped pastries filled with chopped pistachios in a soft, sweet semolina paste; and sütlü nüriye, *pastry layered with almond shavings and soaked in a milk syrup.* Baklava *can be made with chopped walnuts, pistachios or almonds. The sheets of pastry must be as thin as possible, which is easier to attain with an* oklava, *a thin rolling pin.* Baklava *should never be stored in the refrigerator, as the fat congeals and the pastry absorbs the moisture and becomes soggy.*
Always serve at room temperature.

SERVES 5–6

8oz/225g plain flour
1 teaspoon salt
2 eggs
2–3fl oz/60–90ml water
1 teaspoon olive oil
2–3oz/60–90g cornflour
3oz/90g butter

FOR THE FILLING

4oz/120g walnuts, finely chopped

FOR THE SYRUP

½ pint/300ml water
1lb/450g sugar
1 tablespoon rose-water

✧ Preheat oven to 400F/Mark 6/200C

✧ Sift the flour with the salt into a bowl. Make a hollow in the middle and drop in the eggs. Draw flour in from the sides and work the eggs and flour into a dough with the water. Knead well for 5–10 minutes, cover with a damp cloth, and leave to rest for 1 hour.

✧ To make the syrup, dissolve the sugar in the water and bring it to the boil. Reduce the heat and simmer for 10 minutes. Stir in the rose-water and put aside.

✧ Now spread the oil around the dough and knead again for 10 minutes, until smooth and light in texture. Sprinkle some of the cornflour on to a flat surface and roll the dough out into a long rectangle. Cut it into 10 equal pieces. Roll out each piece as finely as possible, sprinkling with cornflour when sticky, in the shape of your baking tin. Pile the thin sheets on top of each other, separated by a dusting of cornflour, then roll them out together, distributing the pressure. Cut them into the shape of your baking tin, if necessary.

✧ Melt the butter in a pan. Brush the baking tin with the melted butter and layer up the sheets of pastry, brushing each one with butter. Sprinkle the fifth or sixth layer evenly with nuts, and continue with the layers. Brush the top with butter and, using a sharp knife, cut the whole pastry into squares or diamond shapes. Place in the oven for 30–40 minutes, until the top is golden-brown.

✧ When it comes out of the oven, brush the top with the rest of the butter. Heat up the syrup and pour it gradually over the pastry, allowing it to soak in. Leave to cool and absorb the syrup.

Su muhallebisi
ROSE MILK PUDDING

The pudding from which the maker of milk puddings, the muhallebici, *gets his name. It is the classic milk pudding, and can be made plain, sprinkled with icing sugar, flavoured with rose-water, cardamom, chocolate or vanilla, or altered in texture by adding* mastika *(p. 220). On special occasions the pudding is set in a*

Su muhallebisi ROSE MILK PUDDING

mould and cut into dainty pieces, which are floated in rose-water and served in a frosted dessert glass. This recipe combines the tastes of rose-water and mastika.

<u>SERVES 4–6</u>

1½ pints/900ml milk

2oz/60g rice flour or ground rice

4oz/120g sugar

1 small piece of *mastika*, pounded with 1 teaspoon sugar

1–2 tablespoons rose-water

2 tablespoons icing sugar

✧ Slake the rice flour with a little of the milk. Put the sugar in a pan with the rest of the milk and bring it to the boil, stirring all the time. Add a little of the hot milk to the rice flour, then pour it into the pan. Still stirring all the time, bring the liquid to the boil again and stir in the *mastika* and the rose-water. Reduce the heat and simmer gently for 25–30 minutes, stirring from time to time, until it thickens.

✧ Pour the mixture into individual dishes or a mould, and leave to cool and form a skin on top. Chill before serving, and sprinkle with icing sugar.

Şekerpare
SYRUPY SPONGE CAKES

Şekerpare means 'sweet' or 'syrupy pieces', which is exactly what these delicious spongy cakes, soaked in syrup, are. Usually prepared by the baklavacı, *the maker of syrupy pastries, when freshly made they are very tempting.*

<u>SERVES 4–6</u>

10oz/300g plain flour

½ teaspoon salt

½ teaspoon baking powder

4oz/120g butter

2oz/60g sugar

1 egg and 1 egg yolk

Şekerpare SYRUPY SPONGE CAKES

FOR THE TOP

12–16 whole blanched almonds

1 egg yolk, beaten

FOR THE SYRUP

1 pint/600ml water

1lb/450g sugar

juice of ½ lemon

✧ Preheat oven to 350F/Mark 4/180C

✧ Sift the flour with the salt and baking powder on to a sheet of greaseproof paper. In a large bowl, beat the butter with the sugar until light and creamy. Beat in the egg and yolk, and shoot in the flour. Knead well, and shape into walnut-sized balls or oblongs. Flatten them slightly and place them at intervals on a lightly greased baking tray. Indent the middle of each one with your finger and fit an almond into the hollow. Brush the surfaces with the egg yolk and place them in the oven for 25–30 minutes, until firm and golden-brown.

✧ Put the syrup ingredients in a pan and bring the liquid to the boil, stirring all the time. Reduce the heat and simmer for 10 minutes. When the *şekerpare* are ready, pour half of the syrup over them and put them back into the oven for 5 minutes. Then take them out and pour over the rest of the syrup, and leave them to cool and absorb the syrup. Serve at room temperature.

Fırında sütlaç
BURNT RICE PUDDING

Sweet rice puddings are popular desserts, and always served cold. Zerde, a delicately flavoured pudding with currants and pine nuts and coloured with saffron, is

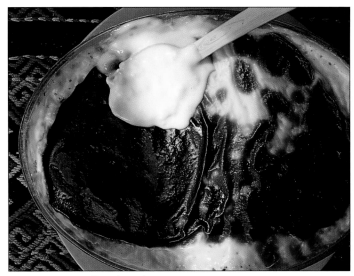

Fırında sütlaç BURNT RICE PUDDING

served at weddings and circumcision feasts, and keşme bulamacı, *a spicy* bulgur *(p. 219) pudding, is eaten as a snack in eastern and southeastern Anatolia. Sütlaç, the classic rice pudding from the Ottoman Palace kitchens, is often flavoured with rose-water and chilled or, as in this recipe, served with the top browned or burnt in a high oven or under the grill. Sütlaç should be moist and creamy.*

SERVES 6

8oz/225g short-grain or pudding rice

2 pints/1.2 litres milk

1lb/450g sugar

1–2 teaspoons vanilla essence

✧ Preheat oven, if using, to 450F/Mark 8/230C

✧ If the rice is sturdy and starchy, soak it for 30 minutes. Drain and rinse well. Put it in a pan and cover with just enough water. Bring it to the boil and cook, uncovered, until almost all the water has been absorbed. Stir in the milk and simmer gently, uncovered, until the mixture thickens. Add the sugar and cook gently for 20–25 minutes, stirring from time to time until it begins to thicken – it should be slightly thicker than pouring consistency, but not solid.

✧ Stir in the vanilla essence, then tip the mixture into a deep oven-proof dish. Brown the top in the oven, or burn it under a conventional grill. Serve at room temperature or slightly chilled.

Tulumba
CRISP PASTRIES IN SYRUP

By adding a little extra flour to this tulumba *recipe before beating in the eggs, the dough can be transformed into other desserts: with oiled hands shape it into balls and punch a hole through the middle, to make 'ladies' navels',* kadın göbeği; *roll it into thin logs and shape into 'Grand Viziers' fingers',* vezir parmağı; *or roll it in the palm of your hand, then flatten and fold in two to form 'sweetheart's lips',* dilber dudağı.

Tulumba CRISP PASTRIES IN SYRUP

SERVES 6
8fl oz/250ml water
½ teaspoon salt
2oz/60g butter
6oz/175g strong plain flour, sifted on to greaseproof paper
2 tablespoons semolina
4 eggs
sunflower oil for deep-frying
FOR THE SYRUP
1lb/450g sugar
½ pint/300ml water
juice of ½ lemon

✧ Prepare the syrup in advance. Put the ingredients into a pan and bring to the boil, stirring all the time. Reduce the heat and simmer for 5–10 minutes. Leave to cool.

✧ Put the water, butter and salt into a pan and bring to the boil. Remove from the heat and shoot in the flour and semolina. Beat well. Return to the heat and continue to beat until the mixture becomes smooth and leaves the sides of the pan. Leave to cool. Beat in the eggs, one at a time, until the mixture shines. Beat in 1 tablespoon of the cold syrup. Spoon the mixture into a pastry bag and attach a fluted nozzle.

✧ Heat the oil in a shallow pan. Squeeze flutes (approximately 1in/2.5cm long) of dough into it, cutting them off at intervals with a knife, until the pan is half full. Shake the pan over a medium heat until the swollen pastries turn golden-brown and float on the surface. Remove, drain on kitchen paper, and drop them into the cold syrup for 10–15 minutes. Repeat with the rest of the dough. Serve immediately.

Aşure NOAH'S DESSERT

Aşure
NOAH'S DESSERT

It is said that when the Flood subsided, Noah created aşure *by using up all the stores of grains and dried fruit in the Ark. Following tradition, it is always made in vast quantities and distributed to neighbours, friends and relatives. In parts of Anatolia* aşure *is made with* bulgur *(p. 219) or* döğme, *a recycled wheat flour made from soaked grains that have been pounded and dried, and barley is used in Istanbul. To make* beyaz aşure, *a white version, the water is replaced by milk. Although easy to make,* aşure *requires some advance preparation.*

SERVES 10 OR MORE

8oz/225g barley, soaked for 24 hours in 4 pints of water
2oz/60g short-grain rice, washed and drained
2oz/60g haricot beans, soaked for 8 hours, cooked and drained
2oz/60g lima beans, soaked for 8 hours, cooked and drained
2oz/60g chickpeas, soaked for 8 hours, cooked and drained
4oz/120g dried apricots, halved, soaked in boiling water for 5 minutes and drained
4oz/120g sultanas or raisins, soaked in boiling water for 5 minutes and drained
2oz/60g currants, soaked in boiling water for 5 minutes and drained
1lb/450g sugar
2 tablespoons cornflour, slaked with a little milk
4fl oz/125ml rose-water

TO GARNISH

2oz/60g dried figs, sliced
2oz/60g dried apricots, sliced
2oz/60g walnuts, sliced
1 tablespoon pine nuts
1 tablespoon currants
2 tablespoons pomegranate seeds (optional)

✧ Cook the barley in the soaking water (top it up if necessary) until tender. Add the rice, chickpeas and beans and bring the liquid to the boil. Reduce the heat and simmer for 10 minutes. Stir in the apricots, sultanas and currants and cook over a medium heat for 10 minutes. Add the sugar bit by bit, stirring all the time, until the mixture begins to thicken. Mix a few spoonfuls of the hot liquid into the slaked cornflour, and return it to the pan. Bring the mixture to the boil again, pour in the rose-water and simmer for 10 minutes. Tip the mixture into a large serving bowl and leave to cool.

✧ Arrange or scatter the garnish over the top. Serve cooled or at room temperature.

Tavuk göğsü kazandibi
BURNT MILK PUDDING WITH CHICKEN BREASTS

We have only the Ottoman Palace kitchens to thank for this wondrous creation. A speciality of the muhallebici, *the maker of milk puddings, this delightful creamy dessert really is made with shredded chicken breasts, which impart an almost undetectable mild meaty flavour and texture. Once the pudding is cooked it can be cooled and eaten plain –* tavuk göğsü *– but for the ultimate satisfaction tip it into a hot thick-based pan, burn the bottom, cut it into pieces and roll them up into logs.*

Tavuk göğsü kazandibi BURNT MILK PUDDING WITH CHICKEN BREASTS

SERVES 6

1 chicken breast

1½ pints/900ml milk

½ pint/300ml single cream

¼ teaspoon salt

6oz/175g sugar

5 tablespoons rice flour

(or a mixture of ground rice and cornflour)

✦ Place the chicken breast in a pan with a little water, bring it to the boil, reduce the heat and simmer until the meat is cooked. Drain and tear it into fine threads.

✦ Slake the rice flour with a little of the milk. Put the rest of the milk into a saucepan with the cream, salt and sugar, and bring the liquid to the boil. Add a few spoonfuls of the hot liquid to the slaked rice flour, and pour the mixture into the pan. Beat vigorously and continue to cook over a low heat, stirring all the time so that it doesn't stick to the bottom of the pan, until the mixture begins to thicken. Beat in the fine threads of chicken and continue to cook the mixture until very thick.

✦ Now tip it into a heavy-based frying pan and place over the heat for 5–10 minutes to burn the bottom of the pudding. Move the pan around so that the pudding is evenly burnt. Leave to cool in the pan, cut into rectangles and lift them out with a spatula.

✦ Roll the rectangles into logs, and serve at room temperature or slightly cooled.

Saray lokması
FRITTERS IN SYRUP

These fritters are generally associated with religious feasting. The multi-shaped lokma *of Izmir are known far and wide. They are most commonly shaped into tiny balls,* saray lokması, *or into rings of different sizes.* Mastika *(p. 220) can be added to the dough to give it a chewy texture, and honey is sometimes dribbled over the warm fritters instead of soaking them in syrup.*

SERVES 6

6oz/175g strong plain flour

1 teaspoon ground cinnamon

pinch of salt

½ teaspoon dried yeast

½ teaspoon sugar

¼ pint/150ml lukewarm water

sunflower oil for frying

FOR THE SYRUP

¼ pint/150ml water

8oz/225g sugar

juice of ½ lemon

✦ Cream the yeast with the sugar in the lukewarm water. Sift the flour with the salt and cinnamon into a bowl, make a well in the centre, and pour in the yeast. Draw in a little of the flour from the sides to make a smooth batter, and sprinkle the surface with flour. Cover the bowl with a damp cloth and leave the batter to sponge for about 20 minutes. (If using *mastika*, crush it with sugar and sprinkle it over the flour at this stage.) Draw in the rest of the flour and add a little extra water to make a smooth, sticky dough. Cover with a damp cloth and leave to prove in a warm place until doubled in size.

◆ Make the syrup. Put the sugar in a pan with the water and lemon juice and bring it to the boil. Reduce the heat and simmer for 5–10 minutes. Leave to cool.

◆ Heat a thick layer of oil in a shallow pan. Drop teaspoonfuls of the dough into the oil, dipping the teaspoon into a cup of water at frequent intervals to prevent stickiness. The shapes don't have to be perfect. Fry them until golden-brown. Drain them on kitchen paper and pop them into the cold syrup for 10–15 minutes. Serve freshly made.

Hoşmerim SOMETHING NICE FOR THE HUSBAND

Hoşmerim
SOMETHING NICE FOR THE HUSBAND

A dish of Anatolian origin, hoşmerim *varies from home to home. Using whatever ingredients are at hand, it is said to be a sweet concoction designed to please the husband. This particular recipe from eastern Anatolia occasionally includes cardamom seeds. The pudding is made with an unsalted* köy peyniri *(p. 219), or* beyaz peynir *(p. 219), soaked in water for 24 hours to reduce the salt content. Ricotta or a soaked feta can be used as substitutes.*

<u>*SERVES 4–5*</u>
1lb/450g unsalted white cheese
2 tablespoons plain flour
8oz/225g sugar
juice of 1 lemon
1 teaspoon lemon rind, chopped
1 teaspoon cardamom seeds (optional)

◆ Preheat oven to 400F/Mark 6/200C

◆ Mash the cheese with a fork and put it into a heavy-based pan, then melt it over a gentle heat. In a separate pan, cook the flour until it turns a strong beige colour. Beat the sugar, cardamom seeds (if using), lemon juice and rind into the melted cheese and cook for 2–3 minutes. Beat in the flour and cook until the mixture thickens. Spoon it into an oven-proof dish, spread it out, and sprinkle more sugar over the top. Bake in the oven for about 30 minutes until well browned and firm to the touch – a hard crust should have formed on top.

◆ Leave to cool and serve at room temperature.

Hoşaf
FRUIT COMPOTE FOR A SULTAN

Fruit compotes are very popular throughout Turkey, ranging from a simple sultana compote, kuru üzüm hoşafı, *to a colourful mix of apricots, figs, prunes and nuts. Perhaps subtly enhanced with rose-water or orange-blossom water,* hoşaf *is frequently served to refresh the palate at the end of a meal – a tradition favoured by the Ottoman sultans, who spooned it over plain pilaf. Such were the refinements that on one occasion Mehmet the Conqueror was served* hoşaf *in a bowl fashioned from the frozen juice, so that the fruit could be served chilled without spoiling its taste and texture.*

<u>SERVES 4–6</u>

4oz/120g sultanas, soaked for at least 6 hours

6oz/175g dried apricots, soaked for at least 6 hours

1½ pints/900ml water

8oz/225g sugar

1 tablespoon orange-blossom water (p. 220)

✧ Drain the fruit, put it in a pan with the fresh water, and bring it to the boil. Reduce the heat and simmer for 10 minutes. Stir in the sugar and simmer for a further 10–15 minutes. Then stir in the orange-blossom water and leave to cool in the pan. Serve chilled.

Yoğurtlu pasta
YOGURT CAKE

Moreish and versatile, this moist cake is delicious served with tea or it can be soaked in syrup and eaten as a dessert, yoğurt tatlısı *– a popular way of using up any left-over yogurt cake. To make the delectable* yoğurt tatlısı, *cut the freshly baked or left-over cake into slices and place them on a flat baking tray or oven-proof dish, smother them in hot syrup (1lb/450g sugar, ½ pint/ 300ml water and the juice of ½ a lemon), and place them in a hot oven (400F/Mark 6/200C) for 10–15*

minutes. Leave them to cool and absorb the syrup, and serve at room temperature with kaymak *(p. 219). The cake can be as plain or as rich in ingredients as you wish to make it. The shape is up to you, but this recipe fits snugly into a 1lb/450g loaf tin.*

<u>SERVES 6–8</u>

8oz/225g self-raising flour

½ teaspoon baking powder

6oz/175g butter

6oz/175g sugar

2 eggs

6oz/175g thick creamy yogurt

a few drops vanilla essence

2 tablespoons desiccated coconut

2 tablespoons sultanas

✧ Preheat oven to 350F/Mark 4/180C

✧ Line the base of a baking tin with greaseproof paper, grease it and dust with flour and sugar.

✧ Sift the flour and baking powder into a bowl or on to a sheet of greaseproof paper.

✧ Melt the butter and leave to cool. In a large bowl, cream the eggs and the sugar together and beat vigorously until light and fluffy. In a separate bowl, beat the melted butter into the yogurt and then add to the creamed eggs and sugar. Stir in the vanilla essence, coconut and sultanas and fold in the flour.

✧ Spoon the mixture into the prepared baking tin and bake in the oven for about 1 hour, until the top is golden-brown and firm to touch. Leave the cake to cool a little in the tin before turning it out on to a wire rack. Enjoy freshly baked, or soaked in syrup as *yoğurt tatlısı.*

FESTIVE SWEETS AND JAMS

The Festival of Sweets, Şeker Bayramı, marks the end of Ramazan. A three-and-a-half-day event, it heralds the celebratory buying and giving of candy-coated almonds, multi-flavoured Turkish delight, and marzipans. The sweet *simit* (p. 93), bread rings, and a special *çörek* – a sweet bun sprinkled with nigella seeds (p. 220) – are made specifically for this celebration.

Helva is one of the oldest sweets, originally eaten as a dessert. *Kar helvası*, made from snow blended with sugar, was popular in the palaces and wealthy homes of Istanbul during the Ottoman Empire, but is now extinct. The tradition of specialist *helva* makers has survived, producing huge sweet blocks of ground sesame seeds, often mixed with whole pistachios or swirled with chocolate. Many of the *helva* dishes made at home are softer, more akin to a dessert, prepared for special occasions such as weddings and funerals. *Helva* should never be kept in the refrigerator, and always be served at room temperature.

Turkey also produces a colourful variety of syrupy jams designed to dribble over bread and *beyaz peynir* (p. 219) in the morning. As whole fruit, or large pieces of fruit, are poached gently in sugar, the resulting concoction is more akin to conserve than what we know as jam – that is, runny and syrupy rather than thick and spreadable. The weight of the fruit usually balances the weight of the sugar, and the tantalizing fruity tastes include apricot, cherry, quince, rosehip, green fig and rose petal. The wizard jam makers of Antalya manage to transform any fruit or vegetable, including watermelons and aubergines, into unique jams. The following recipes make a generous introductory amount of jam for a family of jam-lovers – increase the quantities if you want to store some away.

Gül reçeli ROSE-PETAL JAM

Lokum
CLASSIC TURKISH DELIGHT

Turkey is famous for its 'delight' which is infinite in variety. Multi-flavoured, soft and gooey, jelly-like and chewy, or tender and melting – each kind is individually named and, if stored in a sealed container, will last up to a year. This recipe, which can also be used for the chopped-nut varieties, is for a classic rose-scented Turkish delight. A little pink colouring is often added to this lokum *and, if you prefer the chewy variety,* add *mastika (p. 220), ground with sugar, to the mixture as it cooks.*

MAKES 20–25 PIECES
1lb/450g sugar
1 pint/600ml water
2 tablespoons rose-water
2oz/60g cornflour
icing sugar for dusting

✧ Prepare any shape of mould, approximately 1½in/4cm deep and 7–8in/18–20cm in diameter, by lining it with a piece of muslin covered with a layer of cornflour.

✧ Put the sugar and the water in a pan and bring to the boil, stirring all the time. Slake the cornflour with a little water, and stir in the rose-water. Add a few spoonfuls of the hot syrup to the cornflour mixture, then pour it into the pan. Keep stirring over a medium heat until the mixture thickens and barely drips from the spoon. The mixture is ready when a little of it dropped into a cup of cold water forms a soft, jelly-like ball.

✧ Pour the mixture into the mould and leave it to cool. Spread a layer of icing sugar on a flat surface and turn the *lokum* on to it. Remove the muslin and brush off the excess cornflour. Cut the block into small squares and roll them in the icing sugar until well coated.

Peynir helvası
CHEESE HELVA

This simple village helva *is soft, soothing and delicious. It is made with unsalted soft cheese, for which ricotta could be substituted.*

SERVES 2–3
8oz/225g *lor* (p. 26) or *köy peyniri* (p. 219)
1 tablespoon plain flour
4oz/120g sugar
1 tablespoon icing sugar

✧ Mash the cheese with a fork and put it in a shallow pan. Stir it over a low heat until it melts into a soft, smooth paste.

✧ In another shallow pan, stir the flour over a high heat until it turns a definite beige colour. Beat the flour and the sugar into the cheese and stir constantly, over a medium heat, until the mixture fluffs up and clumps. It is ready when it lifts off the bottom of the pan in one piece.

✧ Sprinkle with icing sugar and serve warm or at room temperature.

Peynir helvası CHEESE HELVA

Un helvası
FESTIVE HELVA

This delicious flour helva *with pine nuts is usually prepared for happy events such as the birth of a child, or a wedding. Concentration is needed for this recipe – at the beginning, you have to stir the contents of two large pans simultaneously.*

<u>*SERVES 6–8*</u>

6oz/175g butter
6oz/175g plain flour
1 tablespoon sunflower oil
2oz/60g pine nuts
8oz/225g sugar
1 pint/600ml milk
¼ pint/150ml water
icing sugar for sprinkling

✧ Sift the flour on to a sheet of greaseproof paper. Melt the butter in a large heavy-based pan. Shoot in the flour and stir into a thick roux. Cook for 4–5 minutes, to colour a little. Stir in the sunflower oil to bind the roux to a smooth paste. Cook until it easily leaves the sides of the pan and turns camel-brown. Stir in the pine nuts and cook for 4–5 minutes until they turn golden.

✧ Meanwhile, keeping an eye on the flour mixture, stir the sugar and milk in a saucepan and bring to the boil. Reduce the heat and simmer for about 10 minutes until the syrup coats the back of the spoon.

✧ Pour the water into the roux in the other pan and stir madly (wear an oven glove to protect against the steam). Pour in the hot milk syrup and again stir vigorously, pressing the balls of roux against the sides of the pan until the mixture forms a thick, gooey paste. Punch the paste with the wooden spoon, flipping it against the sides of the pan, and cook until the pine nuts start to fall out of the mixture, which should be soft and spongy with a nutty taste.

✧ Reduce the heat to very low. Cover the pan with a dry dish-towel and press the lid firmly on top – for safety, make sure you lift the towel flaps up over the lid. Leave to steam gently for 15–20 minutes, to extract the moisture. Remove from the heat and leave to cool. Serve warm or at room temperature.

✦ To serve, scoop the *helva* out of the pan in thin layers, on to plates, and sprinkle with icing sugar. Eat with a fork, pressing the back of it down into the soft, spongy *helva* to attach it.

İrmik helvası
FUNERAL HELVA

Made with semolina, this helva *is carried to the graveside and offered to the mourners. It is also popular on happier occasions.*

<u>SERVES 8–10</u>
1lb/450g semolina
8oz/225g butter
2 tablespoons pine nuts
1½ pints/900ml milk
8oz/225g sugar
1–2 teaspoons ground cinnamon (optional)

✦ Melt the butter in a saucepan. Stir in the pine nuts and semolina, and cook until lightly browned. Reduce the heat and add the milk. Mix well, cover the pan with a dry cloth, press the lid down tightly, instantly pull the towel flaps up over the lid and simmer until the milk is absorbed. Then stir in the sugar until it has dissolved. Cover again with cloth and lid, remove from the heat and leave to stand for 1 hour. Mix well with a spoon, serve, and sprinkle with cinnamon.

İrmik helvası FUNERAL HELVA

Antep fıstık ezmesi
PISTACHIO MARZIPAN

Nut marzipans are popular as sweets, rolled into balls or logs. The pistachio paste is particularly delicious.

SERVES 6–8
8oz/225g blanched pistachios
8oz/225g icing sugar
1 tablespoon rose-water

✧ Pound the pistachios to a paste. Add the sugar and blend well (or pound in an electric mixer). Bind with the rose-water, and knead for 10 minutes. Roll the mixture into a long stick and cut it into pieces. Leave in the refrigerator or a cool place for 2–3 hours before serving.

Gül reçeli
ROSE-PETAL JAM

The exquisite rose-petal jam conjures up the ancient tastes of India and the Middle East. It is a delicately perfumed, runny jam, packed with scented rose petals, which can be picked from the old-fashioned cottage garden rose.

1lb/450g fresh pink or red rose petals
½ pint/300ml water
1lb/450g sugar
juice of 1 lemon

✧ Cut the white ends off the petals, rinse them and drain well. Put the petals into a pan with the water and bring it to the boil. Strain, set the petals aside, and pour the water back into the pan. Add the sugar and bring the liquid to the boil, stirring all the time. Reduce the heat and simmer for 10 minutes. Then stir in the lemon juice and rose petals and simmer for a further 10–15 minutes, until the syrup is thick. If the petals have not imparted a strong perfumed taste, stir in 1 tablespoon of rose-water. Leave to cool in the pan, then spoon into scalded jars.

Kuru incir reçeli
DRIED FIG JAM

This is a popular winter jam from Bursa.

Kuru incir reçeli DRIED FIG JAM

1lb/450g dried figs, chopped roughly
1lb/450g sugar
1 pint/600ml water
juice of 1 lemon
2 tablespoons pine nuts

✧ Put the sugar and water in a pan and bring to the boil. Reduce the heat, stir in the figs and lemon juice, and simmer until the figs are tender and the syrup thickens. Stir in the pine nuts and continue to simmer for 5 minutes. Let it cool in the pan, then spoon into scalded jars.

Yeşil incir reçeli
GREEN FIG JAM

This jam is made with the tiny unripe green figs, which taste of honey when cooked with sugar. They are left whole floating in a runny syrup.

1lb/450g fresh young green figs, trimmed and peeled
1lb/450g sugar
½ pint/300ml water
juice of ½ lemon

✧ Put the sugar and water in a pan and bring to the boil, stirring all the time. Reduce the heat, stir in the lemon juice and the figs, and simmer gently until the syrup thickens and the green colour of the figs intensifies. Leave to cool in the syrup, then transfer to scalded jars. Let the jam stand for 2–3 days before eating.

Patlıcan reçeli
AUBERGINE JAM

An unusual jam from Antalya which, surprisingly, tastes of bananas. It is best made with the tiny, slim young aubergines.

2lb/900g tiny aubergines, peeled, with stalk removed
2lb/900g sugar
1 pint/600ml water
juice of 1 lemon

✧ Soak the aubergines in cold water while preparing the syrup. Put the sugar and water in a pan and bring to the boil, stirring all the time. Reduce the heat, drain the aubergines, and add them to the syrup with the lemon juice. Simmer gently until the syrup thickens and the aubergines turn a deep shade of brown. Leave to cool in the pan, then spoon into scalded jars. Let the jam stand for 2–3 days before eating.

Yeşil incir reçeli and *patlıcan reçeli* GREEN FIG JAM and AUBERGINE JAM

DRINKS

The verb 'to drink', *içmek*, can also mean 'to smoke' or 'to take an oath', and if you ask for 'a drink', *içki*, it usually implies an alcoholic one. But if you ask for a *şerbet*, you will be given a cool, refreshing syrup-based drink. The word *şerbet* is probably derived from the Arabic, *sharab*, and versions of the drink can be found throughout the Middle East. At Ottoman feasts sherbets were served between courses to refresh the appetite, a custom that is still maintained at weddings and other ceremonial occasions. The most common sherbets are made from sour cherries, pomegranates, mulberries, oranges, lemons, almonds, rose petals and rose-water. To mark the birth of a child a red milky drink, *lohusa şerbeti*, delicately spiced with cloves and cinnamon and sweetened with blocks of sugar that have been dyed red, is drunk with a blessing to the mother: '*Sütün bol olsun*', 'May your milk be plentiful.'

Although tea was introduced to Turkey as recently as the nineteenth century, it has become a national institution. Originally from China, tea has blended into the Turkish culture with ease. For anyone who has visited or lived in Turkey, the image of tea drinking is firmly planted in the memory. It is invariably drunk from tulip-shaped glasses, a legacy of the 'Tulip Period' associated with the reign of Ahmet III (ruled 1703–30), when tulip designs became popular on tiles and other artefacts. Glasses of tea are usually served with lumps of sugar – either stirred in, or placed in the mouth and the tea is then sucked through them.

Those of us who enjoy coffee are all indebted to its discovery in Yemen. It came to Turkey in the sixteenth century and was gradually spread by the Ottomans throughout the Empire. Now widely adopted, it is often drunk in the middle of the morning and after a meal, but in parts of rural Anatolia coffee is still reserved for special occasions. Traditionally it played a role in the selection of a bride, *gelin görücülük*, when the daughter of a household would serve coffee to her prospective mother-in-law and future husband, giving them the opportunity to inspect her beauty and grace. This ritual is still practised in parts of Anatolia today.

Ayran
YOGURT DRINK

Cool, refreshing and healthy, ayran can be made in seconds at home and is also sold in bottles and cartons. Along with şalgam, a drink made from turnip juice, it is popular as an accompaniment to fast food and kebabs. It can be served with ice and sprinkled with mint.

SERVES 4–6

1 pint/600ml cold thick yogurt

1 pint/600ml cold water

salt

dried mint (optional)

✧ Beat the yogurt in a bowl until smooth. Add the water and continue to beat vigorously until well blended. Season it with salt to taste, and keep it chilled if you are not drinking it immediately. Pour the *ayran* into a jug or tall glasses and, if you wish, sprinkle a little mint over the top.

Limon şerbeti
LEMON SHERBET

Cool and refreshing, lemon sherbet can be found in every fast food bar, train and bus station, and in sweet-pastry shops. Mint leaves and orange peel can also be added to the simmering liquid.

1 pint/600ml cold water

1lb/450g sugar

½ pint/300ml lemon juice

rind of 2 lemons, grated

✧ Put the sugar, lemon juice and rind into a pan with the water. Stir until the sugar is dissolved and bring the liquid to the boil. Reduce the heat and simmer uncovered for 20–25 minutes. Strain the liquid into a bowl or jug, then leave it to cool. Pour the cool syrup into a jar or bottle and seal tightly with the lid, cap or cork. Store in a cool place and, once opened, keep in the refrigerator.

✧ When you feel like a sherbet, spoon the syrup (1 tablespoon per person) into a glass or jug and dilute with cold water. Serve chilled, with ice.

Gül şerbeti
ROSE SHERBET

Less common, but favoured as a ceremonial drink. It can be made with rose-water or scented rose petals, and coloured with red food dye.

1 pint/600ml cold water

1lb/450g sugar

2 tablespoons lemon juice

4 tablespoons rose-water

✧ Stir the sugar, lemon juice and water in a pan and bring the liquid to the boil. Simmer gently until it thickens and coats the back of the spoon. (If using food colouring, add it at this stage.) Stir in the rose-water and simmer for a further 2–3 minutes. Leave the syrup to cool in the pan. Pour into a jar or bottle and seal tightly. Store in a cool place and, once opened, in the refrigerator.

✧ Dilute 1 tablespoon per person with cold water, and serve chilled, with ice.

Vişne suyu CHERRY JUICE

liquid to the boil, reduce the heat, and simmer for 10–15 minutes. Strain into another pan, press all the liquid out of the cherries and discard them. Simmer the liquid gently until the syrup is thick and coats the back of the spoon. Leave it to cool in the pan.

✤ Pour the syrup into a jar or bottle, seal tightly, and store in a cool place. Keep in the refrigerator, once opened. Dilute 1–2 tablespoons per person with water, and serve chilled, with ice.

Kayısı suyu
APRICOT JUICE

Unlike the sherbets, kayısı suyu *is thick and fruity. Made from dried apricots, it has a pulpy texture and is quite filling – a pleasant addition to a summer breakfast.*

Kayısı suyu APRICOT JUICE

Vişne suyu
CHERRY JUICE

A bold drink as well as a pretty colour, cherry juice is available all year round in cartons and bottles. Made with sour cherries (morello cherries work as a substitute), it is lovely on its own or with a splash of vodka.

1lb/450g sour cherries, washed and stoned
2lb/900g sugar
½ pint/300ml water

✤ Place the cherries in a deep pan and pile the sugar on top of them. Leave to weep for 2–3 hours.

✤ Stir the cherries and sugar with the water over a medium heat, until the sugar dissolves. Bring the

8oz/225g dried apricots
1½ pints/900ml cold water
honey or sugar

✧ Cover the apricots with enough water to just immerse them, and leave to soak for 3–4 hours. Drain them, push them through a sieve, then add the cold water (or blend them with the water in an electric mixer). Add extra water if you like, and sweeten with honey or sugar to your taste.

Boza
BULGUR JUICE

A curious drink, made from fermented bulgur. Regiments of boza-filled glasses, lined up in pudding-shop windows, appear in the winter, then quickly vanish in the spring. Few people bother to make it at home any more, as it is also sold by the bozacı *who pulls his cart laden with copper jugs full of the thick yellow liquid through the streets.*

4oz/120g *bulgur* (p. 219)
1oz/30g short-grain rice
4 pints/2.4 litres water
8oz/225g sugar
½ teaspoon fresh yeast
1 teaspoon cinnamon, finely ground

✧ Wash the *bulgur* and the rice, and put them into a pan with the water. Bring to the boil, reduce the heat and simmer with the lid on for about an hour, until the *bulgur* and rice have cooked to a pulp.

Push the pulp through a sieve, to get a smooth purée. Put the purée back into the pan and add the sugar. Stirring all the time, bring to the boil and cook for 2–3 minutes. Pour it into a bowl and leave it to cool a little.

✧ Blend the yeast with 1 tablespoon of the warm purée, and leave it to froth. Then blend the yeast mixture with the rest of the purée in the bowl, cover it and leave it to ferment at room temperature for at least 8 hours, until bubbles appear on the surface.

✧ Pour the *boza* into stout glasses and sprinkle with cinnamon. It is usually accompanied by *leblebi*, roasted chickpeas.

Salep
ORCHID-ROOT DRINK

This is a hot milk drink, delicately flavoured and thickened with finely ground orchid root. It is popular in the winter, and remarkably soothing for sore throats and tickly coughs. Traditionally, milk and sugar are simmered with a small amount of orchid root in a large copper urn until the mixture thickens. But orchid root is expensive, and an instant salep mix is now available.

SERVES 2
¾ pint/450ml milk
2 tablespoons sugar
2 teaspoons orchid root, finely ground
½ teaspoon cinnamon, finely ground

✧ Heat the milk in a pan and stir in the orchid root and sugar. Keep stirring, and reduce the heat as soon as the milk begins to boil. Simmer for about 5 minutes until the milk thickens. Pour it into cups, sprinkle with cinnamon and serve hot.

Çay
TURKISH TEA

Traditionally tea was made in a samovar. This is often an elaborate vessel with a compartment for burning coals at the bottom of an internal tube, which heats the water in the 'kettle' section that wraps around it, on top of which rests a small teapot in which the tea brews over

Çay TURKISH TEA

the rising heat. The teapot and tea glasses are topped up with boiling water from a tap at the side of the kettle section. Although the samovar is still used, most people prefer the practical, if crude, modern version which consists of a small tin or enamel teapot, sitting on top of a large tin teapot which, in turn, is heated over a flame.

Rize, on the Black Sea coast, keeps Turkey supplied with tea, which is invariably made strong – a measure of 1 teaspoon per person – but individual glasses can easily be weakened with the constant supply of boiling water from the lower teapot. Although lemon peel is sometimes added to the tea-leaves, the method of brewing remains the same. Turkish tea is never drunk with milk.

✧ To make the tea, fill the larger pot with water and put over a flame. Select the tea-leaves of your choice, then put the required quantity into the smaller pot, with ½ teaspoon of sugar and 1 tablespoon of water to moisten them, and place it on top of the larger pot. When the water has boiled, fill the smaller teapot, replace it on top of the larger one, and put them over a low flame. Let the tea brew for a further 4–5 minutes, then pour some into a tea glass and top it up with the boiled water from the lower teapot. In this manner, tea can be drunk all day if the bottom pot is filled regularly with water and the tea is refreshed from time to time with new leaves and a little extra sugar.

Ihlamur çayı
LINDEN TEA

Made from the dried leaves and blossom of the linden tree, this tea is believed to be good for colds and the digestive system. Usually each glass is served with a wedge of lemon to squeeze into it.

juice of ½ lemon
handful of dried linden leaves and blossom
cold water
honey

✧ In a double-pot system (see left), put the linden leaves and blossom in the bottom of the small pot, pour the lemon juice over them and place the pot on top of the larger pot, which you have filled with water. Bring the water to the boil, fill up the small teapot and simmer for 1–3 minutes.

✧ Strain the tea into glasses, sweeten to taste with honey, and refresh with a squeeze of lemon.

Elma çayı
APPLE TEA

Becoming increasingly fashionable are the aromatic infusions of rose petals, camomile, lemon, orange blossom, mint, rosemary, ash blossom and wild sage. One of the most common is apple tea, which can be instantly prepared from processed granules, but it is healthier and more refreshing if it is made from apple slices baked in the oven and dried.

FOR A STRONG BREW

3oz/90g dried apple, sliced or flaked

1 small piece of cinnamon bark

2–3 cloves

a few dried rose petals (optional)

1 pint/600ml cold water

honey or sugar

✧ Put the apple, rose petals and spices in a pan with the water, and bring to the boil. Reduce the heat and simmer for 15–20 minutes. Sweeten to taste with honey or sugar, and strain into tea glasses.

Adı çay
WILD SAGE TEA

Small parcels of dried leafy branches of wild sage are sold in the markets of Turkey, but the plant itself grows all over the hills of the southern coast. An invigorating tea, it is simply made by infusing the leaves in the upper teapot of a double-pot system (see p. 216) and adding water, or by dipping a branch upside down in a glass of boiling water for a few minutes until the flavour has been released.

Adı çay WILD SAGE TEA

Kahve

TURKISH COFFEE

A great deal of importance is given to coffee-making. Sometimes the task falls to the only member of the household who possesses the right touch. Brazilian coffee beans are the favourite, passed through the grinder two or three times to achieve the correct fineness of powder. The coffee is measured by the spoon, 1 teaspoon per person; the water by the tiny cylindrical cup, 1 cup per person. It is made in a cezve, *a long-handled, tin-lined brass pot which differs in size depending on the number of cups to be catered for. The choice of how you have your coffee ranges from* sade, *no sugar,* az şekerli, *slightly sweet, and* orta şekerli, *medium-sweet, to* tatlı, *sweet – all must be served with froth on top. In some parts of Anatolia cardamom seeds are crushed into the ground coffee to enhance the taste.*

Kahve TURKISH COFFEE

MAKES 1 ORTA ŞEKERLI
1 coffee cup of cold water
1 teaspoon fresh coffee, finely ground
1 teaspoon sugar

✧ Put the cupful of cold water into the *cezve* and spoon the sugar and coffee on top. Using a teaspoon, quickly stir the sugar and coffee into the surface of the water to give the froth a kick-start, taking care not to touch the bottom of the *cezve* with the spoon. Put the *cezve* over a medium flame and heat through, gradually stirring the outer edges of the surface into the middle, creating an island of froth. Pour about one third of the coffee into the cup to warm it up, and return the *cezve* to the heat. Continue to use the teaspoon to gather the froth into the middle. Just as it is about to bubble up, take the *cezve* off the heat and immediately pour the rest of the coffee into the warming cup. The coffee must be served hot, with sufficient froth on top, and should be left to stand for a minute before drinking to let the coffee grains settle. (Froth enthusiasts spoon a little extra froth into the cup before pouring the coffee.)

GLOSSARY

beyaz peynir ✧ A firm or soft white cow's-milk cheese, matured in salted water for a year. There are numerous varieties of this cheese, which is often sold in Middle Eastern stores as Turkish feta. Although not quite the same, it can be replaced by a Greek, French or Danish feta for the purpose of the recipes in this book. (See also p. 26.)

bulgur ✧ Cracked wheat, sometimes used as a rice substitute. It is available in Middle Eastern and health food stores, and the more cosmopolitan supermarkets.

çemen ✧ Ground fenugreek, ground cumin, crushed garlic and ground *kırmızı biber* (see right) are mixed together with a little water to form a paste to coat *pastırma* (see p. 220).

ezme ✧ A smooth *meze* dish, usually made from cooked vegetable flesh pounded to a pulp and mixed with yogurt or olive oil.

güveç ✧ An earthenware pot used for cooking vegetable, fish and meat casseroles, which are then served in it. Traditionally the pot was buried in the hot ashes of an open fire or outdoor kiln to cook the contents.

kaşar peyniri ✧ A hard, tangy cheese made from sheep's milk. A strong, dry Cheddar, Parmesan or pecorino are the best substitutes.

kaymak ✧ A thick, rich cream made from the milk of cows or water buffalo, used as a filling for desserts or eaten with them. Fresh clotted cream is the nearest alternative.

kırmızı biber ✧ A ubiquitous spice made from mild chilli peppers. It can be made at home by crushing the long dried peppers and rubbing them in oil. You can roast these oiled flakes in an oven or in a heavy-based pan over a high flame until almost black. The spice is also bought in finely ground form, which is usually hot. If you cannot get the correct *kırmızı biber* in Middle Eastern and Italian shops, it is best to create a comfortable mixture of sweet paprika and cayenne to adapt to the recipes. (See also p. 38.)

köfte ✧ Refers to any dish of pounded flesh (meat or fish) or vegetable pulp, mixed with herbs and spices, shaped into balls or oblongs, and fried or grilled. The most common are the meat *köfte*, which are infinite in variety throughout Turkey and its neighbouring countries.

köy peyniri ✧ A village cheese, made every week from the milk of cows, sheep or goats. It is softer and creamier than *beyaz peynir*. For the recipes, you can substitute ricotta or feta. (See also p. 45.)

kuyrukyağı ⬦ Sheep's tail fat, used for cooking meat and grains in parts of Anatolia. Ordinary or clarified butter can be used as a substitute in the recipes

mahlep ⬦ A flour made from the ground small, pale kernels of the black cherry. It gives a particular flavour to biscuits and cakes. It is sometimes available in Middle Eastern stores.

mastika ⬦ The hard gummy resin from the acacia tree, which is most commonly used in ice-cream to give it a chewy texture. It is a popular chewing gum, too. *Mastika* is also the name given to the mastic-flavoured *rakı* (p. 36). Mastic crystals, which are easily crushed with sugar to release the smell of the acacia bark, are sometimes stocked in Middle Eastern stores.

meze ⬦ A nibble or savoury dish to have with a drink, or the first course (entrée) to a meal. (See also p. 47.)

nigella ⬦ A black aromatic seed often sprinkled on breads and pastries. It also gives a distinct flavour to some fish, chicken and vegetable dishes. It is sometimes available in Indian and

Middle Eastern stores, often incorrectly labelled 'black cumin'. (See also p. 38.)

orange-blossom water ⬦ The fragrant essence of orange blossom used to flavour milk puddings and sweet pastries, available in delicatessens, Middle Eastern, Indian and health food stores.

pastırma ⬦ A cured, dried fillet of veal coated with *çemen*, a paste of ground cumin, fenugreek, ground *kırmızı biber* and garlic; it is cut into thin slices and eaten on its own or in savoury pastries. Sometimes available in Middle Eastern stores.

pekmez ⬦ A thick, dark syrup made from the juice of grapes, pomegranates or dates. The grape and date syrups are used to sweeten dishes, in particular the simple unsweetened milk and wheat-flour puddings of Anatolia, but the pomegranate syrup is slightly sour. A popular mixture of *tahin* (see p. 221) and grape syrup is eaten on bread. Pomegranate syrup is made in the villages of Anatolia for local consumption, but a variety of grape and date syrups is available in Italian, Middle Eastern and health food stores.

pide ⬦ A soft bread pouch, sometimes with a crisp crust, used for mopping up

olive oil and garlicky yogurt. Small, thin *pide* are stuffed with grilled *köfte*, onions, tomato and yogurt as a snack. (See also p. 94.)

pilâki ⬦ A fish or bean stew made with olive oil and onions and served cold.

rose-water ⬦ The fragrant essence of rose petals used to flavour milk puddings, sweet pastries and syrups. It is also used for cosmetic purposes and is available in some delicatessens, Indian, Middle Eastern and health food stores.

salep ⬦ The ground root of the early purple orchid from eastern Anatolia, which thickens milk and is used to make a hot, sweet, nourishing winter drink (p. 214). Pure ground *salep* is expensive and difficult to find, but an instant *salep* drink is available in some Middle Eastern stores.

simit ⬦ Bread rings made from plain bread dough or a sweet, heavier dough, and rolled in sesame seeds. They are often munched as a snack.

sıvı tas ⬦ The standard natural set yogurt made from the full-fat milk of cows, sheep or goats. If you don't make it yourself, use a thick set yogurt from any supermarket. (See also p. 44.)

sucuk ✧ A spicy beef sausage often spiked with garlic and cumin – similar to salami.

sumak ✧ A small, sour, dark-red berry of the *Rhus coriaria* species, a member of the cashew family which grows wild all over Anatolia. The berries can be soaked in water, then pressed to squeeze out the juice, or roughly ground. The juice or ground berries are added to some fish, meat and vegetable dishes to give them a slightly tart flavour. Ground *sumak* is added to salads and grilled meats, and can be found in Middle Eastern stores.

süzme ✧ Thick, creamy yogurt made from *sıvı tas* (see p. 220) which is hung overnight in a muslin cloth and left to drain. If you don't make it yourself, look for a thick strained yogurt in some of the more cosmopolitan supermarkets. (See also p. 44.)

tahin ✧ A thick, oily paste made from crushed sesame seeds, often mixed with *pekmez* (see p. 220) for breakfast, or used in dressings and sauces for salads and grilled fish and chicken. It is available in dark and light versions – a matter of personal preference – in a variety of supermarkets, delicatessens, Middle Eastern and health food stores. (See also p. 65.)

tandır ✧ Traditionally, a pit dug in the earth and used as an oven. Different versions made out of clay and stone can be found in use all over Anatolia.

tarator ✧ A garlic and nut sauce used with steamed vegetables, and grilled or fried fish. It is usually made with walnuts or hazelnuts but works well with almonds, pistachios and pine nuts for certain dishes.

tava ✧ A frying pan; or any fried dish.

tepsi ✧ A deep baking tray, often round, used for savoury and sweet pastries.

yahni ✧ A basic meat stew with onions, served hot.

yufka ✧ A traditional Anatolian flat bread baked in thin sheets on a griddle. The sheets can be stored for weeks, stacked in a dry place and reconstituted with a splash of water. *Yufka* can be eaten as a snack, cut and rolled into savoury pastries, layered and baked into savoury pies and an Anatolian sweet pastry. Sheets of filo can be used as a substitute in some recipes.

zeytinyağlı ✧ A vegetable dish prepared with olive oil and served cold. The olive oil forms an intrinsic part of the dish.

INDEX

Note Unaccented letters precede accented ones: e.g. *kokoreç* comes before *köfte*, currants before *çam fıstık*.

acı domates ezmesi 56
Adana kebab 153
Adana kebabı 39, 153
adı 30
adı çay 217
ahtapot salatası 47
allspice 37
almond cream 191
almonds 32
Anadolu ıspanak ezmesi 58
Anadolu patlican 52
anason 37
Anatolian curd soup 83
Anatolian meat snack 91, 95
Anatolian unleavened bread 97, 98
anchovies in vine leaves 68, 69
anchovy pilaf 127
aniseed 37
Antakya mercimek köftesi 109
antep fıstık 32
antep fıstık ezmesi 207
apple tea 216
apricot(s) 28
    cream-filled 191
    juice 213
    yogurt dip 57
Armenian rice with pumpkin 128
Arnavut ciğeri 151, 152
artichokes in olive oil 2, 118
aside 121
aslan sütü 36
aşure 184, 197
aubergine(s) 24
    and cheese purée 166
    baked, with mint yogurt 52
    casserole 109
    fried, with yogurt 51, 52
    in tomato sauce 72
    jam 25, 208, 209
    moussaka 150, 151
    pilaf 128, 129
    purée with mint and almonds 63, 64
    smoked, with yogurt 48, 49
    stuffed, in olive oil 114
    stuffed with lamb 159
    stuffed with quails 176
    with chicken thighs 170, 173
    with chilli in yogurt 66

    with onion and tomato 107
ayran 41, 43, 212
ayva tatlısı 185, 186

badem 32
baked aubergine with mint yogurt 52
baked cheese 54
baked layered pastries 91, 98
baked prawns 144
baked savoury noodles 99, 100, 101
baklava 15, 18, 89, 169, 182, 183, 192
balık kebabı 134, 135
balık köftesi 139
balkabağı baklavası 192
balkabağı çorbası 78, 79, 85
balkabağı tatlısı 85, 185
basil 30
bean(s)
    and lentil balls 109
    barlotti, in olive oil 117
    green, in olive oil 119
    paste with dill 70
    salad 74
beef
    Adana kebab 153
    meatballs in tomato sauce 166
    tartare meatballs 70
beetroot salad with yogurt 66
beğendi 165, 166
beyaz aşure 197
beyaz peynir 26, 33, 43, 45, 47, 48, 60, 65, 68, 104, 108, 187, 200, 203, 219
beyin salatası 74
boiled savoury noodles 100, 101
börek 18, 90
boza 214
brain salad 74
bread(s) 89
    Anatolian meat snack 95
    Anatolian unleavened 97, 98
    corn 93
    daily 91
    filled Anatolian 96
    rings 93, 203
    soft pouches 94
    village 92

bulgur 80, 113, 122, 123, 128, 149, 169, 195, 197, 219
    juice 214
    patties 51
    pilaf 123, 124
bulls' testes 158
bumbar dolması 150
buryani 122, 127
bülbül yuvası 192

cabbage leaves filled with chestnuts 105
cacık 77, 79, 155
cardamom 37
carrot(s)
    and lentils in olive oil 116
    purée with yogurt 48, 50
    rolls with apricots and pine nuts 106
celery and coconut salad 61
ceviz 32
cezve 218
charcuterie 26
cheese 26, 43
    and courgette patties 104
    and melon 48
    baked 54
    helva 204, 205
    in vine leaves 60
    pastries 46, 62, 98
    sponges in syrup 187, 188
    village 45
cherries 28
cherry
    juice 213
    pilaf 123
    summer pudding 189
chestnuts 32
chicken
    and okra casserole 174, 175
    breast milk pudding 198
    in sesame sauce 176
    in spicy orange sauce 177, 179
    liver pilaf with pine nuts and almonds 130
    shredded, with walnut and coriander 172
    thighs in aubergine 170, 173
chickpea
    and potato paste 76
    hot purée with pine nuts 55

pilaf 125
purée 54, 55
stew 113
chilli tomato paste 56
cinnamon 37, 38
Circassian(s) 30, 122, 172
Circassian rice 122
classic chewy ice-cream 189
classic fish stew 136
classic meatballs 155
classic Turkish delight 204
cloves 38
coffee, Turkish 218
compote, fruit 200
coriander 30, 38
corn bread 82, 93
courgette(s) 31
    and apple in hazelnut sauce 71
    and cheese patties 104
    flowers, stuffed 113
cracked wheat
    pilaf 123, 124
    salad 51
    with spicy lamb 131
cream-filled apricots 191
crisp pastries in syrup 196
cucumber with mint yogurt 77
cumin 37, 38
currants 28

çam fıstık 32
çarliston biber 35, 53, 54
çay 215
çebiç 169
çemen 26, 38, 219, 220
çemen otu 38
Çerkez 30, 122
Çerkez fasulye 172
Çerkez pilavı 122
Çerkez tavuğu 172
çılbır 59
çiğ köfte 70
çingene pilavı 65, 158
çiroz 47
çoban salatası 67, 109
çöp şiş 150
çörek 38, 203
çöreotu 38

dağı kekik 30
deli bal 31

dereotu 30
dilber dudağı 155, 196
dill 30
dil peyniri 26
dolma 18, 103
dolma bahar 37
döğme 197
döner 15
dried fig jam 28, 207
dried okra soup 86
duck, Uncle Tahir's 180, 181
düğün çorbası 79
dürüm 97, 192

eggs
    poached, with yogurt 59
    with minced lamb 169
    with vegetable ragoût 108
ekmek 89
ekmek kadayıf 89
ekşili köfte 161
elma çayı 216
Ermeni köftesi 165
Ermeni pilavı 128
et mangal 149, 158
etli dolma 149
etli yaprak dolması 167, 168
ezme 47, 219

fasulye piyazı 74
fava 70
fenugreek 38
festive helva 205
fig(s) 28
    jam, dried 28, 207
    jam, green 28, 208, 209
    with bay leaves 190
fındık 32
fırında kalamar dolması 137
fırında mantı 99, 100, 101
fırında sütlaç 195
fish
    balls with sunflower seeds 139
    grilled, with dill yogurt 145
    kebabs in vine leaves 134, 135
    roe purée 68
    salt-baked 147
    stew, classic 136
fish spice 40
fried octopus 140

fried vegetables in yogurt 64
fritters in syrup 199
fruit 27
fruit compote 200
funeral helva 206

garlic 29
gözleme 54, 90, 96, 98, 103
Grand Vizier's fingers 196
grapes 29
green beans in olive oil 119
green fig jam 28, 208, 209
grilled bulls' testes 158
grilled fish with dill yogurt 145
grilled pepper and fresh peach
    salad 65
grilled peppers with yogurt 35,
    53
gül dondurması 186
gül reçeli 37, 202, 207
gül şerbeti 212
güllaç 184
güneşli yoğurt 57
günlük ekmek 91
güveç 219
güveçte piliçli bamya 174, 175
gypsy salad 65

hamsi sarması 68, 69
hamsili pilav 127
haşhaş 38
havuç ezmesi 48, 50
havuç köftesi 106
haydari 30, 57
hazelnuts 32
helva 32, 183, 203
    cheese 204, 205
    festive 205
    funeral 206
helva pide 90
herbs 30
hindi takuk 171
hindustan cevizi 122
honey 31
hoşaf 121, 200
hoşmerim 200
hot humus 55
hot yogurt soup 80
humus 54, 55
hünkâr beğendili köfte 166

ıhlamur çayı 216
ıspanak kökü salatası 74
ıspanaklı gözleme 62, 96, 98
ıspanaklı tepsi böreği 91
ızgara balık 145
ızgarada boğa yumurtası 158

ice-cream, classic chewy 189

iç pilavı 130
içli köfte 160
imam bayıldı 107
incir tatlısı 190
irmik helvası 206
işkembe çorbası 36, 81, 150

jam
    aubergine 25, 208, 209
    dried fig 28, 207
    green fig 28, 208, 209
    rose-petal 37, 202, 207

kabak çiçeği dolması 31, 113
kabak helvası 31
kabak mucveri 104
kadayıf 183
kadın göbeği 17, 154, 196
kadınbudu köfte 154
kahve 218
kakule 37
kalamar 61
kalamar tavası 61
kar helvası 203
karadeniz pidesi 90
karanfil 38
karides güveç 144
karışık et dolması 168
karışık turşu 73
karnıyarık 159
kaşar peyniri 26, 144, 166, 219
kavun ve peynir 48
kavurma 122, 130, 149, 150,
    157
kavurma dana pirzola 157, 158
kayısı suyu 213
kaymak 184, 191, 201, 219
kaymaklı kayısı 191
kebab 18
    Adana 153
    fish 134, 135
    lamb, with tomato, peppers
        and onions 149, 154
    tile-baked 156, 157
keçup 51, 150
kekik 30
kelle paça çorbası 149
kereviz salatası 61
keşkek 149
keşkül 191
keşme bulamacı 195
kestane 32
kestane şekeri 32
kestaneli lahana dolması 105
Kıbrıs böreği 111, 112
Kıbrıs salatası 65
Kıbrıslı üzümlü pilav 126
kıkırdak poğaçası 150
kırmızı biber 26, 35, 37, 38, 39,

47, 83, 85, 99, 149, 151, 153,
    172, 219, 220
kırmızı biberli ahtapot 140
kırmızı lahana çorbası 79
kırmızı mercimek çorbası 81
kırmızı soslu patlıcan 72
kısır 51
kıymalı semiz otu 169
kıymalı yumurta 169
kız memesi 17, 155
kız memesi kadayıf 183
kızarmış biber 35, 53
kızarmış peynir 47
kimyon 38
kiraz 28
kiremit 141
kiremitte alabalık 140, 141
kiremitte kebab 156, 157
kişniş 30, 38
klasik köfte 155
klasik mantı 99, 100, 101
koç yumurtası 158
kokoreç 15, 149, 150
köfte 18, 28, 63, 80, 94, 122,
    149, 155, 219, 220
    carrot 106
    classic 155
    fish 139
    in egg and lemon sauce 161
    in tomato sauce with
        aubergine purée 166
    ladies' thighs 154
    mother-in-law's 160
    picnic 162, 163
    tartare 70
köfte spice 39, 40
köy çorbası 82, 89
köy ekmeği 92
köy peyniri 26, 42, 43, 45, 54,
    104, 187, 200, 219
Kurdish pilaf 123, 124
kuru bamya çorbası 86
kuru incir reçeli 28, 207
kuru köfte 162, 163
kuru üzüm hoşafı 200
kuskus 128, 131
kuş üzümü 28
kuyrukyağı 34, 149, 154, 171,
    220
kuzu böreği şişte 154
kuzulu bulgur pilav 131
kuzu ve ayva yahnisi 164
künefe 183
kürt bulgur pilavı 123, 124

ladies' navels 196
ladies' thighs 154
lahana kapaması 169
lahmacun 91, 95

lamb
    and sultana pilaf 126
    and quince stew 164
    classic meatballs 155
    kebab with tomato, peppers
        and onions 149, 154
    ladies' thighs 154
    meatballs in egg and lemon
        sauce 161
    minced meat loaf 165
    minced, with eggs 169
    mother-in-law's meatballs
        160
    moussaka 150
    picnic köfte 162, 163
    roasted 169
    stuffed aubergine 159
    stuffed vegetables 168
    stuffed vine leaves 167
    tile-baked kebab 156, 157
    with cracked wheat 131
lamb's lettuce salad 46, 52
lapa 122
leblebi 36
leeks in olive oil 119
lekerda 47
lemon sherbet 212
lemons 28
limon şerbeti 212
linden tea 216
liver spiced with cumin 151, 152
lohusa şerbeti 211
lokma 184
lokum 32, 204
lor peyniri 26, 43, 54
lüfer yahnisi 136

mackerel stuffed with nuts and
    spices 138
mahlep 28, 93, 220
mantı 90, 99
marrows 31
mastika 36, 91, 189, 193, 199,
    204, 220
maydanoz 30
meat loaf, minced 165
meat spice 40
meatballs
    classic 155
    in egg and lemon sauce 161
    in tomato sauce with
        aubergine purée 166
    picnic 162, 163
melon and cheese 48
menemen 108
meyhane 47
meze 15, 25, 28, 33, 34, 36, 47,
    103, 109, 151, 185, 219, 220
mıhlama 26

mısır ekmeği 93
midye dolması 135
midye tavası 15, 60
midyeli pilâki 73
mihaliç 26
milk pudding, rose 193, 194
milk pudding with chicken
    breasts, burnt 198
mint 30, 57
mint yogurt dip 57
mother-in-law's meatballs 160
musakka 150
mushrooms with garlic and
    spices 57, 58
muska böreği 62
mussels
    fried in beer batter 60
    in tomato sauce 73
    stuffed with pine nuts 135

nane 30
nar pekmez 29
nazuktan 63, 64
nigella 38, 203, 220
Noah's dessert 197
nohut yahnisi 113
nohutlu pilav 125
noodles 99
    baked 99, 100
    boiled 100
nuts 32

octopus
    fried 140
    salad 47
oklava 89, 192
okra and chicken casserole 174,
    175
okra soup, dried 86, 87
olives 33
olive oil 34
    artichokes in 118
    barlotti beans in 117
    carrots in 116
    green beans in 119
    leeks in 119
    stuffed aubergine in 114
onions 34
orange and onion salad 68
orange-blossom water 220
orchid root drink 214
oregano 30

pancar salatası 66
parsley 30
pastırma 26, 38, 96, 219, 220
patates bastısı 110, 111
patates ezmesi 111
patlıcan bastısı 109

patlıcan bildircin 176
patlıcan ezmesi 48, 49
patlıcan musakkası 150, 151
patlıcan reçeli 25, 208, 209
patlıcan sarması 170, 173
patlıcanlı pilav 128, 129
pekmez 39, 63, 220, 221
pepper(s)
   and peach salad 65
   grilled, with yogurt 53
pestil 27
peynir helvası 204, 205
peynir tatlısı 187, 188
peynir ve kavun 48
peynirli güveç 54
pickles 36, 73
picnic meatballs 162, 163
pide 54, 55, 58, 90, 94, 103, 109,
   176, 220
piliç döner 171
pilaf (*pilav*) 121, 122
   anchovy 127
   Armenian 128
   aubergine 128, 129
   cherry 123
   chicken liver with pine nuts
     and almonds 130
   chickpea 125
   Circassian 122
   cracked wheat 123, 124
   cracked wheat with spicy
     lamb 131
   lamb and sultana 126
pine nuts 32
pistachio marzipan 207
pistachios 32
poached eggs with yogurt 59
pomegranates 29
poppy seeds 38, 74
portakal salatası 68
portakalı piliç 179
potato casserole 110, 111
prawns, baked 144
pul biber 38
pumpkin in syrup 185
pumpkin soup 78, 85

quails stuffed into aubergines
   176
quince and lamb stew 164
quinces in syrup 185, 186

rabbit casserole 178, 179
rakı 36, 37, 47, 48, 220
Ramazan *pide* 90
red lentil soup 81
red pepper 38

revani 186
reyhan 30
rice pudding, burnt 195
roasted kid or lamb 169
rose(s) 36
   milk pudding 193, 194
   -petal jam 37, 202, 207
   -petal sorbet 186
   sherbet 212
   -water 37, 220

saç böreği 90, 96
saffron (*safron*) 39
sage 30
sakızlı dondurma 189
salad
   beetroot, with yogurt 66
   brain 74
   celery and coconut 61
   cucumber with mint yogurt
     77
   grilled pepper and fresh
     peach 65
   gypsy 65
   lamb's lettuce 46, 52
   orange and onion 68
   shepherd's 67
   spinach root 74
   tomato, with tahin 65
   white bean salad 74
salep 189, 214, 220
salma 122
salt-baked fish 147
saray lokması 198
sarhoş kalamar 145
sarmısaklı mantar 57, 58
sarmısaklı sos 89, 134
sarmısaklı yahni 150
sefer tası 162
semiz otu kıymalı 169
semiz otu salatası 46, 52
semolina sponge in syrup 186
sesam 39
sesame bread rings 93
sesame seeds 39
sheep's tail fat 34, 149, 154, 171,
   220
sheep's trotters in yogurt 164
sıcak humus 55
sigara böreği 46, 62, 97, 98
sıvı tas 41, 43, 44, 220
simit 39, 93, 203, 220
something nice for the husband
   200
spices 37
spinach
   balls with yogurt 63

-filled Anatolian flat bread
   96
root salad 74
   with yogurt and pine nuts
     58
squid
   fried in beer batter 61
   stuffed with herbs 137
   with olives in red wine 145
stuffed aubergines in olive oil
   114
stuffed courgette flowers 113
stuffed figs with bay leaves 190
stuffed sardines with pine nut
   sauce 143
stuffed vine leaves 75
su muhallebisi 193, 194
sucuk 26, 96, 149, 221
Sultan Reşat pilavı 128
Sultan's moussaka 150, 151
sumak 39, 221
summer cherry pudding 189
summer vegetable stew 112
sunflower oil 40
sunflowers 40
sübye 121, 183
sütlaç 195
sütlü nüriye 193
süzme 41, 44, 57, 221
sweetheart's lips 196
syrupy sponge pastries 194

şakşuka 64
şalgam 212
şekerpare 194
şerbet 211
şiş kebabı 149, 154
şöbiyet 182, 192

tahin 28, 39, 48, 54, 76, 105, 145,
   220, 221
tahin soup 84
tahinli domates salatası 65
tahinli karadeniz çorbası 84
tahinli piliç 176, 177
Tahir amcanın ördeği 180, 181
tandır 141, 147, 169, 221
tandır çorbası 79
tarama 68
tarator 32, 61, 134, 145, 221
taratorlu kabak 71
taratorlu sardalya dolması 143
tarçın 38
tarhana çorbası 83
tartare meatballs 70
tatlı yahni 150
tavşan yahnisi 178, 179

tavuk göğsü 171, 198
tavuk göğsü kazandibi 9, 198
tea, apple 216
   linden 216
   Turkish 215
   wild sage 217
tepsi böreği 62, 97, 98
terbiyeli köfte 161
testi kebab 157
thyme 30
tile-baked kebab 156, 157
tile-baked trout in cabbage
   leaves 140, 141
tomato(es) 40
   chilli paste 56
   salad with *tahin* 65
topik 76
tripe soup 81
tulum 26
tulumba 196
Turkish coffee 218
Turkish delight 204
tuzlanmış balık 147
tuzsuz 26
türlü 112

Uncle Tahir's wild duck 180,
   181
un helvası 32, 205
uskumru dolması 10, 115, 138

üzüm pekmez 28

veal chops with lemon and
   oregano 157, 158
vegetable(s)
   fried, in yogurt 64
   summer stew 112
   ragoût with eggs 108
   stuffed with meat 168
vezir parmağı 196
village bread 92
village cheese 45
village soup 82
vine leaf and yogurt pie 111,
   112
vine leaves 41
   anchovies poached in 68, 69
   fish kebabs in 134, 135
   grilled with cheese 60
   stuffed with rice 75
   stuffed with meat 167
vişne 28
vişne suyu 28, 213
vişneli ekmek tatlısı 189
vişneli pilav 123

walnuts 32

white bean salad 74
wild sage tea 217

yalancı dolma 9, 37
yalancı ıspanak köftesi 63
yalancı patlıcan dolması 114
yalancı yaprak dolması 41, 75
yalova ezmesi 66
yaprak sarması 60
yayla çorbası 80
yaz türlüsü 112
yeni bahar 37
yeşil incir reçeli 28, 208, 209
yogurt 41, 43
   and vine leaf pie 111, 112
   apricot dip 57
   cake 201
   drink 212
   mint dip 57
   soup 80
   with aubergine and chilli 66
   with baked aubergines 52
   with beetroot 66
   with cucumber and mint 77
   with fried aubergine 51, 52
   with fried vegetables 64
   with grilled fish 145
   with grilled peppers 53
   with poached eggs 59
   with sheep's trotters 164
   with smoked aubergine 48,
     49·
   with spinach and pine nuts
     58
   with spinach balls 63
yoğurt çorbası 79, 80
yoğurt tatlısı 201
yoğurtlu paça 164
yoğurtlu salata 201
yoğurtlu patlıcan 51, 52
young girls' breasts 17, 155
yufka 62, 89, 90, 97, 98, 103,
   150, 183, 221

zerde 39
zeytin salatası 47
zeytinyağı 103
zeytinyağlı 34, 103, 116, 118,
   221
zeytinyağlı barbunya 117
zeytinyağlı enginar 2, 118
zeytinyağlı fasulye 119
zeytinyağlı havuç 116
zeytinyağlı kereviz 118
zeytinyağlı pırasa 119